Guide to Cape Cod

Guide to Cape Cod

*Everything you need to know
to enjoy one of New England's
perfect vacation destinations*

by Frederick Pratson

A Voyager Book

The
Globe
Pequot
Press

Chester, Connecticut

Library of Congress Cataloging-in-Publication Data

Pratson, Frederick John.
  Guide to Cape Cod.

  (A Voyager book)
  Includes index.
  1. Cape Cod (Mass.)—Description and travel—
Guide-Books.   I.Title.   II. Series.
F72.C3P73   1988   917.44'920443   87-37364
ISBN 0-87106-784-6 (pbk.)

Manufactured in the United States of America

First Edition/First Printing

FOR PATRICIA, WHO HAS SHARED CAPE COD WITH ME.

Contents

Life on Cape Cod

Visiting Cape Cod

Activities and Attractions

About the Author

Frederick John Pratson is author of several books, among them *Guide to Atlantic Canada, Guide to Eastern Canada, Guide to Western Canada, Consumer's Guide to Package Travel Around the World, Land of the Four Directions, The Sea in Their Blood,* and *Special World of the Artisan.* He has published articles in many major magazines and newspapers. The author is a member of various professional organizations, including The Society of American Travel Writers and Washington Independent Writers. Mr. Pratson is a native-born New Englander and lives with his family in Falmouth on Cape Cod.

To The Readers of This Guide

Every effort has been taken to make this guide up-to-date and accurate. Some information can change, however, such as telephone numbers, hours and seasons of operation, and places going out of business or changing their names; in addition, errors can inadvertantly be made. As a result, we cannot and do not assume responsiblity and liability for such changes and errors. To continue to improve the quality of this guide, we would appreciate knowing of any errors or changes as well as suggestions of places we should consider including or eliminating in our next edition. Send your suggestions and comments to Frederick J. Pratson, *Guide to Cape Cod,* Globe Pequot Press, Chester, Connecticut 06412.

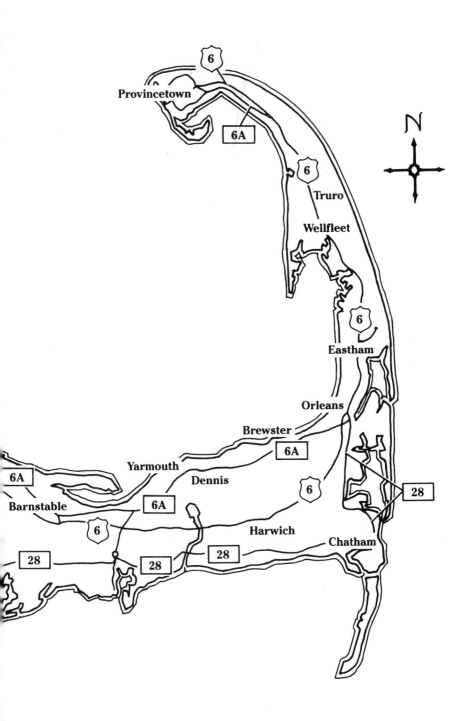

Life on Cape Cod

"The Cape"—a Personal View

To many of us who live along or near the densely populated northeastern seaboard of the United States, the sobriquet "the Cape" means only one vacation place—Cape Cod in Massachusetts. The Cape, however, is also a favorite or much desired vacation destination for travelers from every other state in the Union, from the provinces of Canada, and from many other countries. As a vacation destination in North America, the Cape ranks in priority—a place one "must see and experience"—along with New York City, the Grand Canyon, Hollywood, Florida, the Rockies, and Niagara Falls.

On this fishhook-shaped peninsula jutting out into the Atlantic are some of the best beaches and warmest waters on the eastern seaboard. That's the main reason why so many come frequently to the Cape. But swimming, sunbathing, and sailing are just part of the Cape's allure. Aesthetics is another. Here are some of the prettiest villages in all of North America, arranged one after the other from the Cape Cod Canal all the way to land's end at Provincetown. The cedar-shingled Cape Cod house, with roses blooming along slats of white picket fence, is emblematic of the Cape. This charming style has been replicated in towns all across the United States and Canada. It reminds one of mother's womb—warm, comforting, secure—or of the family home one actually had or dreams of having—a place of acceptance, innocence, and happiness.

Although the Cape has rustic-nostalgic pastiche, it also has, as does Grossinger's in the Catskills, "everything" for a super vacation: top quality inns, B&Bs, hotels, resorts, and motels; outstanding restaurants serving every manner of cuisine from freshly caught seafood to extraordinary concoctions à la Française; leading stars and budding talents performing at playhouses, nightclubs, bistros, and coffee houses; every kind of shopping from budget-busting boutiques and intriguing antique shops to for-fun-and-save-a-buck flea markets; art and crafts galleries galore; golf, sailboarding, surfing, tennis, bike touring, seaside-trail hikes, horseback riding, nature walks, deep-sea fishing, diving, triathlons, marathons, college baseball, and so on; summer camps, writers' and artists' workshops, and courses in just about every aspect of music, the visual arts, and dance; historic homes, fascinating museums, cruises, and whale-watching trips; and still more. And if you want to do nothing at all except relax in solitude by the sea while sipping vintage Bordeaux and listening to Mozart, there's a place that's just perfect for you here on the Cape.

First and foremost, Cape Cod is a family vacation land. In fact many visitors first came here on family vacations and have been returning ever since; many plan to retire or to begin new, more personally satisfying careers here. The Cape is a romantic place. Here people meet, get married, and honeymoon. Here couples come to rekindle the flames of a cooling romance or to renew themselves during priceless moments strolling a deserted beach or sitting before a blazing hearth. The Cape is where singles, regardless of sexual preference, can experience joy, peace, inspiration, and tolerance. And the Cape is where the elderly can discover sights, smells, tastes, and solid values reminding them of times that, in these parts, have never gone out of style. There's a special world on the Cape for everyone: the owner of a Rolls Royce and a Hinckley yacht, the scientist, the intellectual, the artist, the factory worker, the farmer, the computer programmer, and the young of every shape, color, and musical orientation.

The Cape also holds its primacy as an ideal place because most vacationers know that on this once hostile landscape Puritan Pilgrims, English-speaking colonists seeking religious freedom, not only settled but persisted and prospered. Here, as part of Plymouth Colony, the American spirit of democracy was first planted, took root, sprouted, and blossomed all over the continent. The nostalgia for the early days of this country is retained on Cape Cod, and people from all over the world come here to bask in this spirit of freedom, rugged individualism, and self-reliance. The Commonwealth of Massachusetts uses this slogan to lure visitors: "The spirit of Massachusetts is the spirit of America." Although a bit audacious and overblown, this sentiment nevertheless does hit close to home, and it hits closest on Cape Cod.

In the early 1960s, while working for a large corporation in upstate New York, I tried to imagine what quality of life I would want for my family and myself if I could make it possible. Here is the scenario that played in my mind: My wife and I would live in a simple manner on the Cape, raise our children within its health-giving and inspiring seacoast environment, and write to pay for our keep. In due time most of this vision did come true. The irony of my life, however, is that I had written about many places in the world until finally one morning I said to myself, "Now is the time to tell others about my home, a stretch of sea-encircled land most favorably endowed by God and by dedicated men and women—the Cape."

Profile of Cape Cod

A Capsule View of Cape Cod

Cape Cod is a sandy peninsula extending from the east coast of Massachusetts into the Atlantic Ocean. It is in the shape of a fishhook or, for some,

3

of an arm bent at the elbow and forming a fist at land's end. Cape Cod is about seventy miles long, from the town of Bourne in the west to Provincetown in the northeast corner, and from one to twenty miles wide. Within the bowl formed by its north and west coasts and the east coast of mainland Massachusetts is Cape Cod Bay. Cape Cod's north and east coasts, at the forearm and fist of the peninsula, are on the open Atlantic Ocean. Most all of its south coast is on Nantucket Sound, a body of water between Cape Cod and the Massachusetts islands of Nantucket and Martha's Vineyard.

The village of Woods Hole lies at Cape Cod's southwestern tip. The Elizabeth Islands, strung out to the southwest from Woods Hole, also belong to Massachusetts. Cape Cod's west/southwestern coast is on Buzzards Bay. The Cape Cod Canal at the west/northwest end is, by popular tradition, considered the beginning of Cape Cod, although a portion of the town of Bourne and a small section of the town of Sandwich are on the mainland of Massachusetts, on the west bank of the canal. Most visitors, however, consider themselves to be officially on Cape Cod once they cross the canal over the Bourne or Sagamore bridges. The islands of Martha's Vineyard and Nantucket are not part of Cape Cod, although year-round ferry access to them is available from the villages of Woods Hole and Hyannis. There is also seasonal ferry access to Martha's Vineyard Island from New Bedford and from Wareham. The Elizabeth Islands, a group of sixteen small islands, are privately owned, except for the island and village of Cuttyhunk, which are accessible by year-round public ferry from the city of New Bedford.

Cape Cod itself is divided into three regions comprising fifteen towns and a number of villages: the Upper Cape, composed of the towns of Bourne, Falmouth, Sandwich, and Mashpee; the Mid Cape with the towns of Barnstable, Yarmouth, Dennis, Brewster, Harwich, and Chatham; and the Lower Cape with its towns of Orleans, Eastham, Wellfleet, Truro, and Provincetown. All Cape Cod towns are on the seacoast and have beaches, village harbors, and other water-related attractions and conveniences. The village of Hyannis is the commercial, retailing, transportation, and tourism center of Cape Cod. Massachusetts Military Reservation is located within the widest portion of the Upper Cape in Bourne and Sandwich.

The Upper and Mid Cape regions have the highest year-round populations on the peninsula. The towns of the Lower Cape are less populated but rapidly growing nevertheless. In fact Cape Cod is one of the fastest growing areas of Massachusetts. Our current year-round population is close to 165,000. The working part of this population is employed in tourism, retail services, fishing, education, and scientific research. Many of our people are retired from various professions and occupations. During the summer season all Cape Cod towns double or even triple their population with the influx of vacation-home owners and tourists. Except at the business centers of towns and villages, there is plenty of room on Cape Cod for people to spread out and discover their special place of peace and enjoyment.

A Blessed Landscape

Cape Cod was created by the great glaciers that spread over much of what is now Canada and the northern United States. The last of these incredible ice sheets covered Cape Cod and the islands of Martha's Vineyard and Nantucket about 25,000 years ago. Approximately 9,000 years closer to our time, the leading edge of the last of these glaciers melted and receded north, revealing massive deposits of rock and soil that had collected on bedrock. These geological collecting points gave Cape Cad its distinctive fishhook shape and formed the Elizabeth Islands and the islands of Martha's Vineyard and Nantucket. The glacier acted first like a bulldozer, pushing material forward as it advanced, and then like a squeegee blade, pulling over and smoothening this debris as it melted back. In geological terms the forward motion of the glacier built a moraine, the high-ridged spine of the Cape. The retreat formed outwash plains, the extensive flat area along the south coast of the Cape.

When you drive the Mid-Cape Highway, Route 6, heading east toward Hyannis, you move along this high spine or moraine. Here on high ground you can see the landscape dropping off into a broad, level plain. The glacier also gouged out the many ponds and kettle holes that pock-mark most of Cape Cod. Initially these large holes in the ground were filled with melted glacier ice water. They have been replenished ever since with fresh water from rain and underground streams and now provide excellent fishing, boating, and swimming. Through the millenniums the surrounding sea itself has helped to shape Cape Cod's unique configuration. The sea has added shoreline and taken it away; it has created elongated sand bars and covered over others; and it has opened channels and closed others, such as Chatham.

Today's Cape Cod landscape is a composite of many beautiful facets: some of the most magnificent sand dunes and high sand cliffs on the Atlantic coast of North America; long stretches of sand beaches; extensive salt marshes; many estuaries, ponds, kettle holes, bays, streams, rivers, harbors, islands, herring runs, inlets, and peninsulas; and thick woodlands, productive farmlands, and world-famous cranberry bogs. While pitch pines and scrub oaks are two of Cape Cod's dominant flora, our peninsula is also replete with stately elms, maples, and beeches. The flora here is gorgeous and fragrant—rosa ragusa (beach rose), bayberry, heather, holly, honeysuckle, rhododendrons, tiger lilies, and lilacs. There are peach and apple orchards, too, as well as gardens so abundant in diverse flowers, vegetables, and fruits that they rival those in Kent, the most exquisitely cultivated region of England.

White-tail deer still roam the diminishing woodlands of Cape Cod. Ospreys, Canada geese, terns, swallows, swans, sparrow hawks, red-winged blackbirds, herons, owls, and a host of other species make Cape Cod their home or stop-off point for a respite while on their annual migratory flights. Within our bays and inlets live and reproduce in abundance horseshoe and fiddler crabs, oysters, quahogs, razor clams, mussels, scallops, periwinkles, and whelks. Out at sea, within sight of shore, are lobsters, swordfish, striped bass, squid, blue fish, sharks (even the great white ones), and the venerable cod. But the crux of this complex and interconnected ecology is the surrounding sea, along with four distinct seasons and the ever-changing weather. The sea surrounds us and it is never too distant from wherever we are on Cape Cod. The sea is moody, unpredictable, fickle. It can give you pleasure and inspiration one day and threaten to take your life the next. As an agent of nature, the sea is indifferent to our expectations and needs, but it is an excellent provider nevertheless.

Millenniums of Human Habitation

No one knows for sure when humans first settled on Cape Cod. There are, however, native people living here today whose lineage on the Cape extends back to when the last Ice Age glacier retreated north and the land once again became acceptable to human habitation, a span of thousands of years. These native people, living together in tribes or clans, were called by many different tribal names. They organized themselves into a broader confederation, or alliance, of tribes that extended far beyond Cape Cod. This alliance was, and still is, known by the name Wampanoag, very much a group of independent states within a nation of self-governing peoples. The Wampanoag nation, in turn, was related to many other nations of native peoples by virtue of a common language, known as Algonquin. They inhabited much of what is now the eastern United States and Canada.

Because of the relatively mild climate and favorable soil conditions, the native people of Cape Cod were highly productive farmers in addition to being hunters and fishermen. Their communal way of life and the distinct

6

culture they developed—arts, music, oral history, and religion—suited them well enough to allow them to live in harmony with nature for millenniums. They placed high value on personal courage, integrity, and friendship, both among themselves and that extended to strangers coming into their midst. They saw themselves not as *in toto* possessors of the land, in a European legalistic sense, but as its trustees. The land was to be used to serve their needs and to be venerated as a blessing from God.

Once the European presence took hold, however, the civilization of the native people on the Cape, as elsewhere on the continent, quickly weakened and faded. The insatiable desire for land on the part of the newcomers, often accompanied by greed and always by legal documents and the force of arms, destroyed the ancient concept of trusteeship and replaced it with absolute ownership according to foreign law. In addition, the colonists brought with them various diseases over which the native population had no immunity nor methods of cure. Their population was decimated. Once-thriving villages became silent and devoid of life. Outraged, in one final attempt to drive out the Europeans, the Wampanoags went to war under the leadership of the charismatic Metacomet, also known as King Philip, son of the great chief Massasoit, who welcomed and protected the first Pilgrims and who helped them to survive. King Philip's war lasted about a year and resulted in slaughter on both sides and ultimate defeat for the native people in 1676, fifty-six years after the landing of the Pilgrims at the place they called Plymouth.

Since that time the native people of Cape Cod have diminished until some believe they had disappeared altogether. Not quite. In Mashpee, for example, they are an important part of the population, as they are at Gay Head on Martha's Vineyard Island. The Wampanoags continue to decide contemporary issues affecting their destiny through their tribal councils. Their annual Mashpee Pow-Wow brings together native peoples from all over the United States and Canada for the purpose of sharing and taking sustenance from their ancient culture.

There is speculation, though no firm evidence, that the first Europeans to sail along the coasts of Cape Cod were Vikings from Scandinavia. There is some remote credibility to this supposition because the Vikings had established a settlement on the northern tip of the island of Newfoundland at what is now L'Anse-aux-Meadows. After traversing the North Atlantic in their long boats and making settlement on Newfoundland, it is entirely plausible for them to have explored the southern coasts of North America. The mystery is why these intrepid explorers did not establish a Viking town in this more congenial climate.

Between A.D. 1500 and 1600 a number of European explorers—notably Portugal's Miguel Corte Real, England's Bartholemew Gosnold, and France's Samuel de Champlain—sailed along Cape Cod's shores. In addition, fishing vessels from Europe, their identity largely unknown to history, came into the area in search of valuable cod. It was not until 1620, however, that English Puritans ("Saints," they called themselves) under the leadership of William Bradford and William Brewster, diverted from their goal of establishing a colony in Virginia by circumstance or the hand of God, made their first landfall in the New World on Cape Cod at Provincetown. They had their first encounter, actually an armed conflict, with the Cape's native people on the beach at Eastham. Continuing across Cape Cod Bay on the *Mayflower*, these Pilgrims stepped ashore on terrain that was to support one of the first, permanent English settlements in North America.

Once Plymouth, their "New Jerusalem," was established and secured, shiploads of additional settlers arrived. Some of these "newcomers" found Plymouth crowded and much of its worthwhile land already taken or selling at too high a price, not unlike today. They moved on to new lands, such as those of Cape Cod. These lands were bought for a pittance or stolen from the native people by a mind-set that considered itself superior and predestined by their deity to bring civilization to a hostile wilderness and prosperity to themselves. These "deals" were sealed on parchment, backed by courts, and enforced by the militia.

With extensive English settlement of Cape Cod gaining momentum ten years after the first Pilgrim landing, the peninsula was amalgamated into Plymouth Colony. Sandwich, Barnstable, Eastham, and Yarmouth became the Cape's first towns. For thirty-seven years Plymouth Colony was administered by a governor residing in the town of Plymouth. In 1657, however, Eastham's Thomas Prence became governor, and the colony's political power now flowed from Cape Cod for several decades. What limited self-governance Plymouth Colony enjoyed was short-lived. King James II attempted to reclaim full and total sovereignty of the American colonies through agents such as Sir Edmond Andros, who was thwarted in carrying out this purpose by the crafty Yankees. The ascension to the throne of William of Orange quieted the restive colonials for awhile; but soon after, Plymouth Colony as such ceased to exist. Plymouth, Massachusetts, Maine, and Nova Scotia colonies were combined into one colony, or province, by royal decree in 1691. The period from 1676 to 1763 saw Cape Cod men fighting in King Philip's War, the so-called French and Indian War, and the British campaigns to wrest control of Canada from the French.

Although Cape Codders considered themselves loyal subjects of the crown, they did not take too kindly to being forced by it and parliament to swallow without protest laws and administrative inconveniences that they considered oppressive and degrading to free men and women. When the Declaration of Independence was proclaimed in 1776, therefore, Cape Codders could be found on both sides—patriots and loyalists. As the bitterness of the conflict grew in intensity, Cape Cod loyalists left their homes and journeyed with others sharing their sympathies north to Canada to begin life anew, while the patriots fought for their liberty under General Washington and his generals. Both the patriots and the loyalists expressed their courage and resolve despite their doing so from different points of view. Years later, when passions had cooled somewhat and tolerance was no longer viewed as treason, some Cape loyalists returned to their home towns, where they resumed life without acquiescence to a foreign king.

No great, epic battles were fought on Cape Cod to rival those at Bunker Hill, Saratoga, Bennington, and Yorktown. In 1779, however, a force of British troops attempted to land at Falmouth. They were sent scurrying back to their ship by local men wielding loaded cannon, primed muskets, and honed cutlasses. During the War for Independence and the War of 1812, Cape Cod towns suffered hardships from British blockades. Cape Codders were prevented from sailing out of their own harbors to fish and to transport their wares. And when captured at sea, some were impressed into manning British ships, often under cruel conditions. When British blockade ships ran low on supplies, it was common practice to send their sailors ashore to take what was needed out of town larders and storehouses, frequently without payment and much to the distress of Cape Codders.

When the wars with Great Britain finally came to an end and both countries entered a sustained period of peace that developed into the closest of friendships, the history of Cape Cod became focused on economics—commercial enterprises and occupations that would provide a decent living and, for the extra diligent, a profit. Right from the beginning, in the early seventeenth century, the Atlantic cod fishery was the big moneymaker and raison d'être for settlement. Being almost completely surrounded by the sea and possessing many fine harbors, usually ice-free in the winter, Cape Cod was a perfect launching pad from which to go out onto the deep waters. A number of Cape Codders fished as far north as the Grand Banks. Some eventually settled in towns and villages throughout the Canadian Maritime provinces and imparted to their culture a bit of Cape Cod. Along with the fishery came the development of such allied industries as sail making, boat building, chandler services, and cartage.

Whaling also began early on Cape Cod. The first settlers found whales that had for no explicable reason beached themselves, as they continue to do in our time. From the blubber the settlers rendered oil, which was used in candle making, as a fuel for lamps, as a lubricant, and for a wide variety of other useful purposes. As the demand for whale oil and other whale products increased, Cape Codders built stouter boats and went after these noble creatures with a frenzy and an eye to good profits. In time the center of the whaling industry shifted from Cape Cod to Nantucket Island

and to New Bedford, but also in time it faded away in all these places due to the large-scale commercialization of fossil fuels.

One important benefit from whaling was that it brought a new person to Cape Cod—the Cape Verdean. During long whaling voyages, typically lasting several years, it was not unusual for discontented, lonely seamen to jump ship, leaving the vessel's master short-handed. The Cape Verde Islands, a Portuguese colony located off the west coast of Africa, were a major resupply point for Yankee whalers. Here the whaling masters were also able to recruit Cape Verdean men to replenish their crews. When the ships came back to their Cape Cod, Nantucket, Martha's Vineyard, and New Bedford ports, many of these Cape Verdean seamen, finding themselves stranded on American shores, elected to stay rather than seek return to their native islands. As a result, the Cape Verdean presence on Cape Cod and in southeastern Massachusetts has existed since the nineteenth century. These industrious people came from one of the most arid archipelagos on the face of this planet, and yet on Cape Cod they became some of our best vegetable and fruit farmers. Today the Cape Verdeans are as indigenous to our communities as the Yankees and the Native Americans.

In addition to the industries of whaling and the fisheries, Cape Codders built speedy packet boats, which became the quickest method of moving goods and people from port to port along the coasts of New England. Cape Codders also became actively involved in the international maritime trade, with some making sizeable fortunes in their journeys throughout the world. Cape Cod's prosperity from these daring, canny ventures can be seen in every one of our towns in the gorgeous homes and estates built by sea captains and land-based merchant investors. They bought the best available life style at the time from the immense profits they earned. Agriculture also contributed to the Cape's economy. Dairy and small crop farms supplied the needs of the local people. The American cranberry-growing and -processing industries began in this region. Cranberry production continues to be an important moneymaker for Cape Codders. Their bogs are familiar features on the Upper and Mid Cape landscapes. The bogs are at their most beautiful in autumn, when the berries, floated on top of water, form acres of brilliant red carpet against deep greens of surrounding woodland and below an ultramarine blue sky. To see this juxtaposition of colors is one of the most memorable visual experiences the beholder can enjoy.

Ecclesiastes 3:1 says, "For everything there is a season, and a time for every purpose under the heaven." And so it was with the traditional way of life on Cape Cod. Although playing a vital role in the forming of America, Cape Cod became kind of a somnolent backwater of the country as other regions pushed, bullied, and built themselves into prominence. Until the advent of large-scale tourism, Cape Cod essentially remained a place of small towns and villages where the Yankee ethos of self-reliance, hard work, religion, neighborliness, thrift, patience, and prudence was the dominant value. In essence Cape Cod was a series of Thornton Wilder's *Our Towns*. Deception and fraud existed, of course, but to a lesser degree than they did wherever life moved along at a more frenetic pace.

In a very real sense those frenzies, pressures, and stresses that plagued Americans in other parts of the country were responsible for the resurgence of Cape Cod. Because Cape Cod retained the attractiveness and the values of America's past in addition to the allures of a gentle climate and seashore, the movers and shakers of this country discovered that they could renew both their spirits and bodies here. Cape Cod became synonymous with relaxation, of letting the wounds heal and the cobwebs fall away; of enjoying friends without many of the stifling, formal conventions of urban society; and of experiencing the magnificent natural environment of the Cape. Cape Cod took on a new luster and became even more fashionable when John F. Kennedy was elected president of the United States and the family compound in Hyannisport became the Summer White House in the early 1960s.

Also attracted to Cape Cod during the summer were artists, writers, actors, philosophers, and scientists. The creatives and the intellectuals came not only to lounge on the beach or in hammocks while sipping gin and tonics but to produce ideas of substantial value. Some of America's greatest talents received inspiration for their work on the Cape. The scientist Louis Agassiz and playwright Eugene O'Neill are but two of many such individuals. With both the affluent and the intellectual giving an enthusiastic imprimatur to summertime on the Cape, others of more modest bank accounts and/or abilities discovered this peninsula to be their most favorite vacation place as well. Cape Cod became accessible to the general public with the building of better highways and widespread automobile ownership. With more people coming onto the Cape, more places of accommodation, restaurants, attractions, entertainments, gift shops, and diversions were developed to serve their needs.

Along with the transformation of Cape Cod into a popular vacationland, another phenomenon took hold. As people fell in love with the natural and human environment of the Cape during the summer, many decided that *this* was the place to spend their retirement years. This phenomenon has not abated. Each year retirees settle in by the thousands, and the permanent population of the Cape continues to grow, as do the various kinds of businesses and professions that serve their needs. In addition to the retirees, the young and middle aged, representing a wide range of professions, crafts, and occupations, have moved onto the Cape. There is also an increasing population of top-level business executives who reside year-round on the Cape but who commute to offices in Boston and New York City. Since the turn of the century, the real estate and land-development businesses have enjoyed an upward curve in sales and prices thanks to this influx. That rose-festooned Cape Cod cottage in Chatham that cost $20,000 a couple of decades ago now goes for at least a quarter million dollars. Those who bought low and held on have surely profited.

In the not-too-distant past, Cape Codders were a relatively homogeneous breed in terms of ethnicity, religion, attitudes, and family longevity on this peninsula. They were the overwhelming majority, and their culture dominated. The typical Cape Codder was a Republican Protestant who made a living at a small entrepreneurial operation. Today's Cape Codders are far more diverse. Their forefathers were Portuguese, Greek, Quebec-French, Polish, Italian, and Irish; they were African and Asian. And residents today are Roman Catholic, Jewish, Mormon, Baptist, Episcopalian, and Greek Orthodox. The majority of Cape Codders now tend to vote Democratic rather than Republican. The Cape Cod ethos has changed so radically that the region now includes one of the country's largest gay communities (at Provincetown), enclaves of million-dollar-plus homes such as those at Oyster Harbors, some of the finest scientific minds in the world doing oceanographic and biological research at Woods Hole, and one of the most active military installations on the eastern seaboard, Otis Air Force base. Cape Cod's "Yeoman" villages of the past are gone, but their glowing nostalgia and lovely appearance remain. The pace of living is faster now, and the roads can get as crowded, slow moving, and grid-locked as in any urban area. And yet one can find places throughout the Cape that are isolated, where there are only the sounds of wind and sea, where beaches seem to extend into distance forever, and where one can confront oneself alone and feel at peace.

The Four Seasons of Cape Cod

Cape Cod is a favorite vacation destination in all four seasons of the year. Holiday weekends throughout the year draw large numbers of visitors. For example, many people have made it their tradition to spend the Thanksgiving and Christmas holidays on the Cape because its early American atmosphere creates the perfect setting and mood. The holiday weekends of Memorial Day, Fourth of July, Labor Day, and Columbus Day are peak periods within peak periods. Because of our relatively mild climate in fall, winter and spring, Cape Cod has become well known for offering year-round golf, an unexpected treat for those who consider New England woefully frigid.

The summer season begins in mid-May and concludes around mid-September, with July and August being the peak months. At the height of summer, temperatures seldom rise above 80°F, although we have a few dog days to remind us that we have not been entirely absolved by nature. We have a generous share of perfect beach weather—bright skies, fluffy clouds, warm water, and comfortable temperatures. We also have "pea-soup" foggy days, however, when figures on the beach become ghostly apparitions in the mist. While we're having foggy days along the coast, though, it's usually oppressively hot, hazy, and humid well inland. Ocean water for swimming is warmest from August to the end of September. There are many of us who continue taking our daily dip in the briny through October. Every kind of leisure-time activity takes place on the Cape during the summer—swimming, boating, surfing, golf, tennis, base-ball, beachcombing, biking, hiking, picnics, fishing, and so on. People come to the Cape to relax, to be themselves, and to shed many of the hangups and formalities that beset them back home.

Unless you are going to some swank affairs, comfortable, casual clothing is all you need to bring—shorts, polo shirts, cotton sweaters, sports jack-ets, light dresses, bathing suits, plus some foul-weather gear (rain jacket and hat). The best restaurants on the Cape like to see men come in wear-ing jackets, but ties are optional; light-fabric skirts, dresses, or trousers, in any pattern or style, are right for women. Most places of business will not allow you in their establishments with bare feet; the same is true for bare-chested men. The churches of Cape Cod would prefer it if women did not come to service wearing short-shorts.

Autumn on Cape Cod is perhaps its most prized time. The weather is usually mild. The water is still warm enough for swimming. The atmos-phere is usually crystal clear and invigorating. The sky and the ocean are rich shades of blue. The flora of the Cape becomes a feast for the eyes in its array of reds, yellow, and oranges. There are fewer people on the Cape, and you thus have more elbow room and less competition for tables at favorite restaurants. The golf links are at their best and so is the sailing. Most places of accommodation lower their prices considerably, and there are sales and bargains everywhere. If you liked the Cape in summer, you'll adore it in autumn. The Thanksgiving holiday has special meaning on the Cape because the very first one in America was celebrated at Province-town. Although the Pilgrims had their first Thanksgiving feast in nearby Plymouth, the first prayers of thanksgiving were offered by them in 1620 at Provincetown before they landed at Plymouth. What could be better than enjoying your Thanksgiving Day feast at an old Cape Cod inn with all the trimmings both in terms of food and heritage. Clothing for a Cape Autumn should also include warm sweaters, a windbreaker, and gloves.

It used to be the perception among outsiders that winter was the Cape's somnolent time, when, seemingly, things and people went into hibernation. While it is certainly true that much of nature goes to sleep in winter, however, this season has traditionally been a highly productive time for the Yankees (real and pseudo) of Cape Cod. It's when we get a chance to do those things we weren't able to do at other times. And our towns and villages are far from being quiet. There are enough social, cultural, civic, sporting, and educational events going on every day to exhaust even the most energetic individual.

If you've ever wanted to walk for miles on a beach totally empty of humans, with a strong wind to your back and the crashing surf to your side, this is the time to come to the Cape. The clarity of light during the winter months is superb. If you need to get away from the stress of your job and city, the Cape in winter will help renew you. Enough fine places of accommodation and restaurants are open to take care of your needs. Just bring warm clothes, including a good parka, and a camera to capture those beautiful facets of Cape Cod that are denied to those who just come here in the summer.

Fickle is the word that best describes spring on Cape Cod. Sometimes spring comes early, sometimes late. Sometimes it seems to elude us all together. The only thing you can count on from a Cape Cod spring is its unpredictability. In April many of the places of accommodation and restaurants that closed up for the winter begin reopening. Along with migratory birds, tourists and residents who spend the winter months in Florida begin arriving with the sprouting up of crocuses and tulips. You see more people on the golf links and more boats going into the water. In a very real sense mid-May is the start of Cape Cod's "new year," when we year-round folks smile a bit more and anticipate the crazy, frenetic season when our narrow peninsula once again welcomes visitors from every state in the Union, every province of Canada, and scores of countries around the globe. We shed our parkas, take out our bathing suits, and figure out which quick-fix diet will get us back into shape with some semblance of self-respect.

Living, Retiring, and Working on Cape Cod

It is inevitable. People such as I (and perhaps it will happen to you) come to Cape Cod, fall in love with the place, and then make plans to move and live here permanently. Since the end of World War II and particularly since the interstate-highway system opened up the country to fast, easy travel, thousands have come here annually seeking their exclusive piece of Cape Cod. The influx has not abated. Population growth on Cape Cod has produced advantages: a greater variety, quantity, and quality of services; a more diverse, affluent, and better educated population; increased commercial and business activities and opportunities; improved schools and medical facilities; and a broader selection of cultural activities. The disadvantages include higher real estate prices, a labor shortage, an increasing demand on town services (water, roads, sewage, police, fire, etc.), and traffic congestion.

Perhaps the most serious impact on the Cape has been the continual rise in real estate prices. Little affordable housing, or homes selling between $90,000 and $125,000, is being built on the Cape. Until 1987 Cape Cod homes appreciated at an annual rate of around 40 percent, but this rate has slowed appreciably for the time being. Most new homes are priced from $250,000 and up. Desirable land is scarce and selling as high as Jacob's Ladder. On the other hand, once you buy property on the Cape, you have a solid investment that will most likely continue to increase in value. Condominiums and vacation homes are also going up throughout the Cape. There are few real estate bargains to be found, but they do exist if you take time to ferret them out.

Just as pilgrims go to Mecca, retirees go to the Cape. The winter climate is relatively mild, and the life style is very comfortable, though not inexpensive. You'll find most of the services you need on the Cape—doctors, dentists, lawyers, and stockbrokers. There are all kinds of educational and cultural programs in which to participate. There are newcomers' clubs, church socials, and fraternal lodges. Every Cape Cod town has agencies and organizations that serve the needs of retired people. Many local businesses have jobs for retirees, and there are countless opportunities for volunteering your talents to assist others and to help improve the quality of life in your town.

The economy is primarily based on service industries. There is a need for more doctors in every specialty, nurses, teachers, carpenters, plumbers, and electricians. The tourist and retail industries are always short of good help, but wages for these jobs are moderate, and the cost of living is high. Because of the building boom, there have been many job openings in the construction trades. The Cape has always attracted entrepreneurs, those who create new businesses or become self-employed as artists, craftspersons, writers, and business consultants. If you are interested in coming to live and work on Cape Cod, subscribe to the *Cape Cod Times*, 775–1200, 319 Main Street in Hyannis. This paper is published every day of the week and lists job openings, real estate for sale and rent, and an in-depth look at what life on Cape Cod is really like through all the seasons of the year.

Cape Cod for Canadian and British Visitors

Among our most favorite visitors are Canadians. They have been coming to the charming villages and warm waters of Cape Cod since the beginning of tourism here. Even before then, Canadian and Cape Cod fishermen and mariners were frequent visitors in each other's harbors. In fact many towns and villages in the Canadian Maritime Provinces (Nova Scotia, New Brunswick, and Prince Edward Island) were either settled by Cape Cod families or gained in population from them in the seventeenth and eighteenth centuries. In addition some Cape Cod loyalists, those siding with the British crown during the American Revolution, settled in the Canadian Maritimes, Quebec, and Ontario.

There are other ties that bind. During the nineteenth and twentieth centuries, thousands of French-Canadians (Quebecois) settled in New England mill towns and factory cities. Some of their American-born progeny established businesses on Cape Cod or came to work here in many different professions and occupations. The same can be said for thousands of English-speaking Canadians who also came to work in New England, known to them as "The Boston States."

If you are interested in your family's genealogy, local historical societies will help you trace your roots on Cape Cod. Today it is quite common to see autos bearing license plates from most of the Canadian provinces. Many businesses catering to tourists fly the Canadian maple leaf flag alongside our stars and stripes. Unfortunately, Canadian money is not accepted here, although Canadian currency can be exchanged for U.S. dollars on Cape Cod at branches of the Bank of Boston and other major banks. Canadians are not required to carry passports when entering the United States unless they are landed immigrants holding other countries' passports.

More and more people from the United Kingdom are coming to Cape Cod for vacations. British accents are heard in every town and village. Present currency-exchange rates definitely favor a visit to the "Old Colony." Although Cape Codders were ardent revolutionaries and builders of the United States, strong Anglophilia has always existed on this hook-shaped peninsula, perhaps more so today than before. The Union Jack is a common sight; a scenic highway commemorates the "Old King," Charles II; there is an inn named after Queen Anne; there are towns named after their counterparts in England; steak and kidney pie, fish and chips, and Bass Ale are on the menus at a number of eateries. If you are interested in British history, you'll find a substantial amount of it on Cape Cod; for we belonged to the crown for 156 years, not an inconsequential period of time. British subjects must carry passports for travel in this country.

Visiting Cape Cod

Getting the Most Value out of Your Cape Vacation

The information provided in this guide has been structured so that it is easy to use and quick to get to when you need to know something fast. For example, two of the most important areas of concern for travelers are where to stay and where to eat. Recommendations of accommodations and restaurants are listed immediately after a description of each town. Categories such as beaches, entertainment, and sports activities, however, have separate listings that reveal at a glance the full range of options available to you on Cape Cod. The Index at the end of this book is also a quick, convenient locator of information. Specific dollars-and-cents information is not given in this guide because it is probable that such figures will not be accurate by the time you read this book. Your home-town travel agent keeps abreast with changes in prices and will be happy to provide you with current figures to make a vacation budget for Cape Cod. The most direct way to know what it will cost is to contact the places of accommodation and other businesses listed in these pages. Addresses and telephone numbers have been provided herein for that purpose.

The majority of people who come to Cape Cod do so as independent travelers. A large percentage, however, enjoy the Cape's many attractions through package tours that provide motor-coach transportation, lodging, meals, admissions, and other services. A package usually saves you money and provides many conveniences and excellent services. You can arrange for Cape Cod touring packages through your home-town travel agent. The following companies are among the best in providing vacation packages to Cape Cod: Brennan Tours, Country Inn Tours, Maupintour, Presley Tours, and Tauck Tours.

Practical Information

Telephone Area Codes: Until July 1988, all Cape Cod towns have (617) as their telephone area code. After July 1988, all Cape Cod towns have (508) as their area code.

Seat Belts: It is the law in the Commonwealth of Massachusetts that all children riding in motor vehicles be secured by seat/shoulder belts. A fine will be imposed for noncompliance. There is no seat-belt law in Massachusetts regarding adults.

Motorcycle Helmets: It is Massachusetts law, enforced by fines, that all persons driving/riding motorcycles wear safety helmets.

Liquor Purchase & Use: It is the law in Massachusetts that persons purchasing liquor in retail outlets, lounges, taverns, restaurants, and the like must be at least twenty-one years of age. If there is doubt about your age, you will be asked to supply legal proof. Massachusetts has strict laws regarding the legal drinking age and imposes penalties on both the purchaser and the seller. The laws are also severe for driving under the influence of liquor or chemicals.

Banking: Cape Cod banks are open daily from 9:00 A.M. to 3:00 P.M., and many branches have extended weekday hours and hours on Saturday. Many banks have automated teller machines. Most cash traveler's checks and provide cash advances on major credit cards. Personal checks can be cashed with proper identification (for example, a major credit card).

Credit Cards or Cash: Visa, MasterCard, and their international equivalents are widely accepted throughout Cape Cod. American Express is also accepted at many establishments. Diners Club, Carte Blanche, and Discover cards are accepted but not as widely as the other three. Some stores, places of accommodation, and restaurants, however, do business on a "cash only" (including traveler's checks) basis. When in doubt, ask before you purchase.

Business Hours: Business hours on Cape Cod typically run from 8:30 or 9:00 A.M. to 4:30 or 5:00 P.M. Retail stores are open from 9:30 or 10:00 A.M. to 6:00 P.M. Many retail stores, however, extend their hours into the evening and are open on Sundays. There are also some supermarkets and convenience stores that operate twenty-four hours a day every day.

Religious Services: Most religious groups have churches, temples, or meeting houses on Cape Cod, and visitors are most welcome to attend their services.

Tipping: For a restaurant bill, excluding the state tax, 15 to 20 percent is appropriate; for chamber maids, two to three dollars per night is fine. Leave small tips for students working in various establishments.

Rental Cars: Hertz, Avis, and National provide rental services in large communities such as Falmouth, Hyannis, and Provincetown.

Accommodations

The system for determining the cost of accommodations used in this guide is as follows: under $50 a night for a double = *Inexpensive;* up to $100 a night for a double = *Moderate;* more than $100 a night for a double = *Expensive.* Single accommodations tend to run about 10 percent less than doubles, but many places do not discount for singles during the high season.

Wicker on front porches, geraniums hanging from rafters, and white picket fences are as characteristic of Cape Cod as fishing boats, ancient anchors and old school houses.

VISITING CAPE COD

High season for most places of accommodation on the Cape is approximately from mid-June to mid-September, although a number of them advertise a lower "off-season" until the beginning of July and do so again after Labor Day. For example, it is not unusual to get a double in a very nice motel in off-season for thirty dollars a night plus tax. July and August are the busiest months. Advance reservations at the best inns, resorts, motels, and B&Bs are essential during those months, although not all beds are taken during this busy period by any means. Many establishments require a deposit in advance and/or major credit card information.

During high season most every place of accommodation charges its top rates. When making reservations, be sure to ask about packages that can provide lower rates and extra services, meal discounts, and various amenities as incentives: A.A.R.P. and auto-club discounts; special rates for children; and meal plans. Your local travel agent is your best source of assistance in recommending appropriate places of accommodation to fit your budget and to make reservations for you. There is no extra cost in using a travel agent, except for extraordinary services.

The Cape Cod Chamber of Commerce will be happy to supply you with information about accommodations on the Cape. Contact the chamber at 362–3225 or write to them at Hyannis, MA 02601.

The following reservation agencies (their telephone numbers are in parentheses) can assist you in booking Bed & Breakfast places on Cape Cod: B&B House Guests–Cape Cod, Box AR, Dennis, MA 02638 (398–0787); Orleans Bed & Breakfast Associates, P.O. Box 1312, Orleans, MA 02360 (255–3824); Bed & Breakfast Cape Cod, P.O. Box 341, West Hyannisport, MA 02672 (775–2772).

Cottages and homes close to beaches are available for rent throughout Cape Cod during the summer season. The cost of renting a fine, fully furnished home with a water view at peak season can range from $1,000 to more than $2,000 a week. Homes available during the months of May, June, September, and October can rent for less. There is also a large selection of more modest homes and cottages that rent from $350 to $1,000 per week, with lower rates in off-season. Most rentals are arranged through real estate agencies located in the various towns and villages on Cape Cod. Your travel agent might have a listing of some rentals, or you are welcome to contact the Cape Cod Board of Realtors, Inc., 450 Station Avenue, South Yarmouth, MA 02664 (394–2277). While the board cannot recommend any specific agency, the folks there will send you a complete roster of member agencies from which to select.

A few more tips: The majority of places of accommodation do not accept pets; during July and August, a number of motor inns require minimum stays of about three days and firm reservations with deposits; most cottages are rented by the week in the high season.

Dining

The restaurants listed in this guide have been selected on the basis of the quality of their food, service, and reputation. They are rated on the basis of two persons dining together at the evening meal; the cost of drinks, wine, tips, and taxes are not factored into this rating, just the food. A restaurant is rated *Inexpensive* if a meal for two totals less than $25; *Moderate* if it costs up to $50; and *Expensive* if it costs more than $50.

You can save money by taking advantage of lower cost "early bird specials" offered by many Cape Cod restaurants. These specials are usually served for an hour starting at around 5:30 P.M. or when the restaurant first opens for dinner. If you are traveling with children, be sure to ask for special kids' menus; they feature appealing dishes that usually cost less than those on the regular menu.

Advance reservations are a must at many Cape Cod restaurants, particularly during the months of July and August, as the Cape's best restaurants are booked even in the off-season. There are also many popular places that accept guests only on a first come–first served basis. To avoid long lines at these restaurants, arrive early.

A few places don't accept credit cards, and others take only certain ones. American Express, Visa, and MasterCard and their international equivalents are most commonly accepted on the Cape.

You'll find almost every kind of cuisine on Cape Cod—continental, North American, ethnic, and exotic. We are fortunate to have a goodly share of internationally acclaimed chefs and relatively unknown ones who are wowing the palates of gourmets and gourmands with their creativity and excellence. Fresh seafood reigns supreme on the menus of most Cape Cod dining places—New England lobster, oysters, clams, quahogs, swordfish, halibut, Boston scrod, Mako shark, and blue fish. If you find Mako shark on the menu, do give it a try. It's one of the most delectable seafoods going, considered by many to be far better than swordfish.

Attractions

Admission to attractions in this guide are designated by the self-explanatory terms—*Admission Charged, Free,* or *Donation Accepted.* Many attractions charging admission offer lower rates for senior citizens, children, and groups.

Cape Cod is well endowed with museums; historic homes, churches, and buildings; special collections; libraries; rides and cruises; and amusements. Attractions giving testimony to the natural and the early human history of this peninsula and to the beginnings of America should receive top priority on your itinerary. Every Cape town and village is an open history book to be seen, studied, and absorbed.

Sources of Information

The following organizations will be happy to provide you with free information about accommodations, dining, attractions, beaches, and special events to help you enjoy your Cape Cod vacation:

New England Vacation Center
International Building,
Concourse 2,
Rockefeller Center
630 Fifth Avenue
New York, NY 10020
(212) 307-5780

Cape Cod Chamber of Commerce
Junction of Routes 6 and 132;
open all year
Hyannis, MA
362-3225

Information Booth at Sagamore
Rotary;
open daily from Memorial Day
to Labor Day
888-2438

Cape Cod National
Seashore Headquarters
Marconi Station
in South Wellfleet,
off Route 6
349-3785

Greater Bourne/
Sandwich Chamber of Commerce
165 State Road
at Sagamore Beach
888-6202

Falmouth Chamber of Commerce
Academy Lane
in center Falmouth
548-8500

Yarmouth Chamber of Commerce
Route 28
in South Yarmouth
398-5311

Harwich Chamber of Commerce
Main Street
Harwich Port, MA
432-1600

Chatham Chamber of Commerce
Main Street
945-0342

Brewster Board of Trade
896-5713; ask for "President"

Orleans Information Booth
Eldredge Parkway
255-1386

Eastham Information Booth
Route 6 near Cape Cod
National Seashore entrance
255-3444

Wellfleet Chamber of Commerce
P.O. Box 571, Route 6
Wellfleet, MA 02667
349-2500

Truro Chamber of Commerce
P.O. Box 26,
Route 6 and Head of
Meadow Road
North Truro, MA 02652
487-1288, 487-9208

Mashpee Information Center
Mashpee Rotary,
Route 28
477–0792

Hyannis Chamber of Commerce
319 Barnstable Road
775–2201

Dennis Chamber of Commerce
Route 28 at Route 134
in Dennis Port
398–3568

Provincetown Chamber of Commerce
P.O. Box 1017,
307 Commercial Street
Provincetown, MA 02657
487–9007

Division of Tourism
Massachusetts Department
of Commerce and Development
100 Cambridge Street
Boston, MA 02202
727–3201

For the convenience of travelers using Route 3 southbound from Boston, there is a Tourism Information Center, 746–1150, located in Plymouth at a rest-and-picnic plaza with easy access on and off this primary road to the Cape. There is also an information center on I-495 just before you come to the Bourne Bridge.

Publications

The following publications are excellent sources of information about what's happening on Cape Cod throughout the year:

The Cape Cod Times, daily and Sunday newspaper, 319 Main Street, Hyannis, MA 02601, 775–1200
Cape Cod Compass, magazine, P.O. Box 375, 935 Main Street, Chatham, MA 02633, 945–3542
Cape Cod Life, magazine, P.O. Box 222, Osterville, MA 02655, 428–5706

The following books will also be helpful in touring and appreciating Cape Cod:

Cape Cod Locator. J. W. Davenport, published by First Impressions; available at stores throughout Cape Cod
Cape Cod Atlas. Published by Butterworth; available throughout Cape Cod
Names of the Land: Cape Cod, Nantucket, Martha's Vineyard, and the Elizabeth Islands. Eugene Green and William Sachse, published by Globe Pequot Press
Cape Cod—A Guide. Donald Wood, published by Little Brown; an excellent source for brief histories of Cape Cod towns
Cape Cod, Henry David Thoreau; *The Outermost House,* Henry Beston; the two great classics about our peninsula

25

Traveling To and Around the Cape

By Car

Most visitors to Cape Cod come by private auto, recreational vehicle, van, or truck. Before the super highway was built, the car ride from Boston to Hyannis could take from four to seven hours, depending on traffic. You came not for the day, as is the case now for many, but to stay for several days or for the entire summer season. Today, the trip can be done in two hours or less, except on weekends and holidays, when it seems as if the entire world is clogging the road to the Cape.

The U.S. interstate-highway system conveniently and quickly connects Cape Cod to everywhere in the country and to the provinces of Canada. If you are traveling from southern Connecticut, New York City, New Jersey, southern Pennsylvania, Delaware, Maryland, Washington D.C., Virginia, and points south and west, take the interstate highways to I-95 North. Continue on I-95 to Providence, Rhode Island. At Providence the highway divides—I-95 continues north to Boston; I-195 heads east to Cape Cod while passing through the historic cities of Fall River and New Bedford in Massachusetts. There are signs along the way, so you won't get lost, as well as plenty of motorist services (restaurants, gas, and motels) at locations off the highway. At the town of East Wareham, I-195 connects with I-495, which takes you to the Cape Cod Canal and the Bourne and Sagamore bridges crossing over to the Cape. This new link was completed in the summer of 1987. It bypasses the lights and business congestion on Route 6 in Wareham and Buzzards Bay.

If your routing (coming from the north or northwest I-495, I-95, I-93, and U.S. Route #1) takes you through or around Boston, get onto State Highway #3 South, which will take you all the way to the Sagamore Bridge at the Cape Cod Canal. Another alternative, if coming from the west and northwest, is to take I-495 South to the Cape Cod Canal at the Bourne and Sagamore Bridges.

Bourne Bridge, at the southwest end of the canal, and Sagamore Bridge, at its northeast end, are the only two land accesses onto the Cape. Bourne Bridge connects with Route 28, which goes along Buzzards Bay and the southern coast of Cape Cod to Orleans. Sagamore Bridge connects with the Mid-Cape Highway, Route 6, which is the Cape's fast road all the way from the canal to Provincetown. Route 6 is a divided, four-lane highway from the canal to Dennis, at which point it becomes a two laner; it broadens in stretches from Orleans to Provincetown. Roads parallel the canal and connect Routes 28, 6, and also 6A, which is the scenic highway along the north coast of the Cape.

The best way to make sense out of these routings is to get a detailed road map of New England at a local gas station or bookshop or from your auto club (AAA, ALA, etc.); or buy the inexpensive Rand McNally *Road Atlas*, which comes in handy wherever you travel in North America. Hyannis, our largest community, is located approximately in the center of Cape Cod. It is 245 miles from New York City; 331 miles from Philadelphia; 470 miles from Washington, D.C.; 355 miles from Montreal; 622 miles from Toronto; 483 miles from Ottawa; 468 from Quebec City; 77 miles from Boston; and 77 miles from Providence.

By Air

Regularly scheduled, commercial air service to and from Hyannis is, at this writing, nothing to cheer about. Airline deregulation and the consolidation of smaller companies into large ones has made Cape Cod an orphan port in the transportation web. Considering the amount of traffic that exists here—business people and others who need to fly between the Cape and Boston and New York City—the quality of air-transport service should be far better than it is. As an alternative, the Plymouth and Brockton Bus Company provides frequent express service between Hyannis and Sagamore to Boston and Logan International Airport, which most of us use when taking flights throughout the country and internationally; call 775–5524 for information. Bonanza Bus Lines also has express service between Woods Hole, Falmouth, and Logan Airport; call 548–7588.

Barnstable Municipal Airport (commercial and private flights), 775–2020, is located off of Route 132 and the Airport Rotary in Hyannis. The following airlines provide service to and from this airport: Delta Business Express, (800) 345–3400, serving Boston and New York City; Continental Express, (800) 525–0280, connecting with flights in the Continental system; and Tri-Air, 771–4888, offering service to Nantucket and Martha's Vineyard, as does Nantucket Airlines, (800) 635–8787. Rental-car agencies at the airport are: Avis, (800) 331–1212; Hertz, (800) 654–3131; and National, (800) 227–7368.

Provincetown Municipal Airport (commercial and private flights) hosts Continental Express, 487–0241, which provides year-round Boston service. Hertz rental cars, (800) 645–3131, are available here. Other air terminals in the vicinity are Cape Cod Airport in Marstons Mills (private flights), 428–8732; Chatham Municipal Airport (private fights), 945–9000; and Falmouth Airport (private flights), 548–9163.

By Rail

It was the train that opened up Cape Cod to tourism. Families who could afford long summer stays at the grand resort hotels or huge private homes, euphemistically called "cottages," that sprung up along our coasts like asparagus in spring came by steam-driven train from Boston, Hartford, New York City, Philadelphia, Washington, and many other cities. They came to escape the oppressive heat and humidity, and on Cape Cod they found relief in cool breezes and pleasant beaches. Enclaves of "high society" quickly formed and coalesced in what had been simple yeoman villages. Through word of mouth the attributes of the Cape rapidly spread, and soon our peninsula was transformed. The time of the trains ended, and they were replaced by autos, buses, and airplanes. It appeared as if riding the rails to Cape Cod had become part of nostalgia. For train enthusiasts and those tired of boring highways and airports, however, all is not lost. As a matter of fact, things are beginning to look bright for us.

AMTRAK Cape Codder has weekend direct rail service to Hyannis from Washington, Baltimore, Philadelphia, New York City, Stamford, and New Haven. This service operates from the end of May to mid-September. Call (800) USA–RAIL for full information on schedules, fares, and reservations. Daily rail service throughout the year from points west to Boston is available on AMTRAK; Bonanza (Falmouth and Woods Hole) and Plymouth & Brockton (Sagamore and Hyannis) bus services provide transportation from there to Cape Cod.

The Cape Cod and Hyannis Railroad has daily service between Boston and Hyannis from mid-May to mid-October. Take the MBTA Rapid Transit Line (the subway) from the city to its Braintree station. Here you catch the train for Hyannis, arriving at the depot located at the east end of Main Street in Hyannis. Call 771–1145 for schedule and fare information.

By Bus

Bus service to Cape Cod from major cities is excellent. Bonanza Bus Lines/Greyhound has daily service to Falmouth and Woods Hole from New York City, Boston (including Boston's Logan International Airport), and many other cities. For schedule information, call New York City, (212) 564–8484; Falmouth, 548–7588; or Woods Hole, 548–5011.

Plymouth & Brockton also has a daily schedule from Boston to Sagamore and Hyannis and offers express service to and from Logan International Airport. For information, call 775–5524 in Hyannis.

Cape Cod Bus Lines, 775–5524, provides service from Hyannis to Provincetown. The B-Bus, 548–0333, operates between Falmouth and Hyannis, Monday through Friday.

By Boat

Bay State and Provincetown Cruises, 487–1741, provides ferry service from Boston to Provincetown daily during the summer and on weekends during the off-season.

The Steamship Authority, 540–2022, carries passengers and vehicles year-round between Hyannis, Nantucket, and Vineyard Haven on Martha's Vineyard and during the summer between Nantucket and Woods Hole. The *Island Queen*, 548–4800, carries passengers and bikes from Oak Bluffs on Martha's Vineyard to Falmouth Heights during the summer. The Hy-Line, 775–7185, carries passengers and bikes from Oak Bluffs to Hyannis during the summer.

The truly regal way of coming to Cape Cod is to sail in on your own yacht. Cape Cod is a seafaring part of America, and its necklace of harbors, many offering marina, chandler, and repair services, is open to the visiting yachtsman. Consult your cruising guides for locations, telephone numbers, harbormasters, and regulations. Also check with your hometown yacht club as to whether it has reciprocal agreements with clubs on the Cape.

Access to the Cape

Because the canal separates our peninsula from the Massachusetts mainland, Cape Cod is virtually an island. There are only two accesses for cars, buses, and trucks: Sagamore Bridge on the north end and Bourne Bridge at the south. Highways parallel both sides of the canal and provide access to both bridges—Route 3 on the Cape Cod side and Route 6 on the mainland side. A third bridge, in the Bourne area, provides a crossover for trains.

The Cape's primary highways are Route 6 and Route 28. Route 6 is also called the Mid-Cape Highway. It runs the entire length of the Cape from the Sagamore Bridge all the way to Provincetown. From the Sagamore Bridge to Dennis, Route 6 is a four-lane, divided expressway providing easy access to towns along the way. It's the fast-track road to Hyannis, Orleans, and Provincetown. From Dennis to Provincetown the road narrows to two lands. This section can be dangerous, so be careful when passing and put on your headlights for safety. Route 28 goes from the Bourne Bridge, along the Cape's southern coast, to Orleans. The section from Bourne to Falmouth is a four-lane, divided expressway, with access to Otis Air Force Base and Camp Edwards at the Otis rotary. At Falmouth it becomes a narrow, two-lane road going through the various towns along this coast. Route 28 is Cape Cod's busiest highway, and, during the summer season, you should expect heavy, slow traffic everywhere.

VISITING CAPE COD

Alternate routes 6A and 28A are the Cape's main scenic highways. Route 28A from the Otis rotary to Falmouth is a lovely drive through villages on the southwest coast. Route 6A from Sandwich to Provincetown, called "The Old King's Highway," is considered by most travelers our best road for experiencing the true essence of Cape Cod. It is largely devoid of the concentrated commercialization that exists on Route 28. The Cape's principal north/south roads are Route 130 from Sandwich to Mashpee, Route 149 from West Barnstable to Cotuit, Route 132 from Barnstable to Hyannis, Route 134 from Dennis to Yarmouth, Route 124 from Brewster to Harwich, Route 137 from Brewster to Chatham, and Route 39 from Harwich to Orleans.

The popularity of Cape Cod has made driving here, to put it mildly, frequently frightful. If you can cope with the heavy traffic in some areas, however, Cape Cod will be an exceedingly rewarding vacation place. Cape traffic is heaviest from mid-May to mid-October. Route 28 is very busy throughout the year. Getting onto the Cape, expect traffic back-ups starting Friday afternoon and continuing through Saturday afternoon. Getting off the Cape, expect delays starting after lunch on Sunday and continuing well into the evening. Allow for extended hours beyond these periods during long holiday weekends. Try to avoid peak traffic periods by coming and going at other times during the day or night. During the summer season, expect congestion just about everywhere.

Expect, too, that every driver around you is equally frustrated and impatient and that some will do foolish things like going through red lights or stop and yield signs. Therefore, drive defensively at all times. Watch out for vehicles coming out of side streets and from the many businesses along your route. Be courteous by allowing vehicles to enter the line of traffic from side areas; it's commonly done on the Cape as a matter of courtesy and survival. While in the centers of villages, be aware that pedestrians have the right of way at crosswalks; you must stop and let them pass. While on the road, watch out for bikers, kids, dogs, hikers, and people in wheelchairs. As there are many elderly drivers on the Cape, be patient with the slow pace of some. Most of our roads have enough curves to cross a sea captain's eyes and many blind spots as well. Passing a slow mover when the way ahead is not clear can be deadly. Always wear seat belts. Make sure you feed the parking meters. The people who give out tickets are especially zealous with ticketing the tardy in summer. It's one of our profitable growth industries.

Cape Cod has many places—package stores, lounges, and restaurants— that sell liquor. Use liquor wisely and never drive under its influence. The legal age for drinking is twenty-one, and most places will ask you to verify your age. Have a designated driver on hand if you overdo it. Massachusetts strictly enforces its drunk-driving laws with heavy penalties and with intensive police surveillance. Using good sense and a great deal of patience, avoiding stress while driving on Cape Cod roads, will help make your vacation here a pleasure to remember.

If you are biking Cape Cod, use designated bike trails, which will take you just about anywhere on the peninsula (see page 50). Whenever possible, avoid roads with heavy traffic and keep well to the side. There is no biking on Route 6, the Mid-Cape Highway. Biking has become such a popular activity that the probability of riders and motor vehicles colliding on busy roads is quite high, and accidents do happen. Most secondary roads are safe for bikers and offer inspiring scenery and fewer hazards. Watch out for pedestrians while riding in villages. Common sense and basic safety procedures will make biking Cape Cod great fun.

There is limited bus transportation on Cape Cod (see "By Bus" section of this chapter). Many villages have taxi services. Limousines with chauffeurs can be rented in Falmouth and Hyannis.

Traveling to Martha's Vineyard and Nantucket

Year-round ferry service to Martha's Vineyard (Vineyard Haven) and summer service to Nantucket is available at Woods Hole (via Route 28 to Falmouth) from the Steamship Authority (540–2022), P.O. Box 284, Dept. 2H, Woods Hole, MA 02543. Advance reservations for vehicles are required; during the summer they are essential well in advance. Passengers on foot or with bikes usually can board without advance reservations. The Steamship Authority also operates year-round service to Nantucket from its terminal in Hyannis. Ferry parking and shuttle-bus service to and from the Woods Hole terminal are available near the terminal (usually full in high season), on Palmer Avenue, and one-quarter mile north of Main Street in Falmouth. The *Island Queen* provides daily service to Martha's Vineyard (Oak Bluffs) from the end of May to mid-October; it takes passengers and bikes but no vehicles. The terminal is located at Falmouth Harbor, 548–4800; parking is available nearby. In Hyannis the Hy-Line company has a convenient schedule of ferry service to the islands of Martha's Vineyard (Oak Bluffs) and Nantucket. Hy-Line, 778–2602, operates from early May to the end of September and is located at the Ocean Street Dock with parking nearby. All island ferries have on-board snack bars.

Information on the popular islands of Martha's Vineyard and Nantucket has not been included in this guide, except for information on how to get them from Hyannis and Woods Hole. The Cape, Martha's Vineyard, and Nantucket are three distinct and separate worlds, and each one is deserving of its own special focus and treatment. This guide concentrates exclusively on Cape Cod, but it is also part of a trilogy of guide books of the Cape and Islands region published by The Globe Pequot Press. The other two excellent, detailed books in this trilogy are *Guide to Martha's Vineyard* and *Guide to Nantucket*, both authored by Polly Burroughs, a long-time resident of Martha's Vineyard. These guides are available at your bookstore or from the publisher at Box Q, Chester, CT 06412.

Health and Safety

The purpose of a vacation/holiday is to enjoy and renew oneself before tackling another prolonged period of labor and stress. Cape Cod can do wonders for your body and soul provided you stay healthy and avoid accidents. The towns of Cape Cod and the Cape Cod National Seashore do everything they can to provide visitors with a hazard-free environment, but some risks cannot be absolutely eliminated. The following health and safety tips are provided to bring you back home happy and relaxed.

Cape Cod is not free of nasty insects, although there is the temptation to say that everything here is just like Camelot: perfect. When hiking in woods, on the beach, or in marsh or shrub areas, check yourself, companions, children, and pets for ticks on clothing and hair. These insects can cause serious illness; but 99+ percent of Cape Cod visitors and residents avoid them by flicking off the critters before they can do any harm. If you find one imbedded in skin, apply the hot tip of a match to its rear end and it should quickly let go, or pull its head out with tweezers. Do not leave its head imbedded in skin, which can happen if you try pulling it out by its body. Avoid getting bitten by voracious green flies, which seem to be more prevalent at marsh and beach areas on hot windless days in midsummer. If you are allergic to insect bites, obtain medical help right away. Also while hiking, be careful not to expose skin to poison ivy, which is one of our common, less desirable plants.

When on the beach, avoid prolonged exposure to the sun. The sun's strong rays can cause intense discomfort, rapid aging of skin, and, possibly, cancer. Sun screens (lotions) should be used for extended periods on the beach and water. Make sure you buy one strong enough to provide both protection and a tan. Invest in better sunglasses that protect your eyes from damaging ultraviolet and infrared light and wear them. A good sun hat is also advised. Don't swim beyond the ability of life guards to rescue you. The waters at some beaches, during tidal and weather changes and high-wave periods, have powerful, deadly undercurrents that are difficult to handle by even the strongest swimmers. Swim in calm, shallow areas and always keep children under close supervision. Also be wary of sharp obstacles hidden in the water. When walking to and from the beach, wear sandals or shoes that protect your feet from the broiling sand and hidden pieces of sharp debris. Don't dig large holes in the sand; they can be hazardous to you and others. Do not climb up and down the high cliffs along Cape Cod National Seashore. They are composed of loose sand and clay materials that crumble easily and can cause a crippling fall. Be aware of tidal changes when hiking out on narrow peninsulas jutting into the sea. A high tide can cover low areas and strand you for several hours. Although storms along our coasts are very dramatic to observe, do not watch them from places where you can be swept into the sea by the wind or struck by falling power lines and tree branches.

Emergencies

For emergencies requiring local police, fire service, or ambulance service, dial "0" for the operator; stay on the line until your call for help is answered by the service you need; and state your problem and what assistance you require. The operator is obliged to connect you to the proper authorities.

Hospitals

Hyannis: **Cape Cod Hospital,** 771–1800, 27 Park Street; twenty-four-hour emergency care
Falmouth: **Falmouth Hospital,** 548–5300, TerHeun Drive, off Route 28; twenty-four-hour emergency care

Clinics

Buzzard's Bay: **Crow's Nest Medical Center,** 759–2519, One Wolf Road
Falmouth: **Falmouth Walk-In Medical Center,** 540–6790, Route 28
Hyannis: **Health Stop,** 771–7520, K-Mart Plaza, Route 132; also **Mid-Cape Medical Center,** 771–4092, Route 28
South Yarmouth: **Mid-Cape Medical Center,** 394–2151, Route 28
South Dennis: **Dennis Medical Center,** 394–7113, Route 134
Harwich: **Medi-Center Five,** 432–4100, 525 Long Pond Drive
Chatham: **Chatham Medical Associates,** 945–0187, 78 Crowell Road
Orleans: **Orleans Medical Center Walk-In,** 255–9577, Route 6A
Wellfleet: **A.I.M. Clinic,** 349–3131, Route 6
Provincetown: **Provincetown Medical Group,** 487–3505, 16 Shank Painter Road

Pharmacies

Almost every town has one or more pharmacies. Some are closed on Sundays. Check the Yellow Pages of the local phone directory for the one nearest you and its times of operation. The Prescription Center in Falmouth, for example, has a twenty-four-hour emergency hotline, 540–2410, for prescription drugs and ·oxygen. Travel tip: always carry prescriptions for essential drugs, which cannot be legally dispensed without them.

Listed below are additional agencies that provide emergency assistance:

U.S. Coast Guard

Woods Hole: 548–5151
Cape Cod Canal: 888–0335
Chatham: 945–0164
Provincetown: 487–0070

State Police

Bourne: 759–4488
South Yarmouth: 398–2323

Information Center for Individuals with Disabilities: (800) 462–5015
Cape Cod Association for Retarded Citizens: 564–4000
Handicapped Children's Clinic: 362–2511, ext. 340
Suicide Prevention—The Samaritans
  Buzzards Bay: 759–2828
  Falmouth: 548–8900
  Hyannis: 771–7770
  Wellfleet: 255–1888
Poison Hotline: (800) 682–9211
Alcoholics Anonymous: (800) 637–6237
Cocaine Hotline: (800) 662–HELP
Battered Women: 428–4720
Cape Cod Rape Crisis Center: 778–4627; weekends, 771–1080
Missing Children's Hotline: (800) 843–5678
Parental Stress Hotline: (800) 632–8188
Parents Anonymous: (800) 882–1250
Gay and Lesbian Crisis Hotline: (800) 221–7044
Provincetown AIDS Helpline: 778–4627; evenings and weekends, 771–1080

Activities and Attractions

Outdoors

Public Beaches

One of the main reasons why so many people prefer coming to the Cape for their vacations is our superb beaches. Although extensive areas of beach front have gone into private ownership, there are still many public beaches, which welcome the short-stay or seasonal visitor. The open, ocean-side beaches of the Cape Cod National Seashore, for example, extend for nearly forty miles in a north/south direction along the forearm of the Lower Cape.

If there is a problem regarding Cape Cod beaches at the height of the summer season, it is parking your vehicle. Parking lots at the popular beaches fill up fast from mid-July to Labor Day. Before and after this period, though, there isn't much of a parking crunch. Parking lots at the main Cape Cod National Seashore beaches are large and can usually handle most of the cars of those wanting to come in. Between Memorial Day weekend and Labor Day, most town-managed beaches charge a parking fee, as do those of managed beaches of the Cape Cod National Seashore. There is no fee for using beach parking lots in the off-season. If you plan on staying at a Cape location for an extended time (a week, month, or the season), most towns will sell you a permit that allows you to park daily at beach lots. The cost of the permit saves you money over having to pay on a day-to-day basis and allows you to use most town beaches.

A number of the larger beaches, both in the towns and along the Cape Cod National Seashore, have sanitary and other facilities. All beaches bar overnight parking, however, except, in some instances, in the case of surf fishermen, who must obtain a special permit. Open beach fires are also banned, except by permit, but you can use a grill or stove in specially designated picnic areas. The operation of over-sand vehicles on beaches is regulated by laws, and permits are required for their use in designated areas. Most permits can be obtained at town offices or at Cape Cod National Seashore visitor centers. A number of places of accommodation and resorts have their own private beaches, and you should consider this feature when selecting a place to stay. Many accommodations also have freshwater swimming pools, whirlpools, and saunas on their premises.

When you are using our beaches, please dispose of your trash in barrels set aside for this purpose. Don't leave broken glass on the beach, even when it's not your own. Don't pull up or pick beach grass, flowers, shrubbery, and other flora, as this vegetation makes our environment beautiful and helps to protect the beach from wind erosion, which is a major problem on the Cape. Always keep a close watch on young children in the water. Don't swim beyond a life guard's ability to rescue you in an emergency. Avoid getting caught in strong riptides and undercurrents. Surfers and sailboarders cannot use life guard–protected beaches at the same time as swimmers. Check with officials on the beach you want to use for regulations and areas open to you (see following section for more information on surfing and sailboarding). The warmest waters for swimming are found at beaches on Buzzards Bay, Cape Cod Bay, and Nantucket Sound. The water is coldest at beaches along the open-Atlantic side, mostly those within Cape Cod National Seashore. Nude sunbathing is not permitted at Cape Cod National Seashore beaches, and this regulation is enforced by National Park Service rangers and local community police.

The following are some of the many Cape Cod beaches open to the public:

Bourne

Monument Beach, off Shore Road on Buzzards Bay

Falmouth

Falmouth Heights Beach, off Route 28 and Grand Avenue on Nantucket Sound

Megansett Beach, in North Falmouth, off Route 28A on Buzzards Bay

Menauhant Beach, in East Falmouth, off Route 28 and Central Avenue on Nantucket Sound

Old Silver Beach, in North Falmouth, off Route 28A and Quaker Road on Buzzards Bay

Surf Drive Beach, in Falmouth, off Main and Shore streets, on Nantucket Sound

Bristol Beach, off Route 28 in the Maravista area of Falmouth Heights on Nantucket Sound

Wood Neck Beach, in the Sippewissett area off Route 28 and Palmer Avenue on Buzzards Bay

Stoney Beach, in Woods Hole

Chapoquoit Beach, in West Falmouth, off Route 28A and Chapoquoit Road on Buzzards Bay

Sandwich

Town Neck Beach, off Route 6A and Town Neck Road on Cape Cod Bay

Mashpee

South Cape Beach, off Great Neck Road on Nantucket Sound

ACTIVITIES AND ATTRACTIONS

Barnstable

Craigville Beach, off Craigville Beach Road on Nantucket Sound
Millway Beach, in Barnstable Harbor, off Route 6A on Cape Cod Bay
Sandy Neck Beach, in West Barnstable, off Route 6A and Sandy Neck Road on Cape Cod Bay

Hyannis

Kalmus Park Beach, at the end of Ocean Street on Nantucket Sound
Orrin Keyes Beach, off Ocean Avenue on Nantucket Sound
Veteran's Beach, off Ocean Street in Hyannis Harbor

Yarmouth

Bass River Beach, off Route 28 and South Shore Drive on Nantucket Sound
Parkers River Beach, off Route 28 and South Shore Drive on Nantucket Sound
Sea Gull Beach, in West Yarmouth, off Route 28 and South Sea Avenue on Nantucket Sound
Seaview, Parkers River, and Thatcher beaches, in South Yarmouth, off Route 28 and South Shore Drive on Nantucket Sound

Dennis

Chapin Beach, off Route 6A and Chapin Beach Road on Cape Cod Bay
Cold Storage Road Beach, in East Dennis, off Route 6A and Cold Storage Road on Cape Cod Bay
Corporation Road Beach, off Route 6A and Corporation Beach Road on Cape Cod Bay
Sea Street, Haig's, and Glendon beaches, in Dennis Port, off Route 28 and Old Wharf Road on Nantucket Sound
Sea Street Beach, in East Dennis, off Route 6A and South Street on Cape Cod Bay
West Dennis Beach, off Route 28 and Lighthouse Road on Nantucket Sound

Brewster

Point of Rocks Beach, off Route 6A and Point of Rocks Road on Cape Cod Bay
Breakwater Beach, off Route 6A and Breakwater Beach Road on Cape Cod Bay

Crosby Landing Beach, off Route 6A and Crosby Landing Road on Cape Cod Bay

Ellis Landing Beach, off Route 6A and Ellis Landing Road on Cape Cod Bay

Linnell's Landing Beach, off Route 6A and Linnell's Landing Road on Cape Cod Bay

Paine's Creek Beach, off Route 6A and Paine's Creek Road on Cape Cod Bay

Robbin's Hill Beach, off Route 6A and Robbin's Hill Road on Cape Cod Bay

Harwich

Red River Beach, in South Harwich, off Route 28 and Neel Road on Nantucket Sound

Atlantic Avenue and Bank Street beaches, in Harwich Port, off Route 28A on Nantucket Sound

Chatham

Cockle Cove Beach, in South Chatham, off Route 28 and Cockle Cove Road on Nantucket Sound

Hardings Beach, in West Chatham, off Hardings Beach Road on Nantucket Sound

Orleans

Nauset Beach, off Shore Road from town center, a town-managed beach within the Cape Cod National Seashore on the open Atlantic

Skaket Beach, off Route 6 and Namaskaket Road on Cape Cod Bay

Rock Harbor Beach, off Route 6 and Rock Harbor Road on Cape Cod Bay

Eastham

Campground Beach, off Route 6 and Campground Road on Cape Cod Bay

Coast Guard Beach, off Route 6 and Doane Road, a Cape Cod National Seashore–managed beach on the open Atlantic

Cooks Brook Beach, off Route 6 and Massasoit and Steele roads on Cape Cod Bay

First Encounter Beach, off Route 6 and Samoset Road on Cape Cod Bay

There are beaches on Cape Cod which are so crowded on hot Summer days that the sand is just about covered over by colored blankets. While at the same time, there are also plenty of beaches where there is no one other than just you and a seascape that goes on forever.

ACTIVITIES AND ATTRACTIONS

Nauset Light Beach, off Route 6 and Cable Road, a Cape Cod National Seashore–managed beach on the open Atlantic
Sunken Meadow Beach, off Route 6 and Sunken Meadow Road on Cape Cod Bay

Wellfleet

Le Count Hollow, White Crest, Cahoon Hollow, and Newcomb Hollow beaches, off Route 6 along Ocean View Drive, town-managed beaches within Cape Cod National Seashore on the open Atlantic
Marconi Beach, off Route 6 in South Wellfleet, a Cape Cod National Seashore–managed beach on the open Atlantic
Duck Harbor Beach, off Route 6 and via town center and Chequesset Neck Road, a town-managed beach within Cape Cod National Seashore on Cape Cod Bay
Indian Neck Beach, off Route 6 on Cape Cod Bay
Mayo Beach, off Route 6 at Wellfleet Harbor on Cape Cod Bay

Truro

Coast Guard Beach, off Route 6 and South Highland and Coast Guard roads, a town-managed beach within Cape Cod National Seashore on the open Atlantic
Corn Hill Beach, off Route 6 and Castle and Corn Hill roads on Cape Cod Bay
Fisher Beach, off Route 6 and County and Fisher roads on Cape Cod Bay
Great Hollow Beach, off Route 6 and Great Hollow Road on Cape Cod Bay
Head of the Meadow Beach, off Route 6 and Head of the Meadow Road, a Cape Cod National Seashore–managed beach on the open Atlantic
Longnook Beach, off Route 6 and Longnook Road, a town-managed beach within Cape Cod National Seashore on the open Atlantic
Ryder Beach, off Route 6 and Prince Valley and Ryder Beach roads on Cape Cod Bay
Pilgrim Beach, in North Truro, off Route 6A on Cape Cod Bay

Provincetown

Herring Cove Beach, off Route 6, a Cape Cod National Seashore–managed beach on Cape Cod Bay

OUTDOORS

Race Point Beach, off Route 6 and Race Point and Province Lands roads, a Cape Cod National Seashore–managed beach on the open Atlantic

In addition to salt-water beaches, there are beaches at fresh-water ponds throughout Cape Cod: Grew's Pond in Falmouth; Picture Lake in Pocasset; Wakeby Pond in South Sandwich; John's Pond in Mashpee; Lovell's and Hamblin's ponds in Marstons Mills; Wequaquet Lake in Centerville; Hathaway's Pond in Barnstable; Dennis Pond in Yarmouth Port; Scargo Lake in Dennis; Long Pond in South Yarmouth; Sandy Pond in West Yarmouth; Walker's Pond in West Brewster; Sheep Pond in Brewster; Long Pond in Harwich; Flax Pond at Nickerson State Park in East Brewster; Pilgrim Lake in Orleans; Herring and Great ponds in Eastham; and Great, Gull, and Long ponds in Wellfleet.

Surfing and Sailboarding

Surfing and sailboarding, popular and rapidly growing sports on the waters of Cape Cod, attract thousands of enthusiasts each year. Both sports, not confined just to summer, go on throughout the year thanks to the insulated wet suit.

Board-surfing waves are found at beaches along Cape Cod National Seashore—Nauset Beach in Orleans, Coast Guard and Nauset Light beaches in Eastham, and Marconi Beach in South Wellfleet. The waves here are at their best during the fall and winter. Beach regulations prohibit surfing at life guard–protected sections, where swimmers congregate. The Salt Pond Visitor Center of the Cape Cod National Seashore in Eastham will answer your questions about regulations, locations, and conditions. One of the best sources on Cape Cod for surfing information, competitions, lessons, board sales and rentals, wet suits, clothing, and related gear is the Cinnamon Rainbows Surf Company in Orleans (255–5832), which is open all year. Cinnamon Rainbows has two locations in town, one near the Orleans–Route 6 rotary and a new shop on Beach Road. Jaspers Surf Shop (255–2662) on Route 6 in Eastham and Nauset Sports (255–4752) on Route 6 in Orleans are two other sources.

Sailboarding (windsurfing) is the booming, "in" water sport on Cape Cod. Every year more and more people are scooting and flying across our waters creating colorful and thrilling sights. Falmouth has become the center for sailboarding on the Cape because of our beaches and because of the young entrepreneurs who own Cape Sailboards (540–8800), open all year and located at 661D Main Street, across from the ADAP auto-parts store in Falmouth. Cape Sailboards is the leader in organizing important competitions with prize money, promoting the sport to a wider public, and being a force for sailboarders purchasing their own beach off Surf Drive in Falmouth. You should contact Cape Sailboards for current information on wind conditions, beaches available, regulations governing them, and safety instructions. They also have a full line of equipment and clothing for sale, equipment rentals, and sailboarding lessons. Cape beaches typically prohibit the launching of sailboards at life guard–protected beaches until late afternoon. Check with town offices or Cape Sailboards for full details. If you are new to the sport, sail only in areas where, if necessary, others can rescue you. Don't sailboard without someone on the beach watching you who has the ability to get help. For prolonged periods on and in the water, insulated wet suits are a must to prevent hypothermia, which can result in death. First-timers, don't go on the water without good instruction on how to handle and maneuver your sailboard nor without knowing effective safety and survival procedures.

Cape Cod National Seashore

(Features: beaches, biking and hiking trails, historic attractions, etc., are detailed under their specific categories in this guide.)

Cape Cod National Seashore is open to the public all year. Nominal parking fees are charged at all beaches during the summer season (either from Memorial Day weekend or the end of June to Labor Day), but parking is free at other times during the year. Permits are required for open fires, overnight beach parking for surf-fishing, and the use of over-sand vehicles. Permits are obtained at visitor centers. Licenses for shellfish gathering are obtained at town offices. Cape Cod National Seashore Headquarters (349–3785) is located off Route 6 at the Marconi Station entrance in South Wellfleet. Headquarters is open daily during January and February, weekdays from March through December. Salt Pond Visitor Center (255–3421) is located off Route 6 in Eastham. It is both the largest and the first one approached by most people to this area of the Lower Cape. Salt Pond is open daily but closed during the months of January and February. Province Lands Visitor Center (487–1256) is located off Route 6 near the junction of Province Lands Road and Race Point Road in Provincetown. Province Lands is open daily from Easter through Thanksgiving.

During the summer season, visitor centers are in operation from 9:00 A.M. to 6:00 P.M., and a diversified program of ranger-conducted interpretive activities is available seven days a week. Special evening programs also originate at the visitor centers. Contact them for their current schedule of programs, activities, and events. Interpretive activities operate on a reduced schedule from Labor Day to Columbus Day. Cape Cod National Seashore visitor centers have rangers on hand to provide information and answer questions. They also have folders, regulations, and maps describing various aspects of the national seashore. They offer interesting audio/visual programs and displays, scenic overlooks, departure points for biking and hiking trails, ample parking lots, rest rooms, picnic areas, conveniences for the handicapped, and seashore-related books for sale.

There are lodgings, campgrounds, restaurants, and stores near the entrances of Cape Cod National Seashore located along Route 6 and in the town centers of Orleans, Eastham, Wellfleet, Truro, and Provincetown. The nearest state-operated campground is at Nickerson State Park (896–3002) on Route 6A in East Brewster.

Authorized on 7 August 1961 during the administration of John F. Kennedy and sponsored by the Massachusetts congressional delegation, Cape Cod National Seashore, an entity of the National Park Service, is a spectacular natural and historic preserve of more than 43,500 acres running along most of the entire forearm of the Lower Cape. Cape Cod National Seashore extends in a north/south direction for forty miles through the towns of Orleans, Eastham, Wellfleet, Truro, and Provincetown. Most of its coastline is along the open Atlantic, but there are also large sections of beach along Cape Cod Bay. Its Atlantic beaches are among the finest on the entire east coast of the United States. They include miles of wide, flat stretches, high sand and clay cliffs, and many acres of massive sand dunes that remind one of great deserts. The Atlantic side of Cape Cod National Seashore is the leading edge of the U.S. mainland against powerful storms that blow in from the northeast. The action of tide and wind keep eating away at this shoreline, while on the other side of the peninsula, on Cape Cod Bay, land is in the process of being built up by these same forces of nature.

There is an abundance of marine life in the waters and intertidal areas of Cape Cod National Seashore—horseshoe and fiddler crabs, razor clams, quahogs, oysters, lobsters, flounder, bluefish, and whales. Within the interior of Cape Cod National Seashore are other complex and fragile ecological zones and habitats: bogs, marshes, swamps, woodland, glacial ponds (kettle holes), and tidal flats; various species of flora; fauna such as white-tail deer, foxes, rabbits, and raccoons; and a wide variety of migratory waterfowl and land birds.

Cape Cod National Seashore also has a rich human history. In South Wellfleet, Marconi built one of his transatlantic-wireless signal stations. At Orleans one of the first underwater cables linking the United States and Europe was laid. The United States Coast Guard evolved from the life-saving operations along this coast. Hundreds of ships were wrecked offshore, including the *Whidah*, containing millions of dollars worth of treasure now being salvaged. On lands within what is now Cape Cod National Seashore, whaling captains had palatial homes, and one of the most impressive of all, the Captain Penniman House, is open to visitors. And along the coastal length of this national seashore are several picturesque lighthouses, beacons of hope and safety for mariners.

In addition to experiencing the glories of the natural maritime environment through your own perceptions, Cape Cod National Seashore rangers conduct fascinating day and evening interpretive programs and take visitors out on short hikes to explore the various interrelated, ecological zones and significant historic sites. Within Cape Cod National Seashore there are excellent beaches for swimming, fishing, sunbathing, picnicking, hiking, exploring, and surfing. There are biking and hiking trails and special trails for motorized or horseback sand-dune riding. At Salt Pond there is a sensory trail for blind hikers. There are also special ranger-conducted interpretive programs for children. Cape Cod National Seashore is one of the best values going on this vacation peninsula, and it's accessible to all the people.

Children's Camps

Because of the unique land and sea environment, historical heritage, and ability to attract top professionals in recreation, Cape Cod camps are well known for the quality of their staffs, programs, facilities, and services. For close to seven decades, thousands of children throughout North America have enjoyed the camping experience on Cape Cod. The residential and day camps listed below are recommended for your consideration. For additional information, contact the Cape Cod Association of Children's Camps, P.O. Box 38, Brewster, MA 02631. (ACA indicates American Camping Association accreditation.)

Camp Avalon, girls, residential, ACA; established 1929, off Fox Hill Road, Chatham, MA, 945–1345. Saltwater sailing camp for girls eight to sixteen; sailing and racing instruction, swimming, tennis, gymnastics, water skiing, trampoline, crafts, and riding; individualized instruction

Animal Friends Summer Camp, coed, day, ACA; established 1945, on Megansett Harbor in North Falmouth, c/o Animal Rescue League of Boston, P.O. Box 265, Boston, MA 02117, 426–9170. Hands-on programs in ocean ecology, farm animals, arts and crafts; for children six to thirteen

Camps Burgess and Hayward, YMCA boys and girls, residential, ACA; established 1928, on Spectacle Pond in Sandwich, c/o 79 Coddington Street, Quincy, MA 02169, 479–8500. Family atmosphere for children eight to fourteen; programs in athletics, archery, tennis, swimming, sailing, boating, water skiing, photography, and other skills

Cape Cod Sea Campus Monomoy/Wono, coed, residential, ACA; established 1922, on Cape Cod Bay, P.O. Box 13, Brewster, MA 02631, 896–3451. The oldest residential camp on Cape Cod; family atmosphere for children seven to fifteen; more than forty land- and water-based activities

Cape Cod Soccer Camp, coed, day; established in 1979, located in Brewster, P.O. Box 747, South Orleans, MA 02662, 240–0917. Staff of professional soccer players, college and high-school coaches; training in all aspects of soccer; age, talent, and playing experience of each camper considered

Camp Good News, coed, residential, ACA; established in 1935, P.O. Box 95, Forestdale, MA 02644, 477–1707. Christian values in a comprehensive, residential camping environment; traditional activities and skills instruction; for children eight to thirteen

Devon Day Camp, coed, day; established in 1985, on Elisha's Pond, in Yarmouth Port, Wingate-Kirkland, Yarmouth, MA 02675, 362–6032. Development of motor and social skills in children four to seven; director a former teacher of early childhood education

The Family School Summer Camp, coed, day; established in 1983, RFD 2, Brewster, MA 02631, 896–6555. Comprehensive day-camp program for children from one month to eight years of age; swimming, gymnastics, arts and crafts, field and racquet sports, archery, farming, nature, dance, drama, carpentry, horseback riding, sailing, and canoeing; family values stressed

Camp Farley, 4-H, coed, residential and day; established in 1934, on Wakeby Pond in Mashpee, P.O. Box 97, Forestdale, MA 02644, 477–0181. Development, by 4-H philosophy, of physical and emotional strengths in campers eight to thirteen; swimming, sailing, canoeing, horseback riding, archery, arts and crafts

Camp Favorite, girl scout, residential, ACA; established in 1962, on Long Pond in Brewster, c/o Patriot Trails GS Council, 6 St. James Avenue, Boston, MA 02116, 482–1078. Major programs of sailing and biking; activities chosen, carried out, and evaluated by the individual camper with the support of adult leaders; for girls eight to seventeen

Camp Namequoit, boys, residential, ACA; established in 1925, on Pleasant Bay in Orleans, Box 306A, Orleans, MA 02653, 255–0377. Sailing camp for boys eight to fifteen; sailing, racing, windsurfing, swimming, archery, riflery, woodworking, and team sports; emphasis on strengthening self-confidence

Wingate Kirkland, coed, residential, ACA; established in 1957, on Elisha's Pond in Yarmouth Port, 105 White Rock Road, Yarmouth, MA 02675, 362–6032. Counselor/camper ratio, 1:4; a child-centered, caring community stressing personal growth; athletics, tennis, swimming, boating, drama, music, dance, campcraft, woodworking, arts and crafts, gymnastics, and journalism; for children eight to fourteen

Camp Lyndon, YMCA, coed, residential and day; established in 1972, 117 Stowe Road, Sandwich, MA 02563, 428–9251. Development of YMCA goals of self-confidence and personal growth; sailing, swimming, archery, gymnastics, computers, horseback riding, nature, crafts, and sports; children three to fifteen

Camp Mitton, coed, day, ACA; established in 1936, between Slough and Walker ponds, in Brewster, 46 Featherbed Lane, Brewster, MA 02631, 385-3224. Stress on understanding of, and appreciation for, Cape Cod's natural environment; sailing, canoeing, fishing, swimming, field and court sports, crafts, archery, and exploring; children six to eleven

Monomoy Day Camp, coed, day, ACA; established in 1963, on Cape Cod Bay, Box 13, Brewster, MA 02631, 896-3451. Recreational access to salt water, a lake, and a swimming pool; sailing, swimming, archery, riflery, arts and crafts, drama, athletics, and computers; children four to fifteen

New Seabury Children's Programs, coed, day; established in 1985, New Seabury Corp., Box A, New Seabury, MA 02649, 477-9400. Within the attractive New Seabury development; sailing, swimming, tennis, and golf; development of social skills and personal growth; for children three to thirteen

Public Golf Courses

Because of our relatively mild climate during the cold-weather months and the fact that what snow falls is usually rapidly absorbed into the porous ground, Cape Cod is New England's best area for four-seasons golf. Unless the weather goes completely off kilter, which happens on occasion, one can count on playing golf on Cape Cod twelve months of the year, perhaps not every day but enough days to satisfy any fanatic of the links. Many of our public golf courses are open all year. Cape Cod courses welcome visitors from near and far. Most have equipment and cart rentals, pro shops, lounges, snack bars and/or restaurants, and other amenities. Although the beaches are our main attraction to visitors, our golf courses are not far behind in appeal.

Bass River Golf Course, 18 holes, High Bank Road in South Yarmouth, 398-9079

Blue Rock Golf Course, 18 holes, off High Bank Road in South Yarmouth, 398-9295

Cape Cod County Club, 18 holes, open all year, off Sandwich Road in North Falmouth, 563-9842

The Captains Golf Course, 18 holes, 1000 Freeman's Way in Brewster, 896-5100

Chatham Bars Inn, semiprivate, 9 holes, Shore Road in Chatham, 945-0096

Chequesset Country Club, 9 holes, Chequesset Neck Road in Wellfleet, 349–3704

Cotuit Highground Country Club, 9 holes, Crocker Neck Road in Cotuit, 428–9863

Cranberry Valley Golf Course, 18 holes, Oak Street in Harwich, 432–4653

Dennis Highlands Golf Course, 18 holes, Old Bass River Road in Dennis, 385–8347

Dennis Pines Golf Course, 18 holes, Golf Course Road in East Dennis, 385–8347

Tara Hyannis Resort Golf Club, 18 holes, West End Circle in Hyannis, 775–7775

Falmouth Country Club, 18 holes, open all year, 630 Carriage Shop Road in East Falmouth, 548–3211

Paul Harney Golf Club, 18 holes, open all year, Route 151 in North Falmouth, 563–3454

Harwich Port Golf Club, 9 holes, South Street in Harwich Port, 432–0250

Highland Golf Club, 9 holes, Highland Road in Truro, within Cape Cod National Seashore, 487–9201

Holly Ridge Golf Club, 18 holes, open all year, off Route 130 and Race Lane in South Sandwich, 428–5577

Iyanough Hills Golf Club, 18 holes, Route 132 in Hyannis, 362–2606

New Seabury Country Club, semiprivate, 18 holes, Shore Drive in New Seabury, 477–9110

Ocean Edge Golf Club, semiprivate, 18 holes, Golf Course Road in Brewster, 896–5911

Pocasset Golf Club, 18 holes, open all year, House Drive off Route 28A in Pocasset, 563–7171

Quashnet Valley Country Club, 18 holes, open all year, off Route 151 and Old Barnstable Road in Mashpee, 477–4412

Round Hill Country Club, 18 holes, Exit 3 off Route 6 in Sandwich, 888–3384

Tennis

There are public and private tennis courts located throughout Cape Cod. In addition to the courts listed below, most resorts and many motels have private tennis courts for use by their guests.

Falmouth Sports Center, Highfield Drive, 548–7433
Falmouth Tennis Club, Dillingham Avenue, 548–4370
South Cape Resort & Club, Route 28 in Mashpee, 477–0726

King's Grant Racquet Club, Main Street in Cotuit, 428–5744
Tennis of Cape Cod, Route 132 in Hyannis, 775–1921
Mid-Cape Racquet Club, White's Path in South Yarmouth, 394–3511
Dennis Racquet and Swim Club, Oxbow Way, 385–2221
Dennis Tennis Club, Main Street, 394–2262
Bamberg House of Tennis Club, Route 6A in Brewster, 896–5023
Chequesset Yacht and Country Club, Chequesset Neck Road in Wellfleet, 349–3704
Oliver Tennis Courts, Route 6 in Wellfleet, 349–3330
Provincetown Tennis Club, Bradford Street, 487–9574
Hawthorne Bissell's Tennis Courts, Bradford Street at Herring Cove Beach Road in Provincetown, 487–9512

There are also public tennis courts at these Cape Cod schools: Falmouth High School, Lawrence School in Falmouth, Mashpee Middle School, Cape Cod Community College, Barnstable High School in Hyannis, Junior High School in Hyannis, Wixon Middle School in South Dennis, Dennis/Yarmouth Regional High School in South Yarmouth, Cape Cod Regional Technical High School in Harwich, Chatham High School, and Nauset Middle School in Orleans.

Best Bike Trails

Biking has become one of the most pleasurable ways of touring Cape Cod. Biking takes you out in the open and gets you close to our beautiful environment. It's difficult to smell our flowers from inside a buttoned-up auto, but on a bike you take in all the wonderful fragrances and sights. It takes longer to go from place to place, but you see everything in more detail and with greater intimacy. Biking has become such an important leisure activity on Cape Cod that most towns and the Cape Cod National Seashore have established special bike trails, some of which are totally isolated from motorized vehicles.

The entire length of Cape Cod is crisscrossed with bike trails. The Boston/Cape Cod Bikeway is in two sections: sixty-five miles from Boston to Bourne on the Claire Saltonstall Memorial Bikeway; and seventy miles from Bourne to Provincetown, with a side route to Woods Hole. For a map of this bikeway, send a self-addressed envelope with thirty-seven cents worth of stamps to: C.T.P.S., 27 School Street, Boston, MA 02108. The Cape Cod Rail Trail, allowing biking, jogging, and horseback riding, is fourteen miles long and extends from Route 134 in Dennis to Locust Road in Eastham. Auto parking is available at Nickerson State Park in Brewster, Route 124 in Harwich, and at the Salt Pond Visitors Center (Cape Cod

National Seashore) in Eastham. A booklet entitled *Bikeways on Cape Cod* is free from the Cape Cod Chamber of Commerce.

Whether on a short or extended bike tour, *always keep to the right of the trail*; don't speed, and look out for other bikers, hikers, and dogs. Most bike trails have paved surfaces, but watch for slippery patches of sand. The terrain is generally flat with some hilly areas. There are several bike rental-and-repair shops on the Cape (a listing of rental places is provided below). The following are Cape Cod's best bike tours. If you want more information about these and other tours, get a copy of *Short Bike Rides on Cape Cod, Nantucket & The Vineyard* by Edwin Mullen and Jane Griffith, available at bookstores or from The Globe Pequot Press, Chester, Connecticut 06412.

Cape Cod Canal in Sandwich—seventeen miles from Bourne Bridge to Sandwich along the canal and to the Sandwich attractions of Heritage Plantation, Glass Museum, and Hoxie House

Bourne—eighteen and one-half miles from Bourne Bridge to North Falmouth through the lovely villages of Cataumet and Pocasset

West Barnstable to Sandy Neck—ten and three-tenths miles from the Old Village Store to Sandy Neck Beach on Cape Cod Bay, one of the most extensive marsh, beach, and sand-dune areas on Cape Cod

Barnstable to Cummaquid—ten and eight-tenths miles along historic Route 6A with its beautiful old homes and adjacent beaches

West Falmouth to Woods Hole on the "Shining Sea Trail"—twenty-six and one-half miles on the trail named in honor of Katherine Lee Bates, author of "America" (". . . from sea to shining sea."); to Woods Hole with its many scientific institutions, Harvard Square atmosphere, and steamship access to the islands of Martha's Vineyard and Nantucket; also to Nobska Point with its famous lighthouse and to Quissett Harbor, one of the loveliest on the east coast

Osterville to Centerville—fourteen miles through affluent Osterville and past some of the grand mansions on Cape Cod

The Cape Cod Rail Trail—nineteen and six-tenths miles from Brewster to the Salt Pond Visitor Center of the Cape Cod National Seashore on what was formerly the main Cape Cod railroad line

West Yarmouth to South Yarmouth—fourteen and one-half miles through sedate sections of Cape Cod and along its busiest stretch on Route 28

West Dennis to Harwich Port—eighteen miles meandering past historic homes and fine harbors on the Cape's south coast

Harwich to West Chatham—fourteen miles along the coast of one of Cape Cod's prestigious towns

West Brewster to Dennis—twenty-one miles weaving past historic homes, the Cape Cod Museum of Natural History, Sealand of Cape Cod, the Drummer Boy Museum, art galleries, and craft shops

ACTIVITIES AND ATTRACTIONS

Brewster to Nickerson State Park—sixteen miles through lovely scenery with several fresh-water ponds; camping in Nickerson State Park

Chatham—twenty-one and one-half miles along a meandering route of pretty byways and the waterways of Chatham; great for exploring a quintessential Cape Cod town

Orleans—thirteen and two-tenths miles from Rock Harbor on Cape Cod Bay to Nauset Beach, a part of Cape Cod National Seashore where intrepid surfboard riders take on the waves

Eastham to Coast Guard Beach—nine and seven-tenths miles (one of Cape Cod National Seashore's bike trails) from Salt Pond Visitor Center to both Coast Guard and Nauset Light beaches along Ocean View Drive

South Wellfleet to Marconi Station—nine and six-tenths miles from the Massachusetts Audubon Society reservation on Cape Cod Bay to Marconi Wireless Station and Marconi Beach within Cape Cod National Seashore

South Wellfleet to LeCount Hollow—nine and seven-tenths miles to Le Count Hollow, White Crest, Cahoon Hollow, and Newcomb Hollow beaches, all within Cape Cod National Seashore along Ocean View Drive, an area of high sand-clay cliffs and broad beaches

Wellfleet to Great Island—six and eight-tenths miles through Wellfleet Center and along the town harbor to the Great Island Trail's head and to Duck Harbor Beach on Cape Cod Bay, both within Cape Cod National Seashore

North Truro to The Highlands—nine and eight-tenths miles within Cape Cod National Seashore from Pilgrim Lake past famous Highland Light (Cape Cod Light), Jenny Lind Tower, Head of Meadow Beaches, and nearby massive sand dunes

Province Lands—eight and three-quarters miles (the major Cape Cod National Seashore bike trail in the Provincetown area) along Herring Cove and Race Point beaches, Beach Forest area, rolling sand dunes, and the Province Lands Visitor Center

Provincetown—eight and one-half miles through Cape Cod's most fascinating and colorful town via Commercial Street and then to Herring Cove and Race Point beaches within Cape Cod National Seashore

Bike Rentals

Bikes can be rented at these Cape Cod locations (some also provide repairs):

All Cape Sales, 627 Main Street, West Yarmouth, 771–8100
Arnold's, 329 Commercial Street, Provincetown, 487–0844
Art's Bike Shop, 75 County Road, North Falmouth, 563–7379
Beach Road Bikes, 10 Beach Road, Orleans, 255–5148

Bike Path Rental, 26 Main Street, Orleans, 255–8050
Bill's Bike Shop, 847 East Main Street, Falmouth, 548–7979
Black Duck Sports Shop, Main Street, Wellfleet, 349–9801
Cove Cycle, Giddiah Hill Road, Orleans, 255–6282
Dennis Full Cycle, 22 Bridge Street, East Dennis, 385–2214
Full Cycle, 39 North Main Steet, Falmouth, 540–4195; 7 Merchant Square, Sandwich, 888–8445
Gabriel House Bike Rental, 24 Mitchell Lane, Brewster, 896–6775
Holiday Cycles, 465 Grand Avenue, Falmouth Heights, 540–3549
Idle Times Bicycles, Route 6, North Eastham, 255–8281
Little Capistrano Bike Shop, Salt Pond Road, Eastham, 255–6515
Summit Ski and Bike Shop, Route 6A, Orleans, 255–7547
Nelson's Bike Rentals, Race Point Road, Provincetown, 487–0034

Best Cape Walks

Henry David Thoreau, the immortal American philosopher of the nineteenth century, was so impressed with his hike along the windswept, sea-shaped forearm of the Lower Cape that he wrote a book about his trek that has since inspired thousands. Thoreau's *Cape Cod* has become an immortal classic of American literature that will continue to captivate readers well into the future. To hike any area of Cape Cod is to experience our magnificent natural environment not only à la Thoreau but in an intensely personal way, close to the land and the sea. Hugh and Heather Sadlier have written an excellent guide to experiencing the Cape on foot. Their *Short Walks on Cape Cod and the Vineyard* is available at bookstores or from The Globe Pequot Press, Chester, Connecticut 06412. When hiking Cape Cod, wear comfortable shoes that protect and support your entire foot. The Cape has many shoe-outlet stores where you can buy quality footwear for hiking at a substantial discount. While on trails, don't pick flowers or pull up beach grass and shrubbery. Don't litter, and it's good form to pick up the litter of others. Watch out for poison ivy. Check clothing and hair and pets for ticks, which can cause Lyme disease. Hikers allergic to insect bites should get immediate medical treatment. It's also good form to be friendly on the trail by extending greetings to other hikers. Life is impersonal enough as it is. A degree of camaraderie on the trail makes the hiking experience more memorable.

The following short hikes (detailed more fully in the Sadliers' book) are among the best on Cape Cod. Each area has trails that provide satisfaction to vigorous hikers and to those who just want to mosey along. Some areas charge a nominal fee for parking or admission during the summer. Elderly persons and young children should be able to hike most of these areas without much strain and discomfort.

ACTIVITIES AND ATTRACTIONS

Ashumet Holly Reservation, run by the Massachusetts Audubon Society, is located off Route 151 in Falmouth and noted for its varieties of European and Oriental hollies; it was originally developed by Wilfred Wheeler. Ashumet Holly is one of Cape Cod's premier attractions. Admission charged. Round-trip distance—one and one-quarter miles.

Lowell Holly Reservation is a 130-acre natural preserve located between Wakeby and Mashpee ponds in the town of Mashpee and reached via South Sandwich Road. This park of diverse plantings was owned and developed by Abbott Lawrence Lowell, a president of Harvard, who donated it to the Massachusetts Trustees of Reservations, a prominent conservation organization. Admission charged. Round-trip distance—two miles.

Wakeby Holly Sanctuary and Recreation Area in Mashpee has trails that take you through fine stands of high holly trees, 150-year-old beeches, tall pines, oaks, and maples. The trail goes beside a formerly productive cranberry bog. There is a nature center here and a beach on Wakeby Pond. Boating and fishing are allowed on the pond, though you need a license for fresh-water angling, which can be obtained at Sandwich town offices. Access is from Route 130 to Cotuit Road. Admission charged. Round-trip distance—two and one-tenth miles.

The Old Briar Patch in Sandwich memorializes Thornton W. Burgess, the creator of Peter Rabbit, Reddy Fox, Hooty Owl, and Paddy Beaver. The Briar Patch Trail brings you into swampy areas and those of tall white pine. It's a lovely walk, during which you may well imagine that Peter and Mrs. Rabbit will appear around the next bend to greet you with their long ears twitching. Access is from Route 6A in Sandwich to Chipman Road to Crowell Road and then into a parking area off Gully Lane. Free. Round-trip distance—two miles.

Talbot's Point Salt Marsh Wildlife Reservation in Sandwich is a peninsula of land that juts into one of the largest salt-marsh areas on Cape Cod. The trails take you through stands of red pine and beech. Access is from Route 6A and Old Colony Road. Free. Round-trip distance—one and one-half miles.

Sandy Neck, located in West Barnstable, is a magnificent ecological composite of high, undulating sand dunes; one of the longest, uncluttered beaches on Cape Cod; broad salt marshes supporting a wide variety of birds and marine life; and the ever-changing moods of Cape Cod Bay's water and sky. At Sandy Neck you can hike for hours, swim, comb the beach for cast-off odds and ends, enjoy a picnic, fish, and get a nice tan. Access is off Route 6A near the West Barnstable and Sandwich town line. Admission Charged for parking during the summer.

Yarmouth Botanic Trails take you from an herb garden into open fields, areas of pines and oaks, and past Miller's Pond. Various species of wildflowers grow along this route. Access is off Route 6A, behind Yarmouth Post Office. Admission charged. Round-trip distance—one and one-quarter miles.

John Wing Trail in Brewster allows you to explore beautiful Wing's Island: thirty-three acres of upland and ninety acres of beach and salt marsh on Cape Cod Bay in Brewster. Access is off Route 6A, with parking at the Cape Cod Museum of Natural History. Free. Round-trip distance—one and three-tenths miles.

Cape Cod Museum of Natural History is in Brewster. Admission is charged to visit the museum itself. North Trail explores the salt-marsh area. Access is off Route 6A and main building of museum. Free. Round-trip distance—one-quarter mile. South Trail takes you through a marsh and into an upland area of fine, old beech trees. Access is off Route 6A, across the highway from the museum complex. Free. Round-trip distance—three-quarters of a mile.

Stoney Brook Mill Sites lie in Brewster, where, during the summer, you can watch grain being milled the old-fashioned way. There's also the tranquility of a mill pond, a herring run, and the beauty of diverse flowers and plantings. Access is off Route 6A and on Stoney Brook Road. Free. Round-trip distance—one-quarter mile.

The Seaside Trail in Chatham runs along the harbor and brings you to salt marshes, dunes, salt-water inlets, and areas of beach plum and salt-spray rose. You can comb the beach for shells and watch the terns and gulls wheeling above. Access is off Route 28, Barn Hill Road, and Harding's Beach Road. Admission charged. Round-trip distance—two miles.

Fort Hill Trail (Cape Cod National Seashore) in Eastham takes you to a whaling captain's house, Nauset Marsh and views of the open Atlantic, Skiff Hill, and along the boardwalks through Red Maple Swamp. Access is off Route 6. Free. Round-trip distance—one and one-half miles.

Buttonbush Trail (Cape Cod National Seashore) in Eastham is a special, sensory trail for the blind along which they can smell, feel, and hear the natural environment around them. Access is off Route 6, starting from the Salt Pond Visitor's Center. Free. Round-trip distance—one-quarter mile.

Nauset Marsh Trail (Cape Cod National Seashore) in Eastham shows you the diverse ecological zones of this area of the Lower Cape: salt pond and estuary, marsh, and upland woods, also the variety of bird, small mammal, and intertidal marine life. Access is off Route 6, starting from Salt Pond Visitor's Center. Free. Round-trip distance—one and two-tenths miles.

Wellfleet Bay Wildlife Sanctuary in South Wellfleet is run by the Massachusetts Audubon Society and offers several hiking trails that explore the woodlands, marshes, and fresh- and salt-water areas adjacent to Cape Cod Bay. This is a good bird-observing area. Access is off Route 6; watch for signs. Admission charged. Round-trip distance—one and one-half miles.

Atlantic White Cedar Swamp Trail (Cape Cod National Seashore) lies in South Wellfleet at Marconi Station Site. The best part of this hike is to walk on a meandering boardwalk through a swamp thick with white cedars and other flora. Access is off Route 6; follow signs to Marconi Station Site. Free. Round-trip distance—one and one-quarter miles.

Great Island Trail (Cape Cod National Seashore) in Wellfleet is a long hike on a peninsula that juts into Wellfleet Harbor and Cape Cod Bay. This area was, in the old days, used by whalers as a station complete with a tavern. It is now a place of sand dunes, beach grass, pitch pines, and magnificent views. Great Island is also a prime bird-observing area. You'll need a sun hat and a canteen of water for this hike. Also watch that you don't get cut off by high tide in the lower areas toward the peninsula's end. Access is off Route 6, through Wellfleet Center, and at the end of Chequesset Neck Road. Free. Round-trip distance—eight and four-tenths miles.

Pilgrim Spring Trail (Cape Cod National Seashore) in North Truro takes you to salt meadows, giant sand dunes, and views of the open Atlantic. It was here in 1620 where the Pilgrims refreshed themselves with the first fresh water since leaving England. Access is off Route 6; watch for sign. Free. Round-trip distance—three-quarters of a mile.

Small Swamp Nature Trail (Cape Cod National Seashore) in North Truro provides a hardy walk during which you observe birds, small mammals, and indigenous flora. It goes over undulating, sandy terrain and offers views of dunes and salt meadow. Access is from the Interpretive Shelter in the Pilgrim Spring area (see above) off Route 6. Free. Round-trip distance—three-quarters of a mile.

Beech Forest Trail (Cape Cod National Seashore) in Provincetown is virtually at land's end on Cape Cod. It traverses sand dunes, explores a forest of beech trees, and goes around a fresh-water pond. Access is off Route 6 and Race Point Road in the Province Lands area. Free. Round-trip distance—one mile.

Fishing, Boating, and Shellfishing

Fishing is one of Cape Cod's most popular activities for all ages. You do not need to buy a license or pay special town fees to fish for salt-water species, which include cod, haddock, striped bass, salmon, tuna, swordfish, flounder, sea bass, ocean perch, halibut, and shark. Most Cape Cod beaches allow surf casting; however, individual towns and the Cape Cod National Seashore require surf-casters to obtain permits for overnight parking at beaches. Towns and the Cape Cod National Seashore require permits for the use of recreational vehicles on beaches. Many beaches are off limits to RVs. Fresh-water fishing is regulated, and you do need a license, which can be obtained at town halls. Children under fifteen are not required to have a license. Blind, mentally handicapped, or paraplegic persons can get fresh-water fishing licenses for free. Cape Cod is well endowed with fishing and boating services—bait-and-tackle shops, boat-rental places, marinas, charter-fishing boats, and boat-launching sites. Most charter–deep-sea-fishing operations provide equipment, bait, snacks and drinks, and fish-cleaning services.

Cape Cod Tides

To those unfamiliar with the ways of the sea, the odd thing about high tides along the Cape Cod shoreline is that they occur at different times at different sections along the coast. For example, when it is high tide at Boston, high tide will not occur at Monument Beach at Buzzards Bay for three more hours. Conversely, when it is high tide at the Cape Cod Canal and at Truro, it is also high tide in Boston. Precise tide tables are available at most stores throughout Cape Cod and are published in the local newspapers. The timing of high and low tides is important to know when planning for boating, fishing, and shellfish gathering.

Deep Sea Fishing Charters

In addition to the charters listed below, most major Cape Cod harbors have a number of other operators providing fishing expeditions and related services:

Apache Sport Fishing Parties, Chadwell Avenue in Sandwich, 888-2907

Patriot Party Boats, Clinton Avenue at Inner Harbor in Falmouth, 548-2626

Aquarius II, Barnstable Harbor, 362–9617

Barnstable Harbor Charter Fleet, 362-3908

Walter W. Ungermann, Barnstable Harbor, 362–3638

The Drifter, Barnstable Harbor, 398–2061

Capt. Joe Eldridge, Barnstable Harbor, 362-3181

Cotuit Charters, Cotuit Harbor, 428–9711

Hy-Line, Hyannis Harbor, 775–7361

Windward Charters, Hyannis Harbor, 362–4925

Wanderview, Hyannis Harbor, 775–7361

Kar-Nik Charters, Hyannis Harbor, 775–2979

A-1 Sport Fishing Charters, South Yarmouth, 398–2486

Champion Line, West Dennis, 398–2266

ACTIVITIES AND ATTRACTIONS

Cape Cod Mistress, Dennis, 385–8267
Albatross Deep Sea Fishing, Sesuit Harbor in East Dennis, 385–3244
Chanterelle, Sesuit Harbor in East Dennis, 385–9316
Day Breaker, Sesuit Harbor in East Dennis, 385–3571
East Dennis Charter Fleet at Sesuit Harbor, 385–5007
Innuendo Charters, Sesuit Harbor in East Dennis, 385–2402
Prime Rate Sport Fishing, Sesuit Harbor in East Dennis, 385–4626
Arlie M, Saquatucket Harbor in Harwich Port, 432–1145
Shanti, Saquatucket Harbor in Harwich Port, 432–7542
Yankee Deep Sea Fishing Parties, Saquatucket Harbor in Harwich Port, 432–2520
Sadie Cod Fishing Charters, at Chatham Fish Pier, 945–0967
Osprey, Rock Harbor in Orleans, 255–1266
Rock Harbor Charter Boat Service in Orleans, 255–9757
Leigh A. Wentworth, Rock Harbor in Orleans, 255–1809
The Naviator, at Town Pier in Wellfleet Harbor, 349–6003
Shady Lady, at MacMillan Wharf in Provincetown, 487–1700

Bait-And-Tackle Shops

The following is a listing of some Cape Cod bait-and-tackle shops:

Maco's, Route 6 in Buzzards Bay, 759–9836
Red Top, Main Street in Buzzards Bay, 759–3371
Cape Marine, Shore Road in Monument Beach, 759–4410
The Tackle Box, Dillingham Avenue in Falmouth, 540–6800
Gun and Tackle, at the harbor on Scranton Avenue in Falmouth, 548–0143
Green Pond Fish'n Gear, Menauhant Road in East Falmouth, 548–2573
Fishing Plus, Canal Road in Sagamore, 888–5197
Biff's, Route 6A in Sagamore, 888–4988
Canal Marine, Freezer Road in Sandwich, 888–0096
Sandwich Ship Supply, Tupper Road in Sandwich, 888–0200
Sports Port, West Main Street in Hyannis, 775–3096
Hyannis Smallboat Marina on Ocean Street, 775–1931
Truman's, Route 132 in Hyannis, 771–3470
The Tackle Box, Village Marketplace in Hyannis, 778–6556
Cape Cod Rod and Reel, Barnstable Road in Hyannis, 775–7543
Bass River Bait and Tackle, Route 28 in West Dennis, 394–8666
Riverview Bait and Tackle, Route 28 in West Dennis, 394–1036
Tackle and Sport Center, Route 28 in Harwich Port, 432–0416
Cliff's Bait and Tackle, Route 28 in West Chatham, 945–3228
Anderson's Hardware, Route 28 in West Chatham, 945–2525

OUTDOORS

Goose Hummock Shop, Route 6A in Orleans, 255–0455
Black Duck Sports Shop, Route 6 in South Wellfleet, 349–9801
Wellfleet Marine, at the Town Pier, 349–2233
Land's End Marine, Commercial Street in Provincetown, 487–0784

Boat Rentals

The following is a listing of some boat-rental operators on Cape Cod:

Maco's, Route 6 in Buzzards Bay, 759–9836
Peck's Boat, Route 28 in Cotuit, 428–6956
Water Sports, Carol Avenue in East Falmouth, 540–4451
Aquarius III, off Mill Way in Barnstable, 362–9617
Cape Cod Boats, Route 28 in West Dennis, 394–9268
Champion Line, Route 28 in West Dennis, 398–2266
Cape Sailing Center, A Dock in Hyannis, 771–9755
Starfish Enterprises, Bayridge Road in Orleans, 255–7317
Goose Hummock Shop, Route 6A in Orleans, 255–2620
Swift Sailing, Route 28 in Harwich Port, 432–5996
Wellfleet Marine, Town Pier in Wellfleet, 349–2233
Bay Sails Marine, Route 6 in Wellfleet, 349–3840
Flyers Boat Rentals, Commercial Street in Provincetown, 487–0898
Jack's Boat Rentals, Route 6 in Wellfleet, 349–9808
Monomoy Sail and Cycle, Orleans Road in North Chatham, 945–0811
Provincetown School of Sailing, Commercial Street in Provincetown, 487–1764

Marinas

The following list suggests some of the many marinas and boat-service operations on Cape Cod:

Bourne Marina, Academy Drive in Buzzards Bay, 759–2512
Perry's Boatyard, Shore Road in Monument Beach, 564–4221
Monument Beach Marine, off Emmons Road, 759–3105
Kingman Marine, Shore Road, Cataumet, 563–7136
Parker's Boat Yard, Red Brook Harbor Road in Cataumet, 563–9366
Fiddler's Cove Marina in North Falmouth, 563–5825
Woods Hole Marine Supply at Water Street, 540–2402
Falmouth Marine at the Inner Harbor, 548–4600
Town of Falmouth at the Inner Harbor, 548–7625
MacDougall's Marine, Falmouth Heights Road in Falmouth Heights, 548–3146

Green Pond Yacht Services, Green Harbor Road in East Falmouth, 548-2635

Edwards Boat Yard, Route 28 in East Falmouth, 548-2216

Little River Boat Yard in Waquoit, 548-3511

Prince's Cove Marina in Marstons Mills, 428-5885

Crosby Yacht Yard in Osterville, 428-6958

Sagamore Bridge Marine, State Road in Sagamore, 888-4403

Sandwich Cape Cod Canal Marina, Freezer Road in Sandwich, 888-2500

Barnstable Marine Service at Barnstable Harbor, 362-3811

Millway Marine at Barnstable Harbor, 362-4904

Lewis Bay Marina, South Street in Hyannis, 775-6633

Hyannis Marine, off Arlington in Hyannis, 755-6662

Ship Shops, Pleasant Street in South Yarmouth, 398-2256

Bass River Marina, Route 28 in West Dennis, 394-8341

Allen Harbor Marine Service, Lower County Road in Harwich Port, 432-0353

Harwich Port Boat Works at Wychmere Harbor, 432-1322

Saquatucket Harbor Marine, Route 28 in Harwich Port, 432-2562

Chatham Yacht Basin, Barn Hill Lane in West Chatham, 945-0728

Oyster River Boatyard, off Barn Hill Road in West Chatham, 945-0736

Mill Pond Boat Yard, Eliphamet's Lane in Chatham, 945-1785

Mayfair Boat Yard, Old Mayfair Road in South Dennis, 398-3722

Northside Marina, Sesuit Harbor in East Dennis, 385-3936

Arey's Pond Boat Yard, Arey's Lane in South Orleans, 255-0994

Nauset Marine, Main Street in East Orleans, 255-0777

Wellfleet Marine at Town Pier, 349-2233

Provincetown Marina, off Commercial Street, 487-0571

Fresh-Water Fishing Places

Inland Cape Cod is speckled with many ponds and lakes offering enjoyable fresh-water fishing. Trout, bass, pickerel, yellow perch, and white perch are the species. Fresh-water fishing is permitted at these locations:

Bourne—Flax Pond and Red Brook Pond

Sandwich—Hoxie Pond, Lawrence Pond, Peters Pond, Pimlico Pond, Shawme Lake, Snake Pond, Spectacle Pond, and Triangle Pond

Mashpee—Ashumet Pond, Johns Pond, Mashpee Pond, Wakeby Pond, and Santuit Pond

Falmouth—Coonamessett Pond, Deep Pond, Grews Pond, Jenkins Pond, Mares Pond, and Siders Pond

Barnstable—Garretts Pond, Hamblin Pond, Hathaway Pond North, Long

Pond Centerville, Long Pond Newtown, Lovell's Pond, Middle Pond, Mystic Lake, Shallow Pond, Shubael Pond, and Wequaquet Lake
Yarmouth—Dennis Pond, Greenough Pond, Horse Pond, Long Pond, and Big Sandy Pond
Dennis—Fresh Pond and Scargo Lake
Harwich—Bucks Pond, Eldredge Pond, Hinckley's Pond, Long Pond, Sand Pond, and Seymour Pond
Brewster—Cahoon Pond, Cliff Pond, Little Cliff Pond, Elbow Pond, Flax Pond, Griffith's Pond, Higgin's Pond, Long Pond, Lower Mill Pond, Upper Mill Pond, Seymour Pond, Sheep Pond, Slough Pond, and Walker Pond
Chatham—Goose Pond, Lovers Lake, Mill Pond, Schoolhouse Pond, and White Pond
Orleans—Baker Pond, Crystal Lake, and Pilgrim Lake
Eastham—Depot Pond, Great Pond, Herring Pond, and Minister Pond
Wellfleet—Great Pond, Gull Pond, and Long Pond
Truro—Great Pond, Horseleech Pond, and Pilgrim Lake

Shellfishing

Most Cape Cod towns allow residents and nonresidents to gather shellfish—scallops, clams, oysters, and the like—for private consumption from specially designated areas and on certain days. Permits to do so are required by law and are obtained at town offices. When going shellfishing, be sure to heed warnings about contamination such as the highly toxic Red Tide, which can cause severe sickness. Cape Cod shellfish beds have been relatively contamination-free in comparison to other areas along the New England coast. The Cape's continuing population growth and concomitant ecological changes, however, may reverse this condition in the near future unless wise action is taken by everyone concerned.

Baseball—The Cape Cod League

If you want to see some of America's best college baseball players in action, take in the games of the Cape Cod Baseball League. They play an eight-week schedule during the summer. From out of the ranks of these players will come some of tomorrow's hottest professional stars. Carlton Fisk is just one among many Cape Cod League alumni, including the late Thurman Munson, who have made it in the big leagues. Local papers publish schedules and game times. Donations are accepted. Individual teams and their home fields are:

Wareham Gatemen, Clem Spillaine Field in Wareham
Falmouth Commodores, Fuller Field in Falmouth

ACTIVITIES AND ATTRACTIONS

Cotuit Kettlers, Lowell Park in Cotuit
Hyannis Mets, McKeon Field in Hyannis
Dennis-Yarmouth Red Sox, Red Wilson Field in South Yarmouth
Harwich Mariners, Whithouse Field in Harwich
Chatham A's, Veterans Field in Chatham
Orleans Cardinals, Eldredge Park in Orleans

Horseback Riding

The equestrian arts have long been enjoyed and diligently practiced on Cape Cod. Cape Cod riding facilities provide a wide range of services and programs—riding trails, instruction from beginner to advanced jumping, day programs in riding, horse boarding, indoor riding facilities, horses for sale, tack shops, and competition sites. Not all of the following stables, however, offer horse rentals for impromptu trail rides. Calling ahead is advised.

Fieldcrest Farm, 774 Palmer Avenue in the Sippewisset area of Falmouth, 548–6671
Haland Stables, Route 28A in West Falmouth, 540–2552
Hidden-Horse Farm, John Parker Road in East Falmouth, 548–4612
Moon-A-Kiss Farm Stables, Twin Oaks Drive in Hatchville, 563–5373
Boxberry Hill Farm, Boxberry Hill Farm Road in Hatchville, 564–4007
Cloverfield Farm, Cloverfield Way in North Falmouth, 563–3447
Spring Hill Farm, County Road in Cataumet, 564–4440
Maushop Stables, Old Mill Road in Mashpee, 477–1303
Holly Hill Farm, Flint Street in Marstons Mills, 428–2621
Dennis Riding School, Arline Road in South Dennis, 385–3030
Salt Meadow Farm, Great West Road in South Dennis, 398–3644
Sweetwater Farms, off Route 124 in Brewster, 896–3773
Deer Meadow Riding Stable, Route 137 in East Harwich, 432–6580
Woodsong Farm, Lund Farm Way in East Brewster, 896–5555
Nelson's Riding Stable, Race Point Road in Provincetown, 487–0034
Provincetown Horse and Carriage, 27 West Vine Street, 487–1112

Sightseeing, Cruises, and Whale Watching

The following services provide sightseeing, cruises, or whale-watching trips:

Martha's Vineyard & Nantucket Steamship Authority, P.O. Box 284 Dept H, Woods Hole, MA 02543, 540–2022. Offers daily sailings to Vineyard Haven on Martha's Vineyard Island and to Nantucket. Advance reservations, essential for the transport of autos, RVs, and trucks, must be made well in advance for the summer season. Parking is available at Woods Hole and at two other locations, off Palmer Avenue and Gifford, with connecting bus service to the terminal.

Island Queen, terminal located at Falmouth Harbor on Falmouth Heights Road, 548-4800. The *Island Queen* is strictly a passenger boat offering daily sailings from Falmouth Harbor to Oak Bluffs on Martha's Vineyard Island. The *Queen,* however, does carry bikes. This pretty vessel is available for island tours and moonlight cruises. Motels and parking are available near its terminal. The *Island Queen* operates from near the end of May to mid-October.

Hy-line Cruises, Ocean Street Dock, Pier #1 in Hyannis, 775-7185. Hy-line provides daily sailings to Nantucket and Martha's Vineyard, Hyannisport and Hyannis Harbor cruises, sunset cocktail cruises, and deep-sea-fishing trips on Nantucket Sound. Operates from mid-April to the end of October.

Cape Cod and Hyannis Railroad, 252 Main Street in Hyannis, 771-1145. Seeing the cranberry bogs, salt marshes, lovely villages, sand dunes, and sparkling seacoast from the window of a train is one of Cape Cod's great touring treats. The Cape Cod and Hyannis Railroad provides sightseeing trips, trips to and from the Boston area, dinner trains where meals and cocktails are served and live entertainment provided, moonlight cruises on the Cape Cod Canal with buffet and drinks, and train and ferry trips to Martha's Vineyard. On the Cape, the train makes stops at Hyannis, Sandwich, and Buzzards Bay. The Hyannis depot is located at 252 Main Street. Service operates from end of May to mid-October.

Cape Cod Canal Cruises, Onset Bay Town Pier in Onset (Route 6, Onset Beach/Point Independence Traffic Light), 295-3883. Two and three-hour cruises through the Cape Cod Canal from Buzzards Bay to Sandwich Basin. Also has Sunday jazz cruises, sunset cocktail cruises, and moonlight-and-music cruises. In operation from spring to autumn. Cruises are also reached from Hyannis on the Cape Cod & Hyannis Railroad.

Windsong Charters, Ocean Street Docks in Hyannis, 775-1630. Sail Nantucket Sound on an 1800s-type gaff-rigged ketch (a thirty-eight-foot two master), the windjammer *Spray.* Bar and snacks on board. Operates from early May to early November. Moonlight sailing on Friday and Saturday evenings.

Cape Cod Charters, Ocean Street Docks in Hyannis, 771-2225. The Friendship sloop is a classic New England sailing vessel, and you can take to the deep blue waters of Nantucket Sound on this beauty through this service. Also has moonlight cruises. Refreshments on board. Operates from mid-May to early September.

Hyannis Whale Watcher Cruises, Barnstable Harbor in Barnstable Village (off Route 6A), 775–1622 or 362–6088. Whale-watching trips on Cape Cod Bay from April through October. On-board food-and-beverage service. Free parking at Iyanough Motor Lodge, Route 132 in Hyannis.

Barnstable Whale Watch Tours, Barnstable Harbor in Barnstable, 362–8500. Whale-watching trips on Cape Cod Bay and other cruises.

Dolphin Fleet of Provincetown, MacMillan Wharf in Provincetown, 255–3857. Whale-watching trips on Cape Cod Bay and other cruises.

Whale's Tail II Cruises, MacMillan Wharf in Provincetown, 487–2980. Whale-watching trips on Cape Cod Bay, cocktail cruises at sunset, and private charters.

Provincetown's Portuguese Princess Whale Watch, MacMillan Wharf in Provincetown, 487–2641. Whale-watching trips on Cape Cod Bay. Galley serves Portuguese food, cocktails, and snacks.

Ranger IV & V, MacMillan Wharf in Provincetown, 487–1582. Whale-watching trips on Cape Cod Bay. Food and drinks on board, also a naturalist to describe the sights.

Hyannis Aviation, Barnstable Municipal Airport in Hyannis, 775–8171. Aerial sightseeing tours of Cape Cod.

Cape Cod Air, Municipal Airport in Chatham, 945–9000. Aerial sightseeing tours of Cape Cod.

Atlantic Clipper, MacMillan Wharf in Provincetown, 487–2274. Daily trips to historic Plymouth and its Pilgrim attractions—Plimoth Plantation, Mayflower II, wax museum, genealogical archives, and more.

Bessy, Town dock in Orleans, 255–8262. Cruises on Nauset Harbor.

The Hindu and the Olad, MacMillan Wharf in Provincetown, 487–0659 or 487–9308. Grand Banks schooners (windjammers) on Cape Cod Bay.

Art's Dune Tours, At Commercial and Standish streets, 487–1950. Jeep tours of the massive sand dunes in Cape Cod National Seashore. Operates from June through September.

Joyce's Sightseeing Dune Tours, 315 Commercial Street in Provincetown, 487–0515. Tours of sand dunes in Cape Cod National Seashore.

Indoors

Performing and Visual Arts

Cape Cod has long been known as the perfect place for artists, writers, musicians, dancers, craftspeople, and philosophers, all of whom come in the summer or live here year-round to find more rewarding inspiration and fewer distractions combined with a casual life style. This influx of highly productive people in the arts has, over several generations, produced a rich cultural environment and outstanding institutions that express the creative spirit. There are many opportunities for the visitor to participate in Cape Cod's cultural life. Every Cape Cod town offers a smorgasbord of cultural programs and activities throughout the year. Visitors and residents alike are encouraged to partake of whatever interests them most. The following organizations represent but a small sampling from this bountiful table:

Annual Cape Cod Writers' Conference, in West Hyannisport, 775–4811 from mid-June to mid-September and 394–0425 thereafter. Established in 1963, the Cape Cod Writers' Conference provides aspiring authors with a variety of courses on how to hone their skills and be more successful in the marketplace. Guest lecturers are highly regarded professionals in their special areas of publishing. The conference runs during a week in mid-August. Sessions are held at the Tabernacle, Craigville Conference Center.

Cape Cod Conservatory of Music, Art, and Dance at Beebe Woods Arts Center, Highfield Drive in Falmouth, 540–0611 or 362–2772. The conservatory, member of the National Guild of Community Schools of the Arts, offers the broadest range of courses in the arts available on the Cape for Children and adults in musical instruments, drama, the visual arts, and dance. Offered here is a myriad of courses, everything from playing the bassoon to the history of art to ballet instruction.

The Falmouth Artists Guild, 744 Main Street in Falmouth, 540–3304 Courses in the visual arts and exhibitions.

Lower Cape School of Art, 48 Pearl Street in Provincetown, 487–0101 Courses and exhibitions in the visual arts.

Cape Cod Chowder Club, Dennis Senior Center, Route 134 in West Dennis, 428–5492. Square and round dancing.

Scottish Dance Group, Woods Hole Community Hall on Water Street, 548–1428.

Bayberry Chamber Players, in Yarmouth Port, 362–2227.

Highland Light Scottish Pipe Band, Lutheran Church, Route 6A in West Barnstable, 428–6878.

Cantores, at the Methodist Church in Wellfleet, 349–3522. A cappella group singing classical and folk songs.

Society for the Preservation and Encouragement of Barbershop Quartet Singing in America, at the Universalist Church in Barnstable, 563–2471.

The Pro Arte Singers, in Sandwich, 888–1967. Classical and contemporary music.

The Provincetown Art Association, 460 Commercial Street in Provincetown, 487–0871. Courses and exhibitions in the visual arts.

ACTIVITIES AND ATTRACTIONS

Entertainment

A long-standing tradition on Cape Cod is free band concerts in the town parks. These concerts, held weekly in Chatham, Buzzards Bay, Dennis, Harwich, Hyannis, Yarmouth, and Falmouth during July and August, are as eagerly awaited, enthusiastically attended, and highly regarded as performances of top stars at the Cape Cod Melody Tent. In addition, cinemas featuring current films are located in Hyannis, Falmouth, West Yarmouth, Orleans, Harwich Port, Chatham, Dennis Port, Wellfleet, Dennis, Provincetown, and Buzzards Bay. Entertainment on the Cape, however, features much more than local bands and movies.

On Stage

During the summer, Cape Cod attracts many of the finest professional entertainers in the world as well as a large number of highly talented individuals hoping to become stars one day. The following list reveals where these people perform:

Cape Cod Melody Tent, West End Circle in Hyannis, 775-9100. The Cape's "Number One Showplace" for top star entertainment—Roberta Flack, Lou Rawls, Dionne Warwick, Willie Nelson, Alabama, Joan Rivers, Ray Charles, Harry Belafonte, Tony Bennett, The Oak Ridge Boys, and many more; performances from late June to first week in September; for schedule and advance tickets—Cape Cod Melody Tent, P.O. Box 1979, Hyannis, MA 02601.

Falmouth Playhouse, Theatre Drive, access off Route 151 or Old Sandwich Road, in North Falmouth, 563-5922. Popular Broadway musicals, such as *Dreamgirls* and *42nd Street,* with well known talent; pleasant restaurant on premises for lunch and dinner.

The Harwich Junior Theater, West Harwich, 432-2002. Summer classes in the theatrical arts for children six and older. Four plays produced by the children every summer.

Ohio University Players, Monomoy Theater in Chatham, 945-1589. The Ohio University Players have been performing for more than thirty summers here to enthusiastic audiences. Their fare includes Broadway musicals, comedies, and serious drama.

Wellfleet Harbor Actors' Theater, Wellfleet Harbor, 349-6835. Production of avant-garde works; performances on weekend evenings.

The Academy Playhouse, Orleans, 255-9929. The academy players take to the stage throughout the year in Orleans. Their offering in summer includes popular comedies and musicals, including works by Gilbert and Sullivan.

Cape Cod Repertory Theater Company, Sheraton Ocean Park Inn in

Eastham, 255–4021. Cabaret shows and revues featuring songs, dances, skits, and jokes.

Cape Cod Symphony Orchestra, 362–3258. A regional symphony orchestra that has received high praise for excellence; performances at various locations from fall through spring.

College Light Opera, Highfield Theater, Highfield Drive in Falmouth 548–0668. The most delightful group of performers on the Cape, all are college students who have been specially selected for their skills and talents from throughout the United States. They revive the best of musicals and light operas by such immortal composers as Gilbert and Sullivan, George and Ira Gershwin, Rudolf Friml, Stephen Sondheim, Cole Porter, Rodgers and Hammerstein, and others.

Cape Playhouse, Route 6A in Dennis, 385–3911. Popular comedies and musicals by leading entertainers such as Sandy Dennis and Michael Learned and, in the past, by stars such as Gregory Peck and Bette Davis; late June to the first week in September; matinees on Wednesdays and Thursdays.

Barnstable Summer Family Theater, Barnstable High School, West Main Street in Hyannis, 362–6333. Shows that will please kids and parents alike, such as *You're A Good Man Charlie Brown* and *Charlotte's Web.*

Woods Hole Community Hall, Water Street (next to the bridge) in Woods Hole, 548–9270. Various entertainments, concerts, folk and ethnic music, and educational programs throughout the year.

Heritage Plantation in Sandwich, Grove Street, 888–3300. Diverse program of jazz, popular, and classical music; in 1987, concerts by Cape Cod Chorale, Jazz Pops Ensemble, Empire Brass Quintet, Krakowiak Polish Dancers, Northern Lights Bluegrass, New Black Eagle Jazz Band, Mastersingers of Cape Cod, and Clan Sutherland & Highland Light Scottish Pipe Bands.

Barnstable Comedy Club, Route 6A in Barnstable Village, 362–6333. Theatrical productions and workshops throughout the year.

Nightclubs

Cape Cod has entertaining night spots of almost every kind—places featuring rock 'n' roll, disco, piano, Irish, country and western, jazz, ethnic, and folk music; and places offering dining and dancing, cabaret entertainment, comedy routines, and floor shows. There's something for the hot-blooded young, the mellow middle-aged, and the still cookin' older folks. Because nightclub entertainment is an ever-changing feast during the summer, ask the desk person at your accommodation for suggestions as to current entertainment offerings and the most popular night spots in the area. A large number of Cape Cod dining places offer live entertainment as part of the menu. You don't have to go far looking for fun. Some of these places are indicated in the

ACTIVITIES AND ATTRACTIONS

Accommodations and Dining sections under the towns in which they are located. It's the law that last call for drinks is at 12:30 A.M., and everything has to be off the table by 1:00 A.M. For safety sake, make sure someone in your party is the "designated sober driver." Listed below is but a brief selection of the many night places for fun and entertainment:

Laurels, Tara Hyannis Resort, West End Rotary, Hyannis, 775–7775
Casino-by-the-Sea, Grand Avenue, Falmouth Heignts, 548–0777
Pilots's Landing, Gallo Road, Sandwich, 888–6977
Wings discotheque at Yesterday's Hotel, Grand Avenue, Falmouth Heights, 548–4530
Christine's Restaurant, 581 Main Street, West Dennis, 394–7333
Compass Lounge, Route 28, South Yarmouth, 398–3668
Gee Willikers, Holiday Inn, Route 132 (Iyanough Road), Hyannis, 775–6600
Guido Murphy's Back Room, 615 Main Street, Hyannis, 775–7242
Pufferbellies, Route 28, Hyannis, 775–1236
Hanger 222 at the Hyannis airport, 771–9181
Improper Bostonian, Route 28, Dennis Port, 394–7416
Mill Hill Club, 164 Main Street, West Yarmouth, 775–2580
Olde Townhouse Cafe, Village Shopping Center, South Yarmouth, 398–6467
Century Irish Pub, 29 Locust Street in Falmouth, 548–0196
Irish Embassy Pub, Route 28 in East Falmouth, 540–6656
Rum Runner's Cafe, 318 Lower County Road, Dennis Port, 398–5673
Sundancer's, 116 Main Street, West Dennis, 394–1600
Capt. John's, Shank Painter Road, Provincetown, 487–3899
Cavern, 225 Cranberry Highway, Orleans, 240–0387
Surf Club, 315A Commercial Street, Provincetown, 487–1367
The Woodshed, 1993 Main Street, Brewster, 896–7771
Cape Pine Lounge, 177 Lower County Road, Dennis Port, 394–8820
Duck Inn Pub, 447 Main Street, Hyannis, 775–3000
Mallory Dock, 477 Yarmouth Street, Hyannis, 771–7511
Rascals Saloon, Route 28, West Yarmouth, 775–7800
Summersalts, Route 28, South Yarmouth, 398–6200
Pied Piper, 193A Commercial Street, Provincetown, 487–1527

Cape Cod Public Libraries

The public libraries of Cape Cod are tranquil places for further enlightenment. Rainy days make a library an uplifting oasis. A library is also a perfect place to take bored children who want to use their intelligence and imagination. Cape libraries are important sources of information for those tracing their family roots or doing research into early American history. Most have special collections relating to the history of their local area and interesting materials (docu-

70

ments, works of art, etc.) that have been donated by residents. The following libraries welcome all readers, residents and visitors alike. If you wish to visit a library and take out books, call ahead for hours of operation and fees charged.

Bourne

Johnathan Bourne Library, Sandwich Road, 759–3172

Falmouth

North Falmouth Public Library, Chester Street, 563–2922
West Falmouth Library, Route 28A, 548–4709
Falmouth Public Library, Main Street, 548–0280; new statue of Katherine Lee Bates, author of the poem "America"
Woods Hole Library, Woods Hole Road, 548–8961
Marine Biological Laboratories Library, Water Street, 548–3705; one of the most famous scientific libraries in the world
East Falmouth Public Library, Route 28, 548–6340
National Marine Fisheries Library, Water Street, 548–5123; the oldest national marine-fisheries library in the United States

Mashpee

Mashpee Public Library, Route 151, 477–0323; interesting documents and materials relating to history of the Wampanoag Indians

Sandwich

Sandwich Public Library, Main Street, 888–0625; closed Sundays and Mondays

Barnstable

Cape Cod Community College, off Route 132 in West Barnstable, 362–2131; in the William Brewster Nickerson Memorial Room, the Cape's most extensive collection of books, documents, and archival materials
Hyannis Public Library, 401 Main Street, 775–2280; a large John F. Kennedy collection
Cape Cod Synagogue Library, 145 Winter Street, 775–2988
Osterville Free Library, Wianno Avenue, 428–5757
Weldon Library, Route 149, 362–2262
Cotuit Public Library, Main Street, 428–8141; ship models and bound classics

Sturgis Library on Route 6A, Barnstable Village, 362–6636; in the 1644 home of Reverend John Lothrop; considered the oldest library building in the country; an excellent collection of genealogical records and maritime-history documents and materials

Centerville Library, 585 Main Street, 775–1787

Yarmouth

Yarmouth Library Associates, Route 6A, Yarmouth Port, 362–3717
West Yarmouth Library, Route 28, 775–5206
South Yarmouth Library Associates, 312 Main Street, 398–6626

Dennis

West Dennis Free Public Library, Route 28, 398–2050
Dennis Memorial Library, Old Bass River Road, 385–2255
Jacob Sears Memorial Library, 23 Center Street, East Dennis, 385–8151

Brewster

Clarence J. Hay Library at the Cape Cod Museum of Natural History, Route 6A, West Brewster, 896–3867
Brewster Ladies Library, Route 6A, 896–3913

Harwich

Chase Library, Route 28, West Harwich, 432–2610
Harwich Port Library, Lower County Road, 432–3320
Brooks Free Library, Main Street, Harwich, 432–1799; collection of John Rogers figurines

Chatham

South Chatham Library, Route 28, no phone
Eldredge Public Library, 564 Main Street, 945–0274

Orleans

Snow Library, Main Street, 255–3848

Eastham

Eastham Public Library, Samoset Road, 255-3070

Wellfleet

Cape Cod National Seashore Library, Park Headquarters, Marconi Station, South Wellfleet, 349-3785
Wellfleet Public Library, Main Street, 349-6009

Truro

Cobb Memorial Library, Route 6A, 349-6895
Pilgrim Memorial Library, Route 6A, North Truro, 487-1125

Provincetown

Provincetown Public Library, 330 Commercial Street, 487-0850

Art Galleries

The jewels in Cape Cod's crown are its art galleries. The quality of work exhibited within them—oils, acrylics, watercolors, mixed media, sculptures, and photography—is comparable in excellence to what one would find in large cities such as New York, Boston, Chicago, and San Francisco. The subject content ranges from realistic scenes of Cape Cod to metaphysical concepts, from still-life studies to portraits of individuals. Both well-established and new talents are represented. You'll find the highest concentration of galleries in Provincetown, long regarded as a dynamic center of American art. Nearby Wellfleet is also growing in importance as more galleries open up for business there. The following is but a partial listing of the many art galleries you will find on Cape Cod. Most are open every day during normal business hours; some are also open in the early evening. Receptions to celebrate the opening of special shows are frequent occurrences at galleries and are highlights of the Cape's social life. During the summer many towns have festive, outdoor art exhibitions, featuring paintings from both professional and amateur artists, where some excellent buys can be had.

Provincetown

J. L. Becker Gallery, 453 Commercial Street, 487-2545
David Brown Gallery, 430 Commercial Street, 487-4424

ACTIVITIES AND ATTRACTIONS

Robert Clibbon Gallery, 120 Commercial Street, 487–3563
DeBerry Gallery, 212 Commercial Street, 487–4231
Eva De Nagy Art Gallery, 427 Commercial Street, 487–9669
East End Gallery, 424 Commercial Street, 487–2913
Eye of Horus Gallery, 7 Freeman Street, 487–9162
Fine Arts Work Center, 24 Pearl Street, 487–9960
Ellen Harris Gallery, 355 Commercial Street, 487–1414
Julie Heller Gallery, 2 Gosnold Street, 487–2169
Impulse, 188 Commercial Street, 487–1154
Long Point Gallery, 492 Commercial Street, 487–1795
Massimo, 416 Commercial Street, 487–0265
Anne Packard Gallery, 621 Commercial Street, 487–3965
Provincetown Art Association and Museum, 460 Commercial Street, 487–1750
Provincetown Group Gallery, 286 Bradford Street, 487–0275
Tennyson Gallery, 237 Commercial Street, 487–2460
Wenniger Graphics Printmaker Gallery, 443–445 Commercial Street, 487–2452

Wellfleet

Blue Heron Gallery, Bank Street, 349–6724
Cielo Gallery, East Main Street, 349–2108
Connoisseur, East Main Street, 349–2108
Hopkins Group Gallery, Main Street, 349–7246
Jacob-Fanning Gallery, Bank Square, 349–9546
Kendall Art Gallery, East Main Street, 349–2482
The Left Bank Gallery, Commercial Street, 349–9451

Orleans

Orleans Art Gallery, Corner of Main Street and Rock Harbor Road, 255–2645
Peacock's Pride Art Gallery, Peacock Alley near junction of Routes 6A and 28, 255–6396
Tree's Place, Junction of Routes 6A and 28, 255–1330

Hyannis

Barber Gallery, 248 Stevens Street, 775–0021
Signature Gallery, Village Marketplace, Stevens Street, 771–4499

INDOORS

Osterville

Alpert Gallery, 843 Main Street, 428-7686
Birdsey on the Cape, 12 Wianno Avenue, 428-4969

Cotuit

Yvette Bouchard Gallery, Route 28, 428-3699

Barnstable

Cape Cod Art Association, Route 6A, 362-2909
Gallery Under the Elms, Route 6A, 362-6069
Robert P. Wheeler Art Gallery, Route 6A, 362-9688

Dennis

Grose Gallery, Route 6A, 385-3434
Ruth Waite Studio Gallery, 239 Main Street in Dennis Port, 394-5869

Falmouth

Cape Cod Gallery of Contemporary Art, 49 North Main Street, 548-4121
Falmouth Artist's Guild, 744 Main Street, 540-3304
Market Barn Gallery, 15 Depot Avenue, behind the Market Book Store, 540-0480

Brewster

Aries East Gallery, Route 6A and Ellis Landing, 896-7681

Chatham

Paul Calvo Art Gallery, 490 Main Street, 945-3932
Creative Arts Center, 154 Crowell Road, 945-3583
McElwain-Falconer Art Studio, 492 Main Street, 945-2867

Harwich Port

Guild of Harwich Artists, 49 Lower Bank Street, 430-0410
Richardson Gallery, Route 28, 432-0720

Crafts

Cape Cod's ethos of self-reliance has produced a tradition of excellence in the crafts that is several centuries old, as old, in other words, as America itself. Past Cape Codders made things of utility, everything from home furnishings to sailing ships; then they added style and beauty to them. Today's Cape craftspersons continue this tradition by emphasizing individual style, the beauty of the object being made, the quality of materials and workmanship, and an unfailing utility. In the past, form followed function. Today both qualities are intertwined. Excellent craftspersons and their work in all media can be found in abundance in every town on Cape Cod. The following, all members of the Society of Cape Cod Craftsmen, are but a few of the many artisans working on Cape Cod:

Bourne

Richard Kaish—bronze jewelry—10 Monument Neck Road, 759–9019

Santuit

Anne Barrett—sheepskin jackets—and Joe Barrett—brass and silver buckles—Route 28, 428–5374

Woods Hole

Vivian Dreisbach—weaving and spinning—P.O. Box 416, 548–2171

Sandwich

June Kershaw—silver and gold jewelry—9 Liberty Street, 888–6251
Douglas Lyon—jeweler—247 Old County Road, 888–4818
Joy Anne MacConnell—cut out silhouettes of people—P.O. Box 149, 362–5167
Nina Baer Sutton—Sandwich glass jewelry—Old County Road, 888–1072
Ruth and Joe Wimbrow—gifts and toys (House of Fine Woods)—43 Atkins Road, 888–6019

West Barnstable

Robert Black, Jr.—weaver (The Blacks Weaving Shop)—Route 6A, 362–3955
Ron Dean—potter (Blue Heron Pottery)—1000 Osterville Road, 428–6085
Hilary Gifford—hand-painted silks—P.O. Box 42, 362–3538
Rick Moran—fine oak furniture—P.O. Box 204, 362–9589

INDOORS

Cynthia Neilson Parker—jeweler—151 South Sandwich Road (Mashpee), 477–6518

Marilyn Strauss—miniature replicas (Salt and Chestnut Weathervanes)—Route 6A at Maple Street, 362–3012

Osterville

Tom Mazzel—Nantucket Lightship baskets—17 Donna Avenue, 428–7166

Centerville

Roy L. Dupuy—woodcarver and shipcarver—1301 Bumps River Road, 775–2215

Mildred White—quilter—415 Main Street, 775–2956

Hyannis

Dave Lamson—fabric picture frames—P.O. Box 1314, 775–7186

Mira-Slava Pissarenko—old-world Easter-egg decoration, Polish paper cutting—25 Brookshire Road, 771–8427

West Yarmouth

Dorothy Bell—stained glass (Dutch Belle)—300 Camp Street, 771–6916

Bob and Mary Davies—Cape Cod Copper Enameling—24 Jay Bird Lane, 775–1821

Dennis

Michael Baksa—goldsmith (Theatre Marketplace)—Route 6A, 385–5733

Claire Chalfin—porcelain beaded jewelry and pottery—90 Shore Drive, 385–3463

Randy & Elaine Fisher—bird carvings—5 Walden Place, 385–2880

Pauline Haskell—uniquely decorated fine leather—5 Gates Path, 385–5056

Kate Thompson—hand-painted silks—200 Main Street, 394–5600

Brewster

Thomas Brennan—custom inlay work, veneers, and marquetry—451 Stony Brook Road, 385–2970

Marion Eckhardt—pottery, batik (Brewster Pottery)—Route 124 and Tubman Road, 896–3587

ACTIVITIES AND ATTRACTIONS

Judith Griffin—batik—1271 Long Pond Road, 896-6657
James and Pamela Talin—hand bookbinding—Route 6A, 896-6444

Yarmouth Port

Barrie Cliff—pewter (Pewter Crafters of Cape Cod)—927 Main Street, 362-3407
Ross Coppleman—fine jewelry (Sunflower Marketplace)—Route 6A, 362-6108
Martha Watson Lorentzen—handmade baskets—2 Jared Lane, 362-5241

Harwich

Pamela Black—pottery, batik (Paradise Pottery)—Route 28, 432-1713
Darigan and Froes—leather (Meadowlark Leather)—P.O. Box 600, 432-4197
Anne C. Ross—enamels—65 Round Cove Road, 432-5188

Harwich Port

Phyllis Kalmer—fine porcelain (Starflower Pottery)—835 Main Street, 432-6277

Chatham

Barbara Doyle—clay (Clayworks)—364 Cedar Street, 945-3189
Kathy and Robert Loring—Nantucket Lightship and pine-needle baskets, scrimshaw, and carvings—P.O. Box 1145, 432-8746
Marcy Pumphret—scrimshaw—333 Old Harbor Road, 945-0782

Orleans

Gail Binney-Winslow—quilter of clothing and wall hangings—Chatham Road, 255-0525
Lisa Boken—potpourri and herbs (Meadowcrafts)—5 Longview Drive, 255-5572
Bonny Campbell-Runyon—herbal wreaths and wall fans (Gatherings)—Portamicut Road, 255-5788
Mikael Carstanjen—pottery (New Horizons)—Peacock Alley, Route 28, 255-8766
Charis Craven—gold and silver jewelry—8 Juniper Lane, 255-1025
Ann Hart—ceramics and jewelry—P.O. Box 232, 255-4187

Mary Havener—pottery and porcelain (New Horizons)—Peacock Alley,
Route 28, 255-8766
Jean Jensen—spinner and weaver (New Horizons)—Peacock Alley, Route
28, 255-8766
Christine Martell—soft-sculpture environments—1119 Main Street,
240-0514
Rosalie and Tom Nadeau—pottery (Peacock's Pride Art Gallery)—Route
28, 255-6396
Bobby and Curt Rosser—New England and Shaker basketry—P.O. Box
888, 255-7073
Mary Stackhouse—pottery and luster jewelry—P.O. Box 951, 255-4938

Eastham

Donna and John Knight—handmade paper (The Glass Eye)—Main Street
Mercantile, Route 6, 255-5044
Melanie Kline O'Donnell—silver and goldsmith (Sail on Silver Girl)—Main
Street Mercantile, 255-7367
Paulette and Hugh Penney—basketmakers (Sunken Meadow Basket-
works)—North Sunken Meadow Road, 255-8962
Dale Michael Wade—traditional baskets with flower motif (Basketworks)—
185 Bridge Street, 255-6328

Wellfleet

Marla Freedman—woodturnings (The Hopkins Group Gallery)—Main
Street, 349-7246
William Nicholson—wood boxes—P.O. Box 736, 255-7389
Janet Petrillo—weaver—P.O. Box 753
Suzanne Requa—stoneware pottery (Salt Marsh Pottery)—East Main
Street, 349-3342
Florence Richardson-Rich—hooked rugs—Commercial Street, 349-3989

Truro

Nancy Lyon—scrimshaw—P.O. Box 358, 349-3487
Thomas Wojtalak—nautical wood sculptures (Harbor Scenes)—Route 6A,
349-6247

Shopping

Many people come to Cape Cod not to stake a claim to a swath of beach but
to shop at our outlet and bargain stores, at our fancy and high-price bou-

Traveling the scenic roads of Cape Cod will bring you to art galleries where the works of local artists and craftspersons delight visitors with their creativity. You'll also find trading posts that were established by the Pilgrims in the 1600s. In a real sense, American free enterprise began right there.

tiques, and at our antique emporiums. Eventually, everyone vacationing on Cape Cod gets bitten by the shopping bug, especially during rainy days or when they feel the need to bring souvenirs to loved ones left back home. Cape Cod has a plethora of stores selling goods that accommodate all spending limits. You can buy "great stuff cheap" and "put on the ritz" for hundreds of dollars.

Hyannis is Cape Cod's major center for shopping. On Route 132—Iyanough Road—there's the Cape Cod Mall, the largest on the peninsula. This enclosed mall has a Jordan Marsh, Filene's, Sears, a large number and variety of specialty boutiques and stores, several eating places, and various services. Across Route 132 from this mall is the Capetown Mall. It has a K-Mart, Radio Shack, and several other stores. A multiscreen cinema is also in this area, as well as a drive-in church. Main Street in Hyannis has many stores, too—army and navy surplus, many souvenir places, clothing stores, and candy shops.

West Yarmouth, Dennis, Falmouth, and Orleans also have large shopping malls. The main shopping streets of Provincetown, Chatham, Osterville, New Seabury, and Falmouth village are also very popular with visitors for their charm and diversity of offerings. Every Cape town has stores of one kind or another, catering to the type of people who live or visit there. Some are "you all come" towns. Others seem to prefer the Gucci and Cartier set.

Stop and Shop is a large supermarket chain serving Cape Cod. Purity Supreme, Angelo's, Heartland, and A&P are other fine multidepartment supermarkets. Food prices are higher on Cape Cod than on the mainland, but there are also many daily bargains and specials. Many of the large supermarkets and some convenience stores are open twenty-four hours every day. A large number of stores are open all day Sunday. Liquor stores are open daily except Sundays.

The following is a listing of some places for good buys or just for the fun of browsing:

Factory Outlets

Christmas Tree Shops—Cape Cod's most popular discount stores offering a variety of merchandise—in Falmouth, Sagamore, Hyannis, West Yarmouth, West Dennis, Yarmouth Port, and Orleans

The Basket Shoppe—baskets and wicker—in Hyannis and West Barnstable

Ocean State Job Lot—a variety of merchandise—in Falmouth and South Yarmouth

Corning Factory Store—Corning Ware and Pyrex—in Sagamore

Dansk Factory Outlet—quality wooden products—in Hyannis

Swank Factory Store—jewelry, leather goods, personal accessories—in Falmouth

Europa—importer of interesting clothing and furnishings—in Hyannis, West Falmouth, and New Seabury

Van Heusen Factory Store—shirts and sportswear for men and women—in Sagamore, Pocasset, East Falmouth, and Chatham

Quoddy Factory Store—shoes for men and women—in Sagamore, East Falmouth, and South Yarmouth

Colonial Candle of Cape Cod—candles and gifts—in Hyannis, Orleans, West Dennis, and Falmouth

Mill Stores—unpainted furniture—in Hyannis, West Harwich, and Dennis Port

Kitchen Etc.—fine dinnerware—in Hyannis

Big & Tall—clothing for men—in South Dennis

Auctions

Eastham Auction House, Holmes Road, North Eastham, 255–9003

Sandwich Auction House, 15 Tupper Road, Sandwich, 888–1926

Flea Markets

Dick and Ellie's Flea Market, Route 28 at the Mashpee Rotary, 477–2721

Wellfleet Drive-in Flea Market, Route 6, South Wellfleet, 349–2520

Antiques

Cape Cod is an antique maven's heaven. The shops are all over the peninsula. Your best bet is to tour around, poke in and out, and keep a sharp eye out for good buys. The following is but a brief listing:

Caleb's Antiques, Route 28A, West Falmouth, 548–4440

Windsor Antiques, 400 Main Street, Chatham, 945–4343

Aurora Borealis Antiques, 104 Queen's Buy Way, Falmouth, 540–3385

The Spyglass, 618 Main Street, Chatham, 945–9686

Simply Lace, Route 28, Peacock Alley, Orleans, 255–8916

Leaning Tree Antiques, 632 Main Street, Dennis, 385–8826

Leona's Antiques, Route 6A, Yarmouth Port, 362–5169

Country Peddlar, Route 28, Dennis Port, 394–5163

Pleasant Bay Antiques, Route 28, South Orleans, 255–0930

Countryside Antiques, Lewis Road, East Orleans, 240–0525

Design Works, 15 Main Street, Cotuit, 428–9114

ACTIVITIES AND ATTRACTIONS

Specialty Shops

The Duck Blind—sport arts and collectibles—Munson Meeting Way, Chatham, 945-2626

White Lace & Promises—fine lingerie—Village Market Place II, Hyannis, 771-8711

Eldred Wheeler—handcrafters of fine eighteenth-century furniture—875 Main Street, Osterville, 428-9049

Stephanie's—"largest collection of swimwear in New England"—382 Main Street, Hyannis, 775-5166

Salt and Chestnut—antique and new weathervanes—Route 6A, West Barnstable, 362-6085

Kensington's—Nantucket Lightship handbags—172 Main Street, Falmouth, 548-7940

Allen Harbor—precision wind and weather indicators—335 Lower County Road, Harwich Port, 432-0353

Simpler Pleasure—unique, quilted travel bags—393 Main Street, Chatham, 945-4040

The Clambake Company—complete clambakes to go—P.O. Box 1677, Orleans, 255-3289

Mason & Sullivan—antique-reproduction clock kits—Higgins Crowell Road (off Willow Street), Hyannis, 775-4643

Goose Hummock Shop—marine and sporting supplies store—Route 6A, Orleans, 255-0455

Raspberry Thistle—fine fabrics for those who sew—79 Main Street, West Dennis, 398-8200

Waquoit Glass Works—creative stained glass—42 Carriage Shop Road, Waquoit (East Falmouth), 548-6215

Bookshops

Cabbages and Kings (children's books), 628 Main Street, Chatham, 945-1603

Bayberry Books, 368 Main Street, Hyannis, 775-8270

Chart House Books, Village Marketplace, Hyannis, 771-4880

Eight Cousins Children's Books, 630 Main Street, Falmouth, 548-5548

Falmouth Booksellers, 281 Main Street, Falmouth, 540-8639

The Market Bookshop, 15 Depot Avenue, Falmouth, 548-5636; 22 Water Street, Woods Hole, 540-0851 (this is the author's personal favorite because it can order and deliver in a short time almost any book in print, even obscure titles)

Sign of the Owl, 13 Wianno Avenue, Osterville, 428-9393

Titcomb's Book Shop, Route 6A, East Sandwich, 888-2331

Tuttle Travel Book Store, 113 Corporation Road, Hyannis, 771–3535
Parnassus Book Service, Route 6A, Yarmouth Port, 362–6420
Harwich Bookstore, 390 Main Street, Harwich Port, 432–0798
Provincetown Bookshop, 246 Commercial Street, 487–0964
Royal Discount Books, Route 134, South Dennis, 398–5659
Yellow Umbrella Books, 501 Main Street, Chatham, 945–0144
Compass Rose Book Shop, Main Street, Orleans, 255–1545
Brown & Clark Booksellers, Mashpee Commons Shopping Center, Mashpee, 477–6545

Calendar of Special Events

Every town on Cape Cod schedules some special event for the enjoyment of residents and visitors alike—bazaars, bingo, festivals, sporting events, parades, firework displays, arts and crafts fairs, band concerts, painting exhibitions, cookouts, clambakes, open houses, and tours. The following calendar lists just some of these events:

April

Seagull Six Spring Classic Race in Woods Hole
Cape Cod Mall Sport and Recreation Show in Hyannis

May

May Day Celebration at the Thornton W. Burgess Museum in Sandwich
Figawi Race (ocean sailboat race) from Hyannis to Nantucket and return
Johnny Kelly Great Hyannis Road Race
Open House at Massachusetts Military Reservation—equipment displays, aerial stunt flying, stunt parachuting; entrances to base off of Otis rotary, Route 151 in Falmouth, and Route 130 in Forestdale
Memorial Day celebrations in all Cape Cod towns

June

Sprint Triathlon at Craigville Beach
Annual Cape Cod Chowder Festival in Hyannis
Annual Heritage Plantation Antique Show and Sale in Sandwich

ACTIVITIES AND ATTRACTIONS

Thornton W. Burgess Society Herb Festival in Sandwich
Crafts Show at the Pilgrim Congregational Church in Harwich Port
Strawberry Festival at Saint Barnabas Church in Falmouth
Portuguese Festival in Falmouth
Scottish Highland Festival at Dennis–Yarmouth High School
Sandwich Boardwalk Ten-Kilometer Run
Pops Concert by the Cape Cod Symphony Orchestra in Hyannis
Blessing of the Fleet in Provincetown
Chatham Harbor Run

July

Independence Day celebrations in all Cape Cod towns
Dennis Summer Concerts Under the Stars
Wampanoag Indian Pow Wow in Mashpee
Barnstable Country Fair, Route 151 in Hatchville area of Falmouth; agricultural and animal displays and competitions, midway rides and games, live entertainment
Seaside Triathlon—one-mile swim, twenty-five-mile bike race, ten-kilometer run; individual and relay participants
Artists and Craftsmen's Guild of the Outer Cape show in Orleans
Nauset Painters Outdoor Art Show in Orleans
Annual Falmouth Arts and Crafts Street Festival
Harwich Professional Arts and Crafts Festival
Weyars Annual Summer Fair and Lobster Roll Luncheon in West Yarmouth
Annual Antique Show and Sale in Harwich Port
Annual Cape Cod Co-Op Arts and Crafts Show in Orleans
House Tour of Historical Homes in Eastham
Orleans Summer Fair
Hyannis Street Festival

August

Puma Falmouth Road Race—7.1 miles, start in Woods Hole and finish at Falmouth Heights
Bobby Byrne's Ten-Kilometer Run for Leukemia
Tuna Tournament in Provincetown
Lower Cape Tennis Open in Orleans

CALENDAR OF SPECIAL EVENTS

Annual Arts and Crafts Fair of the Society of Cape Cod Craftsmen in Orleans
Annual Renaissance Arts and Crafts Fair in Dennis
Cape Cod Writer's Conference in Craigville
Dennis Festival Days
Cape and Islands Chamber Music Festival in Wellfleet, Woods Hole, and other communities

September

Windmill Weekend in Eastham
Fall Art Festival in Provincetown
Bud Light Endurance Triathlon—2.4-mile swim, 112-mile bike race, 26.2-mile run; Craigville Beach
Bourne Scallop Festival in Buzzards Bay
Harvest Festival at New Alchemy Institute in Falmouth
Harwich Cranberry Festival
Franlinia Festival at Ashumet Holly Reservation in Falmouth
Annual Bird Carver's Exhibit at Cape Cod Museum of Natural History in Brewster

October

Annual Yarmouth Seaside Festival
Annual Fall Antique Show in Dennis
Columbus Day holiday

November

Cape Cod Marathon in Falmouth
Thanksgiving festivals in many Cape Cod towns
Festival of Lights in Hyannis

December

Victorian Christmas Open House at Thornton W. Burgess Museum in Sandwich
Annual Falmouth Christmas Parade
Christmas festivals in many Cape Cod towns

Popular Attractions

Cape Cod is well endowed with all kinds of attractions besides beaches. Some are educational; others are just for fun; each provides interesting experiences for all ages. There's so much to do on Cape Cod that even bad-weather days can be fascinating and enjoyable.

The Major Sites

Cape Cod National Seashore, Lower Cape from Chatham to Provincetown. Attractions include beaches, bike and hiking trails, historical and ecological interpretive programs, fishing, surfing, historic homes and sites, and visitor centers. See pages 44–46 and other sections in this guide for more detailed information.

The National Marine Fisheries Service Aquarium, Woods Hole, 548–7684. This aquarium is Woods Hole's best treat for visitors. Antics of seals in the outdoor pool delight all ages. Indoors there are tanks with live species of fish and shellfish common in North Atlantic waters; exhibits on the East Coast fishery; and pools where kids can pick up and inspect lobsters, crabs, and many other live sea creatures. Open daily from mid-June to mid-September. Side door allows access to visitors in the off-season. Free.

Marine Biological Laboratory, Woods Hole, 548–3705, ext. 405 (call at least one day in advance to be included on a tour). Although summer is its busiest season, with scientists and students converging here from all over the world to do research and study, MBL nevertheless extends itself to the general public by offering daily tours. It is the only scientific institution in Woods Hole to do so. You'll visit a laboratory, talk to a researcher, and see both the holding tanks where live marine specimens are kept and a slide show on what MBL is and how it contributes to science. Tours during the summer only. Free.

The New Alchemy Institute, 237 Hatchville Road in East Falmouth (watch for direction sign off Route 151 and Sandwich Road), 563–2655. New Alchemy is a world-famous research-demonstration farm focusing on organic gardening, energy conservation, and resourceful living. You are welcome to walk through the farm on your own or take a guided tour. There are special day programs for children and various special events. New Alchemy has a visitor center and a farm store that sell, respectively, books on wise ecological management and organic gardening and fresh produce grown on its lands. Open all year. Fee charged for guided tours and special programs.

POPULAR ATTRACTIONS

Peach Tree Circle, Palmer Avenue in Falmouth. If you want to see the work of master gardeners, come and tour the fields at Peach Tree Circle. On just a few acres there are extensive flower beds, vegetable areas, and orchards. Three is a wide diversity of plantings keyed to their right maturation time within the growing season. Adjacent to the fields is an al fresco tea house serving light meals and homemade baked goods. Flowers, fruits, and vegetables from the gardens are also sold here. The gardens are open throughout the growing season. There is no charge to stroll about.

Falmouth Historical Society, Palmer Avenue near the Village Green, 548–4857. The historical society supervises two important buildings in Falmouth: the Julia Wood House, with its beautiful furnishings and garden; and the Conant House, a museum filled with rare glass and china, sailor's valentines, and items belonging to Katherine Lee Bates, author of the poem "America the Beautiful." Miss Bates first published her poem on 4 July 1895 in *The Congregationalist*. It was later set to the music of *Materna*, composed by Samuel A. Ward in 1882. Miss Bates's house can be seen on Main Street, but it is not at present open to the public. Guided tours of the Conant and Wood houses are available. Open mid-June to mid-September in the afternoon. Admission Charged.

New England Fire & History Museum, Route 6A in Brewster, 896–5711. This fascinating museum features hand- and horse-drawn fire equipment; old firemarks, helmets, and trumpets; a diorama of the "Burning of Chicago—1871"; an old-time fire house; an eighteenth-century New England Common; an old-fashioned apothecary shoppe; and a 1929 Mercedes-Benz Nurburg 460. It also has the Arthur Fiedler (late conductor of the Boston Pops) fire-memorabilia collection. Open Memorial Day weekend to Columbus Day weekend. Admission Charged.

The Cape Cod Museum of Natural History, Route 6A in Brewster, 896–3867. This excellent museum has exhibits on whales, geological survey maps, Indian artifacts, sea shells, minerals, birds, and fossils. It also has a working weather station, a live-turtle tank, and salt-water tanks containing several species of marine invertebrates and fish. The museum's Clarence Hay Library is one of the finest natural-history circulating libraries in New England. The museum is also at the starting point of three interesting walking trails: North Trail—ecology of the salt marsh; South Trail—cattail marsh and mature stand of American beech; and Wing Island Trail—salt marsh and beach area on Cape Cod Bay. A visit here is highly recommended for those of all ages. Open all year. Admission Charged.

Drummer Boy Museum, Route 6A in West Brewster, 896–3823. Dramatic scenes show the saga of America's War for Independence, from the time of Paul Revere and the Sons of Liberty in Massachusetts to the final battle for freedom at Yorktown in Virginia. This is a worthwhile stop for history buffs and a fascinating experience for all ages. The museum is near Cape Cod Bay and its beaches. A picnic area and a gift shop are on the premises. Open mid-May to mid-October. Admission Charged.

Sandwich Glass Museum, 129 Main Street in Sandwich, 888–0251. This unique museum exhibits beautiful decorative and table glassware produced by companies operating in Sandwich from 1825 into the twentieth century. Featured are pressed lacy glass with a stippled background; pattern glass of various designs in colors of amethyst, canary, green, and blue; and enameled, etched, and cut glass. There are also historical items from the lives of Daniel Webster, actor Joseph Jefferson, Thornton W. Burgess, and historian Frederick Freeman. Open daily from early April to late October; open all other months except January and holidays during November and December. Admission Charged.

Hoxie House, Route 130 in the center of Sandwich. Here is Cape Cod's oldest house and one of the oldest dwelling places in all of North America. It was built in 1637, or only seventeen years after the first landing of the English Pilgrims at Plymouth. The Hoxie House features an authentic saltbox roof, which has become a rare sight on Cape Cod. Open from mid-June to the first of October, Monday through Saturday.

Thornton W. Burgess Museum, Water Street, next to Dexter's Grist Mill in Sandwich, 888–4668. Author and naturalist Thornton Burgess was the creator of the best loved tales *Peter Rabbit* and *The Briar Patch*. This museum honors Mr. Burgess's life and work and his immortal characters— Peter Rabbit, Digger the Badger, Reddy Fox, Jimmy Skunk, and Chatterer the Red Squirrel. Burgess wrote more than 170 books and 15,000 daily columns. On exhibit is the largest known collection of Burgess's writings and original Harrison Cady illustrations. The museum holds a story hour, using live animals, daily at 1:30 P.M. Open April until Christmas. Donations Accepted.

Green Briar Nature Center, Discovery Hill Road off Route 6A in East Sandwich, 888–6870. Green Briar Nature Center not only has a live Peter Rabbit but also a Briar Patch trail along which you can walk. One of the best parts of this center is the mammoth kitchen where on any given day fresh jams, jellies, and relishes are cooked and poured into glass jars. The aromas and tastes are, as you can imagine, great seducers; respond to them by buying a few of your favorite jams. The center, open year-round, also offers a number of lectures, field trips, and workshops for the enjoyment of nature and the good life it offers. Donations Accepted.

Heritage Plantation of Sandwich, Grove and Pine streets, off Route 130, in Sandwich, 888–3300. Heritage Plantation is Cape Cod's finest and most beautiful privately operated attraction. It features a round Shaker barn, which contains a priceless collection of thirty-four mint-condition antique cars built from 1899 to 1937—Mercer, Stutz, Cord, Packard, Pierce-Arrow, Peerless, an American-made Rolls Royce, and Gary Cooper's snappy yellow 1930 Duesenberg Model J Tourester. There is also an old Cape Cod windmill, a military museum, a collection of antique firearms, military miniatures, Indian artifacts, a collection of American-flag replicas, an art museum, an old-fashioned carousel restored and running, exhibits of early tools, American folk arts, and one of the country's largest displays of original Currier and Ives lithographs.

Heritage Plantation is situated on seventy-six acres of landscaped grounds, flower beds, and nature trails. There are more than a thousand varieties of trees, shrubs, and flowers. During May, June, and July, thousands of Dexter rhododendrons bloom, and in summer 550 varieties of daylilies turn the grounds into blankets of bright, warm colors. The plantation presents three major exhibits a year. It also has a varied program of live entertainment. Don't leave Cape Cod without visiting Heritage Plantation. It's that special. Open daily from mid-May to the end of October. Admission Charged.

State Fish Hatchery, Off Route 6A in Sandwich, 888–0657. Trout by the thousands and in all sizes are raised here to inhabit the streams of Massachusetts and provide a fine sport for anglers. You are welcome to walk among the holding tanks and get close looks at the trout in their various stages of development. Fish-food pellets are available in vending machines for feeding the trout, an enjoyable experience for all ages. Open daily throughout the year. Free.

The Cape Cod Canal, Visitor Center on Academy Drive, off Main Street, in Bourne, 759–5991 or for additional information, 759–4431. The Cape Cod Canal extends seventeen and four-tenths miles in a southwesterly direction from Cape Cod Bay to Cleveland Ledge at Buzzards Bay. It has a controlling depth of thirty-two feet at mean low water and a minimum bottom width of 480 feet. It is the world's widest sea-level canal. In 1985 the Cape Cod Canal was designated a National Historic Engineering Landmark.

The first white man to see good sense in building a canal linking Cape Cod Bay with Buzzards Bay was Myles Standish, of Pilgrim fame, back in the early 1600s. He figured that the canal would help to increase trade between Plymouth Colony and the other European colonies, such as New Amsterdam (New York City), that were developing along the Atlantic seaboard. Several generations later George Washington also saw the economic and military advantages of a canal at Cape Cod. A canal would not only make sea transport between Boston and southerly ports faster and cheaper but also safer. Until a canal was actually built, thousands of vessels were lost on dangerous shoals and in fierce storms trying to make it around the Cape.

ACTIVITIES AND ATTRACTIONS

It was not until the early 1900s that the first Cape Cod Canal was completed and ready for service, thanks to the vision and bankrolling of the millionaire August Belmont, who incidentally had familial roots on the Cape. The Cape was linked to the Massachusetts mainland by two drawbridges over this early canal. Belmont, however, lost money on this venture because the canal did not generate the volume of traffic anticipated. It had major limitations, being too narrow and allowing only one-way traffic, and the drawbridges caused a number of accidents to ships attempting to get through. In 1928 the canal was bought by the federal government, and the U.S. Army Corps of Engineers was given the task of making it better. The corps realigned and deepened the canal so that it could accommodate two-way traffic. Army engineers developed and continue to improve upon a state-of-the-art traffic-control system as well as a system to monitor tide and wind conditions, which ensures safe navigation.

Under the direction of the engineers, the present Bourne and Sagamore bridges were constructed and opened to motor-vehicle traffic in the mid-1930s. These bridges are high enough to allow the largest ship to pass with more than enough clearance. Today the Cape Cod Canal is used by both commercial shipping and pleasure craft. You, too, can sail through the Cape Cod Canal on a tour boat operating from Onset (see page 65 for details). There are canal overlooks plus rest and picnic areas flanking both sides of the canal. Visitors center open Monday through Friday. Free.

The Aptucxet Trading Post, Aptucxet Road in Bourne, 759–9487. In 1627 the leaders of Plymouth Colony had a trading post built here for the purpose of exchanging their goods for furs brought in by Indians and white trappers. Within a short time, this commercial enterprise was sending a considerable amount of furs worth many thousands of pounds in British currency to merchants in the "olde country." The trading post was rebuilt by the Bourne Historical Society in 1930 on the original foundation. It now contains many artifacts from early white settlers and Indians, a salt works, and a grist mill. There is also the railroad station that was built for President Grover Cleveland, who spent his summer vacations in Bourne; inside is a model of the Cape Cod Canal. Open mid-April to mid-October. Closed Tuesdays. Admission charged.

Pairpoint Glass Works, 851 Sandwich Road—Route 6A in Sandwich, 888–0251. Pairpoint Glass Works uses age-old glass-blowing-and-shaping techniques to create beautiful and useful objects. You can watch master craftsmen at work and purchase their creations at the store on the premises. Pairpoint continues a long-honored Sandwich tradition, and a visit here is highly recommended. The blowing room is open Monday through Friday. Free. Store open daily.

Pilgrim Monument and Museum, Town Hill off Bradford Street in Provincetown, 487–1310. The Pilgrim Monument commemorates the landing of the Pilgrims in America in 1620, *an event that took place before they set foot on Plymouth Rock.* If the land had been more more receptive to agriculture here at land's end on Cape Cod, Provincetown could have been the Pilgrim's first settlement. The monument rises 352 feet above sea level, and it is considered the highest granite structure in the United States. There is an observation area on top, reached by stairs, from where you can see Cape Cod Bay, the open Atlantic Ocean, the sand dunes of Provincetown and North Truro, the curving land of Cape Cod at its most northerly point, and the distant shoreline of mainland Massachusetts. Conversely, the monument, on a clear day, can be often seen from the mainland, across Cape Cod Bay, off Duxbury Beach.

At the base of the monument is a museum containing exhibits depicting Pilgrim life, their ship the *Mayflower,* and the signing of the Mayflower Compact, which took place in Provincetown harbor. The museum also has memorabilia of both Admiral Donald B. MacMillan, the famous Arctic explorer and long-time resident of Provincetown, and Eugene O'Neill, the immortal American playwright who spent many summers in Provincetown and was a central figure in its cultural life. Open all year. Admission charged.

Ashumet Holly Reservation and Wildlife Sanctuary, Ashumet Road off Route 151 in East Falmouth, 563–6390. This forty-five-acre sanctuary was given to the Massachusetts Audubon Society by Wilfred Wheeler, who brought together and made flourish many species of American, European, and Oriental hollies. This beautiful and tranquil sanctuary is also lush in season with magnolias, dogwoods, rhododendrons, and wild flowers. Easy hiking trails take you through the stands of hollies and other plantings and around a lovely pond. During the summer, Ashumet Holly sponsors sightseeing cruises to the Elizabeth Islands. In addition various courses are taught during the year—for example, Oriental brush painting and dried-flower arranging. In late September Ashumet celebrates its Franklinia Festival, one of the few trees to flower in autumn and named in honor of Benjamin Franklin. Activities include hay rides, guided walks, slide programs, and refreshments. Open all year. Admission charged.

Wellfleet Bay Wildlife Sanctuary, Route 6 in South Wellfleet, 349–2615. An extensive wildlife sanctuary on Cape Cod Bay operated by the Massachusetts Audubon Society, Wellfleet Bay features a number of self-guided nature trails to marsh, beach, woodland, and island areas. There are interesting courses and lectures on natural history and conservation. This facility sponsors the best tours of the tern and other seabird habitats of remote Monomoy Island. It also operates a summer day camp for children. A gift shop is on the premises. Open all year. Admission charged.

Cranberry World Visitors Center, on the harbor in Plymouth, 747–1000. Although off the Cape, Cranberry World offers fascinating exhibits showing how cranberries were cultivated historically, how they are harvested now, and how they are processed into different kinds of delicious foods. Free samples of cranberry drinks are offered. Cranberries are Cape Cod's major agricultural crop, and Cranberry World in Plymouth tells the story best.

The best time to see the harvesting of cranberries on Cape Cod and in other southeastern Massachusetts areas is from mid-September to the end of October. The old way of harvesting was done by stoop labor using a wooden hand rake with an attached box; the berries were scooped up and collected into the box. Today the cranberry bogs are flooded, and the cranberries float to the top, forming brilliant scarlet lakes; the berries are then harvested by machines. It's a very interesting and colorful sight, so bring your camera. Cranberry bogs can be seen throughout the Upper Cape and the Mid Cape. They are easily identified as low, flat, open areas with vegetation growing close to the sandy soil, and appearing like a thick, green carpet. The bogs are extensive spaces, rectangular in shape and bordered by two-to-three-foot-high dikes.

Most cranberry growers do not mind if you hike their bogs. Stay on top of the dikes and don't walk on the bogs themselves, however, as your footsteps will crush the plants and their fruit. Cranberry World is open daily from the first of April to the end of November. Free.

The Edaville Railroad, Route 58 in Carver, 866–4526. This major attraction is located a few miles to the northwest of Cape Cod, with the easiest access being off Interstate 495. Edaville is famous for its "old time" huff-and-puff trains, which provide exciting rides around local cranberry bogs. There are also many other rides and family entertainments. Open from the first weekend in May to January third. Closed Thanksgiving Day and Christmas Day. From the end of October to January third, Edaville holds its popular Christmas Festival of lights, music, and special events. Admission charged.

The Town of Plymouth, Via Route 3 North. A visit to our peninsula would not be complete without experiencing the source from whence many of the early settlers of Cape Cod came and where the first Thanksgiving Day celebration was held. Here you will see famous Plymouth Rock with its "1620" inscription; *Mayflower II,* a full-scale replica of the original Pilgrim ship; Plimoth Plantation (746–1622), a re-creation of the first Pilgrim settlement—open daily April through November, admission charged; Plymouth National Wax Museum (746–6468), dramatic scenes of the Pilgrim adventure in the New World—open daily March through December, admission charged; the impressive statue of Sachem Massasoit, which has become a rallying point for today's Indians; Mayflower Society House; Pilgrim Maiden statue; Pilgrim Monument; Brewster Gardens; Pilgrim

Mother statue; Pilgrim Hall Museum, containing important historical artifacts of the early settlers; the 1640 Richard Sparrow House, the oldest in
Plymouth; the 1666 Jabez Howland House; Coles Hill Pilgrim burial
ground; and the 1809 Antiquarian House.

Historic Homes and Other Noteworthy Places

Bourne Area

Leonard Wood Homestead, Shore Road in Pocasset. The early home of
General Wood—commander of Theodore Roosevelt's "Rough Riders" in
the Spanish American War, governor-general of the Philippines, and candi-
date for U.S. president—it is currently under private ownership.

Cataumet Methodist Church, County Road in Cataumet. Built at a
nearby location in 1765 and originally a missionary church among the
local Indians, the church conducts services that are open to the public.

Wampanoag Indian Burial Hill, Bournedale Road in Bourne. Christian, "praying" Indians were buried here until the early nineteenth century. A man named King Saul was the last one. Many of the Indians in this
area were converted to the faith by Thomas Tupper and Richard Bourne.

Massachusetts Maritime Academy, at the end of Academy Drive in
Buzzards Bay. The Commonwealth's major training facility for seafaring
officers, the academy carries on a centuries-old maritime tradition in Massachusetts. Visitors are welcome; good views of ships entering and leaving
the Cape Cod Canal are plentiful.

Falmouth, Woods Hole

Bourne Farm, Route 28A in West Falmouth. This beautiful, working,
forty-acre farm features a restored 1775 farmhouse, barn, and other buildings; fields cultivated with various vegetables; a truly magnificent pump-
kin patch open to all in autumn; walking trails; and peach, pear, and apple
orchards. The farm is a delightful oasis of tranquility. Free.

Friends Meeting House, Route 28A in West Falmouth. Quaker worship
was held in this area as far back as 1720. The present building was built in
1775. An old Quaker graveyard flanks the meeting house, and across the
highway are old horse-carriage stalls used by the Friends. You are welcome to attend worship.

Saconesset House (Ship's Bottom Roof House), Old Homestead Road in
West Falmouth. Both the home, built in 1678 by Thomas Bowerman, a
Quaker, and the grounds are history books revealing how a Cape Cod farm

looked and operated more than three hundred years ago. Open from mid-June to late September. Admission charged.

Endeavor House, (548–1400, ext. 2663), Woods Hole Oceanographic Institution Exhibit Center, School Street in Woods Hole. Interesting exhibits feature some of the oceanographic research conducted by WHOI. Open June to Labor Day, Monday to Saturday. Free.

Bradley House Museum, (548–7270), Woods Hole Road next to Library in Woods Hole. Historical memorabilia of Woods Hole can be viewed from the end of June to mid-September. Admission charged.

First Congregational Church, on the Village Green in Falmouth. This quintessential New England church, built in 1708, features a brilliant white exterior, high steeple with weather vane, and a bell made by Paul Revere. Services are open to the public.

Mill Road Cemetery, off Mill Road in Falmouth. Historic burial ground contains the remains of early settlers and Revolutionary War soldiers. The cemetery is located near where Mill Road meets the main road to Woods Hole. There is a wooded lane that leads to this historic place, set a short distance from the road.

Saint Barnabas Church, on the Village Green in Falmouth. This beautiful Episcopal church reminds the visitor of similar structures gracing the small villages of England. You are welcome to attend services.

Church of the Messiah, Church Street in Woods Hole. This lovely Episcopal church is beloved by the scientists and residents of the Woods Hole area. You are welcome to attend services.

Sandwich

Nye Homestead, Old County Road in East Sandwich. This unique house dates from 1685 and features exposed construction details to give you an idea of how well people in that period built their homes. The antique furnishings are of interest to most visitors. Open from July to mid-October; closed Saturdays and Sundays. Admission charged.

Thomas Dexter's Grist Mill, Town Hall Square. This seventeenth-century mill has been restored to good working order. It grinds cornmeal fine enough to make excellent muffins or Indian pudding, and you can buy this delicious fixin' right at the mill. Open mid-June to mid-October.

Quaker Meeting House and the Steven Wing House, Spring Hill Road in East Sandwich. Worship has been held here continually since 1657, making this site the oldest meeting place for Quakers in this hemisphere. The present meeting house was built in 1815. Visitors are welcome. Also in this area is the historic Steven Wing House, a portion of which was built in 1641. It is furnished with colonial and Victorian period antiques. Open from mid-June to mid-October. Admission charged.

Mashpee

The Old Indian Meeting House, at Meeting House Pond, near cemetery off Route 28 in Mashpee. Considered to be the oldest standing place of Christian worship on Cape Cod, this meeting house was built in 1684, moved to this location in 1717, and served the spiritual and social needs of the so-called "praying" Indians of the Upper Cape for many generations. Open mid-June to beginning of September on Wednesday, Friday, and Saturday. Free. For more information, call Tribal Office at 477-1190.

Wampanoag Indian Museum, (477-1536), Route 130 in Mashpee. This interesting museum is housed in a 1793 building. It features early Indian artifacts and exhibits portraying Wampanoag life. Open from May to the beginning of October on Friday, Saturday, and Monday; open all year by appointment. Free.

Barnstable Area

Colonial Court House, (362-4682), Route 6A in Barnstable Village. This was the English king's court house in the eighteenth century. English justice was administered from here, as was opposition to the king's rule. The court house contains many historic items and memorabilia from the recent bicentennial celebration.

Captain Jonathan Parker House, on Parker Road in Osterville. Built in 1795 and now housing the Osterville Historical Society, this lovely Cape Cod home features displays of Victorian furnishings, Sandwich glass, nineteenth-century photos of Osterville life, a children's room with dolls, and many other period artifacts. Open from late June through September on Thursday and Sunday, 3:00 P.M. to 5:00 P.M. Admission charged.

Crosby Yacht Yard, via West Bay Road from center Osterville. The famous Crosby Cat Boat, a favorite of fishermen and leisure sailors, originated here in the mid-1880s. There's a plaque in honor of Horace Crosby here. The yacht yard now provides services to some of the most expensive sailing vessels found anywhere in the United States.

Dottridge Homestead, Ocean View Avenue in Cotuit. Built in the early 1880s, this home contains period furnishings and memorabilia. The house was moved to Cotuit from Harwich over log rollers pulled by oxen. Open from late June to Labor Day on Thursday and Sunday (afternoon). Donations accepted.

Saint Francis Xavier Church, South Street in Hyannis. This fine Roman Catholic church has long been associated with the Kennedy family, especially with Rose Kennedy, the beloved matriarch. John F. Kennedy worshipped here, and there's a plaque in honor of his memory on a pew in the chapel. You are welcome to attend services.

The Kennedy Compound, in Hyannisport. This is a private enclave of homes belonging to the Kennedy family. Rose Kennedy resides here. The compound is closed to the public, although harbor tours (see chapter 8) will take you by it.

John F. Kennedy Memorial, Ocean Street in Hyannis. The memorial is in a park overlooking Lewis Bay, and it consists of the presidential seal, a decorative fountain, and a pool. This memorial is emblematic of the late president's love for the sea and for sailing.

Trayser Memorial Museum, Route 6A in Barnstable Village. Originally built in the mid-1800s as a customs house and used in more recent times as a post office, the museum contains memorabilia relating to the history of Barnstable. Adjacent is an old-time jail; graffiti from incarcerated sailors can be seen on its walls. Open from the first of July to mid-September; closed Sunday and Monday. Admission charged.

Mary Lincoln House, Main Street in Centerville. Built in 1840, this house contains rare Sandwich glass, Revolutionary War uniforms and many other period costumes, bird carvings by Elmer Crowell, ship models, and beautiful quilts. Open from the first of June to early October; closed Monday and Tuesday. Admission charged.

Sachem Iyanough's Grave, Route 6A in Cummaquid. This is the burial site of the famous Indian chief who assisted the Pilgrims when they scouted settlement and trade possibilities in Barnstable. Iyanough was forced to seek refuge from Myles Standish and his force, who were exacting retribution against those native people who dared to challenge white dominance in this "new-found-land."

Reverend John Lothrop House/Sturgis Library, (362–6636), Route 6A in Barnstable. Built originally in 1644 by Reverend John Lothrop, the famous minister and patriarch of Barnstable, this house was expanded in 1782 by Captain William Sturgis, a mariner of considerable note. The library contains important genealogical material and the original 1605 Lothrop Bible. Open all year.

West Parish Meetinghouse, Route 6A and Meeting House Way. Considered to be the oldest Congregational church in America (established in Scituate, Massachusetts, in 1634 and in Barnstable in 1639). The West Parish Meetinghouse was originally built in 1717; it was restored in the 1950s. The cock at the top of the steeple was made in England and has overlooked this bit of Cape Cod since 1723, and the meeting house's bell was made by Paul Revere in the first decade of the 1800s. West Parish Meetinghouse is an architectural classic.

Yarmouth

Bass Hole in Yarmouth. It is speculated by those who wish such events to be true that the Viking warrior Thorvald, Leif Ericsson's younger brother, was killed by local Indians here. No evidence pertaining to the Vikings, however, has ever been found. In the mid-1800s this area was the site of a major shipbuilding enterprise operated by the Bray family. Today nature has taken over and converted the area back to its natural beauty, but you can imagine that the sails of Viking long boats are out on the horizon.

Winslow Crocker House, Route 6A in Yarmouth Port. A Georgian design home built in 1780, the house contains many exceptional antiques and is a prime showplace for the Society for the Preservation of New England Antiquities (617-227-2956). Open from the first of June to mid-October; closed Monday, Friday, and Saturday. Admission charged.

Friends Meeting House, Station Avenue in South Yarmouth. Built in 1809 after local persecution of the Quakers ceased, the meeting house offers services open to the public.

Captain Bangs Hallet House, (362-3021), off Route 6A in Yarmouth Port. This early Greek Revival home of a sea captain engaged in the China Trade houses a fine collection of early maritime artifacts and memorabilia: logs, charts, and chronicles; antique furnishings; and a 1740 kitchen. Open from early July to Labor Day. Admission charged.

Church of the New Jerusalem, Route 6A in Yarmouth Port. This lovely Swedenborgian church, which possesses an exceptional organ, is noted for the emphasis on music during services. You are invited to attend worship.

Judah Baker Windmill in Yarmouth. Built in 1791 and kept in operation as a moneymaking operation until 1891, this windmill was also used in a signaling system to announce the arrival and departure of Boston/Cape Cod packet ships.

Pawkanawkut Village Graves, Indian Memorial Drive in South Yarmouth. On this site was an Indian village that existed until the late 1700s. The Indian inhabitants were killed off by smallpox, and their remains are buried in unmarked graves according to ancient custom.

Yarmouth Port Village Pump, Summer Street in Yarmouth Port. Built in 1886, the pump served as the main source of fresh water for the village. Pumps such as this one were common in Cape Cod towns in the nineteenth century.

Dennis

Jericho House Museum, Trotting Park Road in Dennis. Built in 1801 for a Cape Cod sea captain, the structure now houses a fine collection of nineteenth-century antiques. An adjacent barn features tools and household implements used during the nineteenth century, exhibits of early salt works and a general store, equipment used in cranberry cultivation and

Your journey along the Cape's roadways will take you back decades before the American War for Independence to visit the first house built on the Cape and to a railroad station used by President Grover Cleveland when he vacationed there.

harvest, and a display of driftwood sculpture. Open from the first of July to Labor Day on Wednesday, Friday, and Saturday from 2:00 P.M. to 5:00 P.M. Donations accepted.

Hockum Rocks, Hockum Rock Road in Dennis. This rock pile was once the home of an Indian hermit who greeted visitors with the salutation, "Ho kum?"—meaning "Who comes here?"

Josiah Dennis Manse, (385–2232), Whig Street in Dennis. Built in 1736 and furnished with period antiques, including Reverend Josiah Dennis's portable pulpit/writing desk, the manse also has a fine collection of books and manuscripts relating to Cape Cod history. The oldest schoolhouse in Dennis is on the grounds of the manse. Open from July through August on Tuesday and Thursday from 2:00 P.M. to 4:00 P.M. Donations accepted.

Scargo Lake and Tower, off Scargo Road in Dennis. This twenty-eight-foot-high tower, built in 1902, offers good views of the surrounding landscape; the grounds contain picnic facilities and nature trails. This area is rich in Indian legends concerning Princess Scargo and that of Maushop, a friendly giant. Here also is the burial ground of the Nobscusset Indians and their chief Mashantampaine.

Shiverick Shipyards (historical plaque), Sesuit Neck Road in East Dennis. This was one of the largest shipyards on Cape Cod during the nineteenth century. Shiverick schooners and clippers sailed the waters of the world.

South Parish Congregational Church, Main Street in South Dennis. Built in 1835, the church had many sea captains in its congregation. Its organ was made in 1762 in London by a craftsman who also built one for the composer George Frederick Handel. The church's chandelier is made of 1835 Sandwich glass. You are welcome to attend worship.

Brewster

Brewster Historical Society Museum, second floor in Brewster Town Hall. The museum houses local historical exhibits. Open July through August, Wednesday through Friday, from 1:00 P.M. to 4:00 P.M. Free.

Harwich

Brooks Academy, Main Street in Harwich. Built in 1804 and used as a school to teach navigation, the academy now houses a historical museum of Indian and maritime artifacts, Sandwich glass, and old manuscripts. Open July through August on Monday, Wednesday, and Friday from 1:30 P.M. to 4:30 P.M. Free. The Old Powder House, adjoining Brooks Academy, used to store gun powder during the Revolutionary War and the War of 1812.

POPULAR ATTRACTIONS

Chatham

Atwood House, 347 Stage Harbor in Chatham. Built in 1752, the home contains period antiques, an extensive seashell collection, Sandwich glass, and Cape Cod books. In an adjoining shed are murals of Chatham painted by Alice Stalknecht-Wight. Open from mid-June to the end of September on Monday, Wednesday, and Friday from 2:00 P.M. to 5:00 P.M. Admission charged.

Chatham Fish Pier, off Main Street. Watch the fishing boats unload their catches of fresh seafood from a special observation deck. Best time to experience this typical Cape Cod event during weekdays is after 2:00 P.M.

Godfrey Windmill, at Chase Park in Chatham. Dating back to 1797, the mill still grinds corn during the summer to the delight of tourists. Open July through August; closed on Tuesday. Donations accepted.

Monomoy Island Wildlife Refuge, off Chatham Harbor and accessible only by boat. Contact the Massachusetts Audubon Society in South Wellfleet, 349–2615, for more information.

Railroad Museum, (945–0783), Depot Road in Chatham. Built in 1887 and now in the National Register of Historic Places, the structure was restored as a country depot and contains railroading memorabilia, models, equipment, and photographs. Open from the end of June to the Friday after Labor Day, 1:30 P.M. to 4:30 P.M.; closed Saturday and Sunday. Donations accepted.

Orleans

First Universalist Meeting House, Main Street in Orleans. Built in 1834, it now houses the Orleans Historical Society and contains exhibits of Indian, local-history, and lifesaving artifacts. Open July through August, Thursday and Friday, 2:00 P.M. to 4:00 P.M. Donations accepted.

French Cable Museum, Route 28 and Cove Road in Orleans. Built in 1890, the structure housed cable and transmission gear for transatlantic communications between North America and France. Open from July to mid-September, Tuesday through Sunday, 2:00 P.M. to 4:00 P.M. Admission charged.

Eastham

Doane Homestead, off Doane Road in Eastham. A marker here denotes where the first English settlers in Eastham established their habitation.

First Encounter Beach, (historical plaque), Samoset Road in Eastham. This is where a party of Pilgrims under the leadership of Myles Standish was attacked by local Indians. The attack took place shortly after the Pilgrims made their first landing in the New World in 1620 and before finally setting ashore at Plymouth. The reason for the attack was that, a few years previous, an Englishman had come into this area, captured some of the Indians, and sold them as slaves to buyers in Spain. The Indians were obviously concerned that these new white men had similar intentions. Although this "first encounter" was a conflict involving flying arrows and discharging muskets, it is said that no one was killed or injured. In a very real sense this "first encounter" was the advent of the decline of Indian cultures in New England.

1741 Swift-Daley House, (255–3380), Route 6 in Eastham. Once the home of Nathaniel Swift, one of the founders of the Swift Meat Packing Company, this historic house is furnished with antiques dating from the late-eighteenth century and other artifacts of interest. Open July through August, Wednesday and Friday, 1:30 P.M. to 4:30 P.M. Free.

Old Cove Cemetery, Cove Road in Eastham. The first cemetery in Eastham, the site contains the graves of early settlers and memorials to three who came over on the *Mayflower*. This area was also the site of the first meeting house in town, which was built shortly after settlement in 1644.

Captain Penniman House, Fort Hill Road in Eastham. A palatial Victorian home built in 1876 by a prominent whaling captain, the house is now an attraction within Cape Cod National Seashore.

Schoolhouse Museum, Nauset Road in Eastham. Built in 1869 and used as a Eastham school until 1905, it now serves as a museum of local history. Open July through August, Wednesday and Friday, 2:00 P.M. to 5:00 P.M. Admission charged.

Eastham Windmill, Route 6 in Eastham. Built in 1680 and still in good working order, the mill is open from the end of June to Labor Day.

Wellfleet

First Congregational Church, Main Street in Wellfleet. The building contains a clock that strikes ship's time and a Tiffany stained-glass window illustrating a ship reminiscent of the Pilgrim's *Mayflower*. You are invited to attend worship here.

Wellfleet Historical Society Museum, Main Street in Wellfleet. This excellent maritime and local-history museum is open from late June to early September, Tuesday through Sunday, 2:00 P.M. to 5:00 P.M. Admission charged.

Samuel Rider House, Gull Pond Road in Wellfleet. Built in the early 1700s, the home is characteristic of a Lower Cape farm of that period.

Open from late June to early September, Monday through Friday, 2:00 P.M. to 5:00 P.M. Admission charged.

Marconi Wireless Station, off Route 6 in Cape Cod National Seashore. From transmission towers built on these cliffs overlooking the open Atlantic, Guglielmo Marconi sent the first transatlantic wireless message in January 1903. There is little left of Marconi's towers. There is, however, a memorial to Marconi and the historic event of his making, as well as an observation pavilion from which to view the panorama of the cliffs and ocean. Open all year. Free.

Truro

Bell Church, Meetinghouse Road in Truro. Built in 1827, the church contains a Paul Revere–made bell in its steeple and Sandwich glass windows. You are welcome to attend services.

Truro Historical Museum at Highland Light, Highland Road in North Truro. An interesting collection of maritime, farming, and whaling artifacts is housed in what was once an early Lower Cape inn. Also here are artifacts from shipwrecks, antique firearms, Sandwich glass, and bird carvings. Open from June to September. Admission charged.

Jenny Lind Tower, off Lighthouse Road in North Truro. The "Swedish Nightingale" used this tower in 1850 to sing to people in Fitchburg, Massachusetts, who couldn't get into a concert that was oversold by unscrupulous wheelers and dealers. The fifty-five-foot tower was brought to Truro by Harry Aldrich and set on high ground as a memorial to his father.

Provincetown

MacMillan Wharf, off Commercial Street in downtown Provincetown. Named in honor of the late Admiral Donald B. MacMillan, famous Arctic explorer and long-time resident, the wharf is where the fishing fleet brings in its catch and where whale watching and Cape Cod Bay cruises originate. Every day it's a busy place and one of the most enjoyable attractions in Provincetown. The annual "Blessing of the Fleet" takes place at MacMillan Wharf toward the end of June.

Oldest Cemetery in Provincetown, Shank Painter Road in Provincetown. A good place for cemetery buffs to wander, the grounds contain many markers from the eighteenth century and a memorial plaque honoring four who passed away when the *Mayflower* was anchored in the nearby harbor in 1620.

Mayflower Compact Memorial, (historic bas-relief plaque), adjacent to Town Hall in Provincetown center. This plaque commemorates one of the earliest documents in American history whereby a group of people sought to govern themselves by majority rule for their mutual prosperity and well being. The Mayflower Compact—or "The Agreement," as the Pilgrims called it—which was signed on board the *Mayflower* in Provincetown harbor on 21 November 1620, is considered by many to be as revered a document of liberty as the Magna Carta, the Declaration of Independence, and the United States Constitution. It was a strong step forward in the development of democracy in the political entity which would emerge as the United States of America.

Heritage Museum, 356 Commercial Street in Provincetown. Housed in what was an 1860 Methodist church, this local museum contains historical artifacts, old lifesaving equipment, fire apparatus, fishing gear, antique furniture, and books. It also features exhibitions of contemporary painting, photography, and sculpture created by area artists. Open from the beginning of April to mid-October. Admission charged.

Seth Nickerson House, 72 Commercial Street in Provincetown. Built in 1746 , this house is considered to be the oldest one in Provincetown; its rooms are furnished with antiques. Open from May through October. Admission charged.

Famous Photogenic Lighthouses

Nobska Light, via Church Street and Nobska Road in Woods Hole. This is my favorite lighthouse on the entire Atlantic coast because of its site high on top of Nobska Point. From here you have magnificent views of Nantucket and Vineyard sounds, Woods Hole, Martha's Vineyard Island, and the Elizabeth Islands. Nobska Light, originally built in 1828 and rebuilt in 1876, is a very important lighthouse because of all the sea traffic sailing about in these waters—island ferries, fishing boats, pleasure vessels, and oceanographic research ships. It's not unusual to see large cruise liners, such as the *QE II,* and tall-masted, full-rigged ships representing a bygone era. There are times during July and August when the sea lanes around here seem as thick with traffic as the cross streets of Times Square in New York City. I, as do many others, also consider Nobska to be one of the most photogenic lighthouses on the Atlantic Coast, because it and its surroundings offer so many points of view. The sunsets from here are breathtaking. Snap a good photo of Nobska, get it blown up, and you'll have one of the finest possible souvenirs of your trip to Cape Cod.

Chatham Light, Main Street in Chatham. Two wooden lighthouses, known as the Twin Sisters of Chatham, were built here in 1808 but were destroyed in the storm of 1879. Mrs. Angeline Nickerson was the keeper after her husband died. The present lighthouse is electronically operated. This is a good location from which to view Chatham Harbor and the barrier beaches of Nauset and Monomoy Island.

Nauset Light, Ocean View Drive, off Route 6 via Cable Road in East-ham. Three stone light towers were built here in 1838, and they became known to mariners rounding the Cape as the Three Sisters. They eventually collapsed due to the eroding soil and were replaced by wooden towers in the 1890s. The current steel tower is automated.

Highland Light, via Highland and Lighthouse Roads in Truro. Highland Light is better known to mariners around the world as Cape Cod Light. It is one of the first lights seen on the American mainland by mariners sailing in from Europe. The first lighthouse was built in 1797 to keep vessels away from the shoals known as the "graveyard of ships." Literally thousands of ships went aground or disappeared around these cliffs. The current, automated lighthouse is a popular attraction within Cape Cod National Seashore. Visitor centers in Eastham, South Wellfleet, and Provincetown will be happy to provide you with more information on visiting lighthouses within Cape Cod National Seashore.

Scenic Drives

Route 6A—"The Old King's Highway". This scenic drive takes you through the towns of Sandwich, Barnstable, Yarmouth, Dennis, Brewster, and Orleans on a journey past lovely, old villages of historic homes, fine inns and B&Bs, gourmet restaurants, marsh lands, beaches, forests, estuaries, antique and crafts shops, museums, and major attractions. Always close by are the beaches and harbors of Cape Cod Bay. Route 6A, along the north coast of Cape Cod, is our longest and most satisfying scenic drive. Along this route you will experience the Cape without a lot of commercialization. The traffic is usually more relaxed and not as thick nor as frenetic as in other parts of the Cape. You can't help falling in love with Cape Cod when you tour Route 6A. This truly is quintessential Cape Cod, where nostalgia and reality blend together in harmony.

Route 28A—Pocasset to West Falmouth—access off the Otis Rotary. This portion of Route 28A, heading toward Falmouth and Woods Hole, takes you through the charming villages of North and West Falmouth, near Old Silver and Chapoquoit beaches on Buzzards Bay, and past fine restaurants and B&Bs, historic sites and homes, old Cape Cod farms, and harbors. In many respects Route 28A here is similar in environment and pace to Route 6A. You can meander along, enjoying the scenery, without the pressures persisting on the major highway. Route 28A will bring you to Palmer Avenue in the Sippewissett area. Sippewissett Road off Palmer is another lovely, scenic drive that takes you past Wood Neck Beach on Buzzards Bay, to Quissett Road and Quissett Harbor, and into Woods Hole Village.

ACTIVITIES AND ATTRACTIONS

Woods Hole to Menauhant. Take Woods Hole Road to the village of Woods Hole. Find a parking place, which may be difficult in this small, extremely busy community, and see the sights (islands ferry terminal, Woods Hole Oceanographic Institution, Marine Biological Laboratories, etc.), visit the shops, and eat a good meal of fresh seafood. Go back on Woods Hole Road and turn right on Church Street, which takes you past the Church of the Messiah, down to the beach, and up to Nobska Point with its well-known lighthouse offering superb views of Martha's Vineyard Island, the Elizabeth Islands, Vineyard Sound, and Nantucket Sound. Walk the cliff and take pictures of the lighthouse. Then continue east on Nobska Road, which merges with Fay Road, then Oyster Pond Road, and then Surf Drive Road. There are beaches along Surf Drive Road on Nantucket Sound. At the end of Surf Drive, turn onto Shore Road and then right onto Clinton Avenue and then Scranton Avenue, which goes along Falmouth Inner Harbor, where here are restaurants, charter fishing operations, and band concerts at Marine Park. Turn right onto Robbins, at the end of the harbor, and then right onto Manchester Avenue, which take you past the Martha's Vineyard Island ferry terminal. This road merges with Grand Avenue and Menauhant Avenue, taking you past some of the most popular beaches in the town of Falmouth.

Mashpee to Cotuit. Not far from Mashpee Circle, heading east on Route 28 toward Hyannis, take a right on Quinaquisset Road and continue until you reach the center of Cotuit. The beauty of Cotuit center is that it is one of the least commercial villages on the Cape, a place where it seems that time has stood still but in a very pleasing way. Tour the center, using Main Street and Ocean View Avenue, and go out to the beach on Nantucket Sound at the end of Main Street; there are many fine vistas along the way. Then go back on Main Street, which will take you past some fine old homes to Route 28.

Osterville to Hyannis. Heading east on Route 28, take a right on County Road which merges into Main. Along the way you will pass or be near facilities for the Cape Cod Symphony (its season runs from fall to spring, with performances in various Cape towns) and Cape Cod Academy, one of several fine, private secondary schools on the peninsula. Main will take you into center Osterville, one of the most affluent communities on the Cape, where you can shop at the Scottish Lion or take a meal at the East Bay Lodge. You can see some of the palatial homes and seaside estates on Wianno Avenue and along Seaview Avenue. West Bay Road will take you to the yacht marinas and to the well-guarded entrance to the exclusive Oyster Harbors section. From Osterville continue east on Main Street, which will bring you to the public beaches at Centerville and from there to Hyannisport and Hyannis center.

POPULAR ATTRACTIONS

Marstons Mills to West Barnstable. Route 149 north/south takes you across the Cape Cod peninsula from Route 28 to Route 6A. This is a rural road with pleasant scenery. Highlights along the way are a herring run with tame waterfowl to feed; West Parish Congregational Church, a classic New England white Protestant church with an aesthetically perfect interior (its first service was held on Thanksgiving Day 1719; services now feature superb choir and organ music); the Weldon Library and an old-fashioned general store. There is also a small, private airport off Route 149 where, occasionally, sailplane rides are offered in the summer.

Chatham Harbor. The center of beautiful Chatham, reached via Route 28, can be toured by motor vehicle or on foot. There are many charming shops, inns, B&Bs, and restaurants in town. Chatham is what "outlanders," or visitors, imagine a perfect Cape Cod town to be like: small, friendly, quaint, weather-beaten shingled, bright, cheery, and at the edge of the sea. Main Street brings you to Chatham Light, the fish pier overlooking Chatham Harbor, and the lower extension of Nauset (barrier) Beach and Nantucket Sound; to the south is Monomoy Island Wildlife Refuge. Following first Shore Road and then Main will take you past Tern Island, a Massachusetts Audubon Society sanctuary; along Chatham Harbor to Norris Road; and then to Morris Island. At the northern end of town, take Fox Hill Road to Nickersons Neck and the Chathamport area. Barn Hill Road, off of Main Street, leads to Hardings Beach.

Ocean View Drive and Wellfleet Harbor Drive. To view the drama of the open Atlantic from top of high cliffs and broad, fine sand beaches, take Le Count Hollow Road, which runs east off Route 6 in South Wellfleet. This road leads to Le Count Hollow Beach. Doubling back from the beach, take your first right onto Ocean View Drive, which parallels the ocean; it brings you to White Crest and Newcomb Hollow beaches. All three beaches are town managed and within Cape Cod National Seashore. Another scenic drive in Wellfleet is on the west side of Route 6; it leads to attractive, downtown Wellfleet, Wellfleet Harbor on Cape Cod Bay, scenic Chequesset Neck Road, the Great Island Trail, and Duck Harbor Beach.

Province Lands. In Provincetown explore the vast sand areas of the Province Lands area of Cape Cod National Seashore by taking Province Land and Race Point roads. These roads also lead to Herring Cove and Race Point beaches, bike and nature trails, horseback-riding stables, and the Province Lands Visitor Center. There are many splendid vistas of sea, rolling sand dunes, and beach grass. Also explore the side roads on either side of Route 6 in North Truro and Provincetown for access to spectacular sand dunes and super beaches.

ACTIVITIES AND ATTRACTIONS

Family Amusements

Sealand of Cape Cod (385–9252), Route 6A in West Brewster. This interesting aquarium center features a number of marine-life exhibits, performing dolphin shows, and seal and penguin pools. There are a gift shop, snack bar, and a picnic area, too. Open daily all year except on Wednesdays from the beginning of October to the beginning of June. Admission charged.

Aqua Circus of Cape Cod (775–8883), Route 28 in West Yarmouth. This marine aquarium and zoological park presents dolphin and sea lion shows. It has a petting zoo of gentle animals for small children and live exhibits of lion, cougar, bear, piranha, alligator, sea turtle, and snakes. There are pony rides, antique fire and farm exhibits, an extensive sea-shell collection, a gift shop, and a picnic area. Open from February to November. Admission charged.

Bassett Wild Animal Farm (896–3224), Route 6A in Brewster. A favorite with small children, Bassett Wild Animal Farm has a number of wild and farm animals. It also offers a petting zoo, hay and pony rides, a gift shop, and an area for picnics. Open from mid-May to mid-September. Admission charged.

Yesteryears Doll Museum (888–1711), corner of Main and River streets in downtown Sandwich. The museum houses a fascinating collection of antique dolls, doll houses, miniature furnishings, and toys. Open from early May to the end of October. Admission charged.

Provincetown Marine Aquarium (487–1040), on Commercial Street in Provincetown. This small aquarium is interesting to all family members. It contains displays of fish and shellfish common to New England waters, harbor seals, and penguins. Open from Memorial Day to mid-October. Admission charged.

Cape Cod Potato Chips (775–3358), Independence Park near the Cape Cod Mall in Hyannis. See for yourself how the world's best tasting, all-natural chips are made. This company is a Cape Cod institution and one beloved by potato-chip gourmets. Self-guided tours Monday through Friday all year, on Saturdays from May through October; free samples and gift shop. Free.

Other Amusements

Sea View Playland, Lower County Road in Dennis Port—miniature golf and coin-operated games
Pirate's Cove Adventure Golf, Route 28 in South Yarmouth
Harbor Glen Miniature Golf, Route 28 in West Harwich
Holiday Hill Mini Golf, Route 28 in Dennis Port

110

POPULAR ATTRACTIONS

Bourne Kart Track, Route 28 in Bourne
Playland, Main Street in Buzzards Bay
Chuck E. Cheese, Airport Shopping Plaza in Hyannis—kids games
Cape Cod Miniature Golf, Main Street in Hyannis
Ryan Family Amusement Center, Route 28 in South Yarmouth and
   Capetown Mall in Hyannis
Hatfield and McCoy's Survival Game of Cape Cod, Pamela Way in East
   Harwich
Family Sports Center, Route 6 in North Eastham

Guide to Towns, Accommodations, and Dining

Cape Cod consists of fifteen towns and a number of villages. The organization of Cape Cod towns and villages is confusing to both visitors and residents alike. For example, there's this anomaly: Barnstable is the county that encompasses all of Cape Cod; it is also a town and a village within this town; the town of Barnstable has thirteen villages, one of which is Hyannis, the most populous community on the Cape and large enough in importance to be a city. There are, however, no cities on Cape Cod, nor will there ever be any as long as Cape Codders remain fixed in the nostalgia of living in small communities, where the fantasy, if not the reality, of society on a human scale is retained.

Every Cape Cod town has a long and distinguished history. Many have been published in thick volumes filled with fascinating information, not only about local persons and events, but also about the very development of the United States from colonial times to the present. Persons interested in their family roots and/or American history can wade through a rich treasure trove contained in the public libraries and historical societies of Cape Cod as well as at Cape Cod Community College in Barnstable, which has one of the largest collections of books and manuscripts.

The following descriptions of individual Cape Cod towns also contain aspects of local history, but they appear only as highlights to emphasize each community's uniqueness. My purpose is not to tell you everything about an individual town, just enough so that, when you explore it on your own, each community will already have a distinct image in your mind.

Bourne

Town offices—24 Perry Avenue in Bourne, 759–3441 Greater Bourne/ Sandwich Chamber of Commerce, 165 State Road in Sagamore Beach, 888–6202 Cape Cod Chamber of Commerce Information Center at MacArthur Blvd. 759–3814.

The following villages, with their postal zip codes, are within the town of Bourne: Bourne—02532; Pocasset—02559; Cataumet—02532; Sagamore—02561; Sagamore Beach—02562; Buzzards Bay—02532; and Monument Beach—02553.

Regardless of what land road you take, Bourne is the "Gateway Town" to Cape Cod. Bourne is located on both the mainland side of the Cape Cod Canal and on the peninsula itself. The two highway access bridges to the Cape, the Bourne and the Sagamore, are in the town of Bourne. Within Bourne are the Massachusetts Maritime Academy in Buzzards Bay and the

Massachusetts Military Reservation, which consists of Otis Air Base; Camp Edwards, a training area for National Guard units; and a base for contingents of the Coast Guard, Marines, and Navy. One of the best military shows in all of New England, often featuring such performing groups as the Navy's Blue Angel precision jet team and the Army's Golden Knights stunt parachute group, takes place at the reservation in late May.

The village of Buzzards Bay, on the mainland side, has several motels and restaurants for the convenience of travelers. Interstate 495 now connects directly with the Bourne Bridge, bypassing congested Route 6 through Wareham. If you need restaurants, service stations, and souvenir shops, the diversion to Route 6 is easy to make from I-495. The village of Sagamore provides access to the Sagamore Bridge, the Mid Cape Highway—Route 6—and scenic Route 6A, "The Old King's Highway," which goes through the charming villages along the north coast of Cape Cod. There are motels, restaurants, and shops in Sagamore. The Christmas Tree Shop at the Sagamore Bridge and a complex of outlet stores across from it have become popular stops for bargain-hungry travelers. The villages of Pocasset, Cataumet, and Monument Beach are reached from the Bourne Bridge via Route 28. The villages continue to retain the traditional rural charm and simplicity of Cape Cod and offer many pleasant scenic drives and vistas.

Historically, Bourne is important to the development of Cape Cod because it contains the isthmus between Buzzards Bay and Cape Cod Bay. Myles Standish, shortly after the Pilgrims established their Plymouth Plantation in 1620, recognized that trade between his colony and those of the Dutch and English along the Atlantic Coast could flourish if a canal could be built connecting the two bays. In the eighteenth century George Washington saw military value in having a canal here. It was not until the beginning of the twentieth century that the first canal was built, thanks to the money and vision of August Belmont. It was a brilliant venture in concept and execution, but Belmont and other investors came close to losing their shirts when the canal produced substantial losses instead of fat profits. The federal government bought the canal, and the U.S. Army Corps of Engineers made it wide enough for two-way traffic and safer for navigation. The Corps also built the Bourne and Sagamore bridges, and they keep improving the systems, which allow vessels to sail through safely and economically.

Bourne was part of the Town of Sandwich until 1884, at which time it separated and became a town in its own right. In the early 1600s a trading post was established by the Pilgrims in Bourne at Aptucxet. Indians and white trappers brought in furs and were paid in the manufactured goods they needed. Aptucxet Trading Post flourished until the middle of that century and then declined in importance as similar trading operations sprouted along the Atlantic Coast and within the wilderness of North America. During early white settlement, Protestant ministers, such as Richard Bourne and Elisha Tupper, converted many Indians to Christianity. Through much of its history, Bourne was an agricultural and fishing town. When the railroad connected the large cities of America with Cape Cod, though, Bourne also became a summer oasis for the wealthy of Boston, Hartford, New York City, Philadelphia, Baltimore, and Washington, D.C. Affluent people from these cities sought to escape oppressive heat and find comfort by a pleasant seaside. Although today the presidency of John F. Kennedy is closely associated with Cape Cod, it was President Grover Cleveland who first established, at his Gray Gables estate in Bourne, a Summer White House on the Cape. Warm waters and cooling breezes of the Bourne coast also attracted many other notables, such as the actor Joseph Jefferson, one of Cleveland's fishing buddies.

With the evolution of better means of transportation, the dominance of Bourne as a preferred vacation place diminished somewhat in favor of other Cape Cod towns. Bourne, however, retains a committed and growing contingent of loyalists who know that everything they want from Cape Cod is right here and not necessarily farther down the peninsula.

Bourne Accommodations

Bourne Scenic Park, Buzzards Bay, 759–7873. *Campground.* Near the Cape Cod Canal. Open from early April to late October; 422 sites.

Quinstar Motor Lodge, Route 28 at the Bourne Bridge, 759–2711. *Motor Inn.* Convenient location on the canal's mainland side. Near several restaurants. Indoor pool, sauna, and whirlpool. Open all year. Moderate.

Windmill Motel, Route 6 at the Sagamore Bridge, 888–3220. *Motor Inn.* Convenient location on the Cape Cod side of the Sagamore Bridge and next to several factory-outlet stores, such as Corning and Christmas Tree. Open all year. Moderate.

Panorama Motor Lodge, South Bourne Bridge Rotary, 759–4401. *Motor Inn.* Convenient location on the Cape side of the Bourne Bridge. Swimming pool. Open all year. Moderate.

Bay View Campgrounds, Route 28, 759–7610. *Campground.* Hot showers, swimming pool, tennis, and playground. Open May 1 to October 15; 415 sites.

Cataumet Motel, Route 28A in Cataumet, 564–5011. *Motor Inn.* Motel and efficiency units. Located in quiet area. Near beaches, golf, and fishing. Open all year. Moderate.

Bourne Dining

Inn at Buttermilk Bay in Buzzards Bay, 23 Nick Vedder Road, 759–6736. An imposing old home overlooking the water and serving excellent seafood and continental dishes. Accommodations are also available in the motel section. Although on the mainland side of the Cape Cod Canal, well worth a diversion for the cuisine and ambience, lunch or dinner. Open all year. Moderate to Expensive.

Sagamore Inn, Route 6A in Sagamore, 888–9707. Well liked by the ✓ local crowd for delicious Italian food. Open from April to October. Inexpensive.

The Commodore Restaurant (formerly the Captain Barlow House), Route 28 in Pocasset, 563–5351. Excellent roast prime rib of beef and seafood. Daily specials. Piano entertainment in the lounge. Open all year. Moderate.

The Courtyard Restaurant and Pub, Route 28A in Cataumet, 563–7002. A very nice restaurant offering an eclectic menu: broiled scallops with sherry-buttered crumbs, marinated boneless breast of chicken grilled with crushed peppercorns, grilled swordfish with dill butter, and cioppino—clams, mussels, white fish, shrimp, and scallops simmered in tomatoes, fresh vegetables, and white wine. Also an equally creative luncheon menu. Open all year. Moderate.

The Chart Room, Shore Road in Cataumet, 563–5350. A comfortable dining room overlooking the water and serving fine seafood and meat dishes. Live entertainment. Open end of May to mid-October. Moderate.

Falmouth

Town offices—173 Main Street in Falmouth, 548–7611 Falmouth Chamber of Commerce, Academy Lane in Falmouth, 548–8500

The following villages, with their postal zip codes, are within the town of Falmouth: Falmouth—02540; East Falmouth—02536; North Falmouth—02556; North Falmouth (Old Silver Beach)—02565; West Falmouth—02574; Woods Hole—02543; Teaticket—02536; Waquoit—02536; Falmouth Heights—02536; and Hatchville—02536.

Falmouth was settled by English colonists in 1660. Its roots were planted by those dissatisfied with the prevailing religious order of the late seventeenth century in the colony. They included a group of dissident Congregationalists, under the leadership of Isaac Robinson, and another strain represented by Johnathan Hatch, whose disgust with the persecution of the Quakers in Barnstable motivated him and many members of the Society of Friends to settle in the western areas of Falmouth.

The gem of Falmouth is its triangular Village Green. It was cleared and set aside as common land in 1749. Here, as a war for independence from Great Britain became inevitable, Falmouth's militia drilled under Colonel Joseph Dimmick and Captain John Grannis. During the war, British ships attempted to send landing parties ashore to subdue the inhabitants of Falmouth and requisition without pay their stores of food and other supplies; but the British were driven off by heavy fire from townsmen defending home and hearth. The British again tried to take Falmouth during the War of 1812, but artillery batteries under the command of Captain Weston Jenkins battered them back and away. During the same war, the captain of the British warship *Nimrod* demanded that Jenkins give up his cannon. Jenkins told him to "come and get 'em!" After a torrid exchange of fire and some minor damage to shore facilities, the *Nimrod* sailed away— without the cannon.

When peace took hold, Falmouth settled down to developing and prospering from its manufacturing industries, agriculture, and fisheries. Within this solid Yankee environment, Falmouth's most noteworthy citizen was born and raised. Katherine Lee Bates later traveled this immense country and was so inspired by what she saw that she composed "America," perhaps our favorite patriotic hymn. In the late nineteenth century, Falmouth emerged from its tranquil insularity into a popular summer vacation town. In addition to the affluent people who could afford extended warm-weather stays here came eminent scientists such as Louis Agassiz, who was among those founding a research colony that became the internationally famous Marine Biological Laboratory in 1888. In the 1930s, Woods Hole Oceanographic Institution was established and is now considered one of the world's premier research facilities in the ocean sciences.

Falmouth, the second largest town on Cape Cod, is a community of contrasts. It is a place of solid, long-established wealth; a center of basic research and stunning discoveries on the leading edge of science; a jock town of runners, swimmers, boaters, and bikers; a place of culture where visual art, dance, music, and theatricals are performed at all levels of expertise; a town of bountiful farms and gorgeous gardens; a collection of picture-book New England villages with lovely churches, historic homes, and peaceful greens; a place of gaudy shopping centers and bargain outlets; a collection of excellent inns, B&Bs, and gourmet restaurants; the main embarkation point for the islands of Martha's Vineyard and Nantucket; and a necklace of beaches both packed sardinelike with humanity and vacant, with hardly a soul to be seen.

Falmouth is a place of infuriating traffic tie-ups and gridlocks, especially on Woods Hole Road, Route 28 in the east end, and downtown, but also of less frequented back roads where the scenery is often far better. It is a community of craftspeople, tradesmen, scientists, artists, professionals, blue-collars, the retired, and the young; of WASPS and ethnics; of Protestants, Jews, Catholics, Buddhists, Agnostics, and Atheists; of loud-mouths and book worms; and of those who inspire and those who create rage. Falmouth is typically American, offering the best and the worst of our society. On the other hand, it is also unique unto itself, so much so that one does not visit for a brief while or an extended stay and remain indifferent and bored

North and West Falmouth and the Sippewissett area are special because they have not been spoiled by the intensive commercialization affecting many parts of Cape Cod. They continue to have the coziness of what most people imagine small communities in New England to be like. They are located along the warm waters of Buzzards Bay, where Old Silver, Chapoquoit, and Wood Neck beaches are open to the public. Even during the height of summer, it is a pleasure to drive along scenic Route 28A and tour the side roads. You really feel that you're on Old Cape Cod in these parts. There are nice B&Bs, restaurants, and shops along the way. In West Falmouth there's a historic Quaker meeting house and cemetery and the 1775 Bourne Farm, restored, continuing in operation, and welcoming you to walk about. On Palmer Avenue, in the Sippewissett area, is Peach Tree Circle with its magnificent gardens, a veritable horticulturist's paradise. Also in Sippewissett is the Cape Codder Hotel, one of the grand old resorts on the peninsula with what many consider the best ocean views on the Cape.

The west end of Falmouth has perhaps the finest example of a coherent Cape Cod village scene. At the center is the triangular village green, circumscribed by a bright white rail fence on which there is a tall pole proudly flying the American flag. At the sides of the village green triangle are many historic homes, including the birthplace of Katherine Lee Bates; the buildings of the Falmouth Historical Society; the white, tall-steepled Congregational church with its Paul Revere bell; beautiful Saint Barnabas Episcopal Church and its lovely grounds; and the main post office, where ordinary people and some of the best minds in the world come daily to collect their mail.

Main Street in downtown Falmouth, from the post office to Shore Street, is flanked by many small shops, restaurants, and offices. This area is the most aesthetically pleasing part of commercial downtown and is enjoyed by visitors for its slow pace, personal service, and human scale. Here are also the public library, statue of Katherine Lee Bates, and town offices. South of downtown are public beaches. East of downtown, Falmouth has its collection of shopping malls, convenience stores, bargain and factory outlets, motels, and fast-food places. Within this area are Falmouth Inner Harbor with its ferry to Martha's Vineyard; band concerts at Marine Park; and beaches, motels, and restaurants at Falmouth Heights. Adjacent areas

The town water pump and the grain mill were essential to life in Cape Cod towns. Today they are romantic reminders of a time of fewer conveniences.

are Maravista, Menauhant, Green Harbor, Davisville, and East Falmouth. Heading north and inland from downtown is rural Falmouth with farms, cranberry bogs, horse stables, golf courses, fresh-water ponds, and such major attractions as the New Alchemy Institute and Falmouth Playhouse. This inland area of Falmouth includes the Hatchville section and borders on the Massachusetts Military Reservation.

Woods Hole, famous throughout the world for its Woods Hole Oceanographic Institution, Marine Biological Laboratory, and summer headquarters of the National Academy of Sciences (at Quissett Harbor), is also a village in the town of Falmouth. It is no exaggeration to say that, during the summer, more distinguished brainpower in the biological sciences converges on Woods Hole than on any other place in the world. Woods Hole is the primary terminal for year-round ferries to Martha's Vineyard and also to Nantucket during the peak vacation season. Woods Hole is a tiny, quaint village with several excellent seafood restaurants and handicrafts shops. Many interesting events are open to the public during the year, including scientific lectures and programs, theatricals, musical concerts from ethnic to folk, art exhibitions, and poetry readings. Most events take place at the community hall, next to the drawbridge, or in facilities at the scientific institutions.

Young people are attracted to Woods Hole because they perceive it to be an avant-garde place, an extension of Greenwich Village and Harvard Square in miniature with easy access to the beach and islands. A walk along Water Street will bring you to a book shop, boutiques, crafts shops, restaurants, a rustic drawbridge, yacht basin, and the buildings of Woods Hole Oceanographic Institution, Marine Biological Laboratory, and the National Marine Fisheries laboratories. The building with the sailing-ship model coming out of its granite facade is Candle House, in which candles were made and whale oil stored. It is now the administrative center for Marine Biological Laboratory. Nearby is a small public park overlooking the harbor. From here you can see the research vessel *Knorr* (when she is home from an expedition), on which Robert Ballard and his team found the remains of the Titanic off Newfoundland.

Straight ahead, beyond the WHOI docks, are Uncatena, Nonamesset, and Naushon islands of the Elizabeth archipelago. Naushon is the largest of the Elizabeth Islands and is privately owned. Boaters, however, can anchor in Naushon's Tarpaulin Cove, where swimming and picnicking, but not fires, are allowed. The buildings and docks farther down Water Street belong to the National Marine Fisheries. One of these is an aquarium open to the public. It its outdoor pool are harbor seals whose antics or wallowings in the sun delight visitors. On Millfield Street, overlooking Eel Pond filled with expensive yachts, is Saint Joseph's Tower, with bells named after the scientists Louis Pasteur and Gregor Mendel. Here also is a tiny flower garden, which invites the walker to rest and contemplate. A short drive or bike ride from Woods Hole center, via Quissett Avenue, will bring you to pretty Quissett Harbor and the seaside walk to The Knobb on Buzzards Bay. Or take Church Street to Nobska Point and its lighthouse overlooking Nantucket Sound and Martha's Vineyard Island.

Two points of caution are worth noting when visiting Falmouth. First, finding a parking space in the center of Woods Hole is extremely difficult. Illegally parked cars are ticketed and towed by aggressive sorts who would make good candidates for Atilla's or Khan's legions. Best bet is to find parking on streets away from the center and then walk to attractions and dining spots. During evenings a parking lot on Water Street, near the drawbridge, is open to the public. Second, make sure you have advance reservations for accommodations during the week in mid-August when the Puma-Falmouth Road Race takes place. Thousands of runners converge on Falmouth during this exciting period, and all tourist facilities in town are stretched beyond their limits.

North Falmouth Accommodations

Sea Crest Resort, Off Quaker Road in Old Silver Beach Area, 548–3850. *Resort.* Fine accommodations with ocean-front location on private portion of Old Silver Beach. Resort offers outdoor and indoor pools, saunas, steam and exercise rooms, tennis, ocean-view dining, dancing and entertainment, and cocktail lounge. A popular Cape Cod resort. Part of this resort is being converted to condos. Open all year. Expensive.

Silver Shores Lodge, Old Silver Beach, 548–0846. *Motor Inn.* Ocean-front rooms at one of the Upper Cape's most popular beaches. Seasonal. Inexpensive to Moderate.

Captains Inn, Old Main Road, 563–6793. *B&B.* Historic Cape Cod estate, large rooms, gardens, croquet, horses; near beaches. Gourmet breakfasts and afternoon tea served. Highly recommended. Open all year. Moderate.

North Falmouth Dining

Bill Weaner's Silver Lounge Restaurant, Route 28A in North Falmouth, 563–2410. Known for friendly, casual dining; steaks, seafood, and daily specials are featured. Open all year. Inexpensive to Moderate.

West Falmouth Accommodations

The Elms, Route 28A, 540–7232. *B&B.* A comfortable home that emphasizes great food. Breakfasts include Irish bread, eggs Benedict, and homemade codfish cakes; also serves dinner. Near Chapaquoit Beach and Woods Hole. Open all year. Moderate.

Sjoholm, 17 Chase Road off Route 28A, 540–5706. *B&B.* Fine accommodations in a quiet, lovely area. Near beaches, Falmouth center, and Woods Hole. A bountiful, all-you-can-eat buffet breakfast featuring Swedish dishes. Open all year. Moderate.

The Ideal Spot Motel, Route 28A at Old Dock Road, 548–2257. *Motor Inn.* Motel and efficiency units near Chapaquoit and Old Silver beaches. In nice village area of boutiques and restaurants. Open all year. Moderate.

West Falmouth Dining

√**Domingo's Olde Restaurant,** Route 28A, 540–0575. Superior continental cuisine and seafood—shrimp scampi, bouillabaisse, mussels prepared in various sauces, and lobster. Open all year. Moderate to Expensive.

Woods Hole Accommodations

The Nautilus Motor Inn, Woods Hole Road, 548–1525. *Motor Inn.* Fine accommodations near Martha's Vineyard ferry terminal. Dining and lounge at the adjacent Dome Restaurant; tennis, swimming pool, and lovely grounds. Seasonal. Moderate to Expensive.

The Marlborough, 320 Woods Hole Road, 548–6218. *B&B.* A lovely home tastefully decorated with many romantic touches, just up the road from Martha's Vineyard ferry and near beaches and bike trail. French spoken here. Breakfast buffet served with many gourmet items, such as ham poached in beer and hot fruit soup. Open all year. Moderate.

The Grey Whale Inn, 565 Woods Hole Road, 548–7692. *Inn.* 1804 home overlooking Woods Hole harbor. Near ferry terminal to islands. Open early April to end of December. Moderate to Expensive.

Sands of Time Motor Inn, Woods Hole Road, 548–6300, *Motor Inn.* Fine accommodations overlooking Woods Hole Harbor. Swimming pool and many other guest amenities. Near Dome Restaurant, Martha's Vineyard ferry terminal, and beautiful ocean drive to Nobska Point. Seasonal. Moderate to Expensive.

Sleepy Hollow Motor Inn, Woods Hole Road, 548–1986. *Motor Inn.* Comfortable accommodations, swimming pool; near beaches, Dome Restaurant, and ferry terminal to the islands. Seasonal. Moderate.

Woods Hole Dining

Shuckers World Famous Raw Bar, 91A Water Street, down Cobble Way, 540–3850. A Woods Hole favorite on Eel Pond for raw and steamed seafood, king crab legs, and lobster. Fresh fruit drinks. Seasonal. Inexpensive. **Dome Restaurant,** Woods Hole Road, 548–0800. An excellent restaurant housed within a unique geodesic dome overlooking Woods Hole harbor and Nantucket Sound. Popular with locals and visitors to the village and the islands. American and continental cuisine—baked seafood Milanese, sole Shannon. Live entertainment—jazz and popular music. Open April to October. Moderate.

Fishmongers Cafe, Water Street, 548–9148. Very popular Woods Hole seafood restaurant overlooking harbor. Seasonal. Inexpensive to Moderate.

Landfall Restaurant, Luscombe Avenue, near Ferry Terminal, 548–1758. A busy but efficient seafood restaurant overlooking the water. Great food—Cape Cod fish-k-bob, seafood Newburg, Nantucket swordfish; maritime decor, good service. Open June through October. Moderate.

Black Duck, 73 Water Street, 548–9165. Here world-famous scientists and ordinary tourists fill up on some of best and varied chowders concocted on the Cape. Also serves gourmet breakfasts and sandwiches. Rustic atmosphere; sundeck for dining overlooking Eel Pond yacht basin. Seasonal. Inexpensive.

Captain Kidd, 77 Water Street, 548–8563. A popular eating and drinking place for the Woods Hole crowd; focus on seafood—pasta and scallops Provençal, grilled native tuna. Closed from January to April. Inexpensive to Moderate.

Falmouth Village Accommodations

Coonamessett Inn, Gifford Street and Jones Road, 548–2300. *Inn.* The Coonamessett is the one of the Upper Cape's finest places for accommodations and dining, and it has been that way for years. It is on the banks of a pretty pond and near a golf course. This is what a New England inn should look like and how it should be operated. Beautiful grounds surround it. Downtown Falmouth and the beaches are within a few minutes' drive. Open all year. Moderate to Expensive.

Cape Codder Hotel, 24 Cape Codder Road (Off Route 28 and Sippewissett Road), 540–1900. *Resort.* The Cape Codder is a traditional turn-of-the-century resort with one of the finest ocean-front locations on Cape Cod. It has broad verandas with rocking chairs, a decent dining room, swimming pool, cocktail lounge, live entertainment and dancing, and many other amenities. If the movie *Some Like It Hot* had been shot in New England, the Cape Codder would surely have been the setting. This grand resort hotel is expected to be converted to condos soon. Open end of May to mid-October. Moderate to Expensive.

Shoreway Acres Resort, Shore Street, 540–3000, *Motor Inn.* A fine, popular place of accommodation located on one of the most beautiful streets in Falmouth. Within easy walking distance of shops, restaurants, and attractions in the village and of Surf Drive Beach. Gourmet dining, indoor pool, sauna, and lovely grounds. Open all year. Moderate.

Sheraton Falmouth, 291 Jones Road, 540–2000. *Motor Inn.* Excellent accommodations near center of town and beaches. Indoor pool, saunas, restaurant, and lounge. This Sheraton has one of the best nightclubs on the Upper Cape, with live entertainment and dancing. Open all year. Moderate to Expensive.

Sippewissett Campground and Cabins, 836 Palmer Avenue in the Sippewissett Area, 548–2542. *Campground.* Also cabins and cottages. Free shuttle service to Woods Hole. Near beaches and downtown attractions and eateries. Open May 1 to end of October; 120 sites.

Best Western Falmouth Marina Motel, Robbins Road at the Harbor, 548–4300. *Motor Inn.* Overlooks scenic Falmouth Harbor. Within walking distance of Martha's Vineyard ferry, restaurants, and shops. Seasonal. Heated pool. Moderate.

The Admiralty Resort, Route 28, 548–4240. *Motor Inn.* Nice accommodations at a convenient location. The Admiralty has been recently enlarged and improved. Swimming pool, restaurant, lounge, and live entertainment. Package plans available. An excellent value. Open all year. Moderate.

The Trade Winds Motel, Robbins Road at the Harbor, 548–4575. *Motor Inn.* Overlooks Falmouth Harbor, within a short walk of Martha's Vineyard ferry, shops, and restaurants. Heated swimming pool and efficiency apartments. Seasonal. Moderate.

Mostly Hall, 27 Main Street at the Village Green, 548–3786. *Inn and B&B.* I pass by Mostly Hall most every day and it never fails to impress me as one of the most palatial homes on Cape Cod. Located anywhere else in the United States, it would be considered a grand mansion. Antiques fill the rooms, which have ceilings close to fourteen feet high. Some German spoken here. Mostly Hall is located across the street from the village green and near all the conveniences of Downtown Falmouth. Open all year. Moderate to Expensive.

The Falmouth Square Inn, 49 Main Street, on the way to Woods Hole, 457–0606. *Motor Inn.* A new place of accommodation near junction of roads to downtown and Woods Hole. Lounge and restaurant; indoor pool and exercise room. One of Falmouth's finest places of accommodation. Open all year. Expensive.

Capt. Tom Lawrence House, 75 Locust Street, on the way to Woods Hole, 540–1445. *B&B.* 1861 sea captain's house located on the road to Woods Hole, near village green and downtown shops and restaurants. Once hosted Jacques Cousteau. Serves full breakfasts featuring many gourmet items. Open all year. Moderate.

The Inn at One Main Street, One Main Street, on the Way to Woods Hole, 540–7469. ***B&B.*** Lovely home built in 1892 located at the beginning of the road to Woods Hole and within steps of the village green and downtown shops and restaurants. Continental breakfasts served; take-out breakfasts supplied to those catching early ferries to the islands. Open all year. Moderate.

Palmer House Inn, 81 Palmer Avenue at the Village Green, 548–1230. ***B&B.*** A comfortable, lovely old home adjacent to the village green and downtown conveniences. Interesting breakfast menu includes Finnish pancakes and cheese blintzes. Open all year. Moderate.

The Village Green Inn, 40 West Main Street at the Village Green, 548–5621. ***B&B.*** Originally built in the eighteenth century, this home was later made more elegant in the nineteenth-century Victorian style. Located across the street from the village green and within walking distances of shops and restaurants. Continental breakfasts. Free beach-parking stickers. Open all year. Moderate.

Cape Colony Motor Lodge, Surf Drive, 548–3975. ***Motor Inn.*** Accommodations with beach on Nantucket Sound. Landscaped grounds, swimming pool; morning coffee. Seasonal. Moderate.

Falmouth Inn, Main Street, 540–2500. ***Motor Inn.*** Formerly a Holiday Inn. A large motel offering good accommodations, indoor pool, restaurant, and lounge. Near downtown, shopping centers, ferry to Martha's Vineyard, and beaches. Owns Falmouth Country Club, championship eighteen-hole course. Golfing packages are available. Open all year. Moderate to Expensive.

Falmouth Dining

Coonamessett Inn, Jones Road and Gifford Street in Falmouth, 548–2300. A visit to Cape Cod should include a lunch or dinner at the Coonamessett. Great food, impeccable service, and lovely interior. The Coonamessett also offers nightly entertainment and dancing. Open all year. Moderate to Expensive.

The Regatta of Falmouth, End of Scranton Avenue at the Entrance to Falmouth Harbor, 548–5400. One of the finest gourmet restaurants on Cape Cod. Delicious American and French cuisines creatively prepared and presented. Freshest ingredients used. Dining room overlooks entrance to Falmouth Harbor. There's docking for your yacht and parking for your Rolls. Reservations essential. Open end of May to end of September. Expensive.

Country Fare, 319 Main Street, 548–9020. Downtown location across from the library. Roast prime rib of beef, quiche of the day, baked scrod with crab sauce, and veal or chicken Parmigiana. Good food and good value. Open all year. Inexpensive.

Golden Swan, 323 Main Street, 540–6580. A favorite Falmouth restaurant with attentive service. Its facade and interior reminds one of a charming place found in a small town in England. The cuisine is continental with emphasis on excellent veal dishes—from wienerschnitzel to shrimp and veal Francaise. Early bird specials. Open all year. Moderate.

The Nimrod, Dillingham Avenue, 548–5500. An extensive menu of seafood and meat dishes. Excellent Sunday brunch that can include broiled sea scallops, baked haddock, and broiled scrod. Fresh baked pies, cakes, and breads. Inexpensive to Moderate.

David's Restaurant, Route 28, heading West from Falmouth Village, 548–7313. David's is Falmouth's gourmet breakfast and brunch restaurant: Belgian waffles, English or Irish style bangers and eggs, sauteed rainbow trout and eggs, grilled tuna or swordfish and eggs, Cajun andouille sausage and eggs, and lobster meat topped with poached eggs. Inexpensive to Moderate.

Eco's Landing, 356 Palmer Avenue, 540–7877. Seafood, chicken, and steak are specialties—broiled bluefish, fried oyster plate. Open all year. Inexpensive to Moderate.

Flying Bridge, 220 Scranton Avenue at Falmouth Harbor, 548–2700. The Flying Bridge, located on Falmouth's inner harbor, has two restaurants: Portofino, serving continental cuisine such as medallions of beef Siena and fettucine Portofino—expensive; and The Cafe, featuring steaks, chicken, seafood, and gourmet pizzas—moderate. Nightly entertainment. Great location for yacht watching. Open all year.

McMenamy's Seafood Restaurant, Route 28, 540–2115. A popular place, located near shopping malls, offering seafood plates, lobster rolls, scallop casserole, and daily specials. Open all year. Inexpensive.

Christopher's Restaurant and Pub Route 28, 540–7176. Popular family dining place offering good value, though the service tends to be slow. Clam chowder and kale soup, Greek lamb and vegetable gyros, hash and eggs, and roast turkey with stuffing. Open all year. Inexpensive.

Falmouth Heights Accommodations

The Red Horse Inn Motel, 28 Falmouth Heights Road, 548–0053. *Motor Inn.* Award-winning flower gardens, swimming pool; location convenient to shops, restaurants, and beaches. Open all year. Moderate.

Park Beach Motel, 241 Grand Avenue, 548–1010. *Motor Inn.* Accommodations located near popular sandy beach. Heated pool and many guest amenities. Seasonal. Moderate.

Falmouth Heights Motor Lodge, 146 Falmouth Heights Road, 548–3623. *Motor Inn.* Conveniently located near Martha's Vineyard ferry and Falmouth Heights beaches. A good value. Seasonal. Moderate.

Falmouth Heights Dining

Lawrence's, Nantucket Avenue in Falmouth Heights, One Block up from the Beach, 548–4441. Reputed to be Falmouth's oldest restaurant (started in the 1890s) and continuing to attract both loyal patrons and newcomers. Cozy interior. Home-style cooking. Lobster a specialty. Also black diamond steak and fisherman's platter. Early bird specials. Open from mid-May to mid-October. Moderate.

East Falmouth Accommodations

Surfside East Resort, 134 Menauhant Road, 548–0313. *Motor Inn.* Popular motel where all units have balconies or patios. Private beach on Nantucket Sound, two swimming pools, putting green, shuffleboard, fishing jetty, children's play area. Efficiency units available. Continental breakfast served. Seasonal. Moderate.

    Green Harbor Waterfront Motor Lodge, Acapesket Road, 548–4747. *Motor Inn.* Excellent family accommodation with many features. Tranquil country setting but close to Route 28 and ocean beaches. Swimming pool, boating, fishing, sun deck, and lovely lawns. Open all year. Moderate.

    John Parker Lakeside Resort Condominium, Parker Road, 548–5933. *Housekeeping Units.* Many features for a family vacation: swimming pool, game room, private beach, boating, fishing, children's playground, and picnic area. Ocean beaches nearby. Open end of June to end of August. Moderate.

East Falmouth Dining

The Big Fisherman, Route 28, 548–4266. A popular seafood restaurant on the road between Falmouth and Hyannis—baked stuffed shrimp, English fish and chips. Open all year. Inexpensive to Moderate.

    Golden Sails, Route 28, 548–3521. A favorite Chinese restaurant on the Cape because of its warm, friendly service. Cantonese, Mandarin, and Szechuan dishes; Hunan beef, chicken, and pork; Moo Shi shrimp. Open all year. Inexpensive.

Sandwich

Town offices—145 Main Street in Sandwich, 888–0349 Greater Bourne/ Sandwich Chamber of Commerce, 165 State Road in Sagamore Beach, 888–6202 Cape Cod Chamber of Commerce Information Center at the Sagamore Bridge Rotary, 888–2438.

The following villages, with their postal zip codes, are within the town of Sandwich: Sandwich—02563; East Sandwich—02537; and Forestdale— 02644.

Settled in 1637, Sandwich is Cape Cod's oldest town. The land was cleared and homes built by Edmund Freeman and his compatriots. They were colonists who came to Cape Cod from Saugus, a community north of Boston. After the landing of the Pilgrims at Plymouth and the successful establishment of their colony, more English emigrants sailed to Massachusetts to become spiritually and materially prosperous. As the population expanded along the mainland coast and good land was taken, enterprising individuals such as Edmund Freeman saw better possibilities for themselves south on Cape Cod. The governor of Plymouth Colony gave Freeman and nine other men permission to create a settlement of sixty families on Cape Cod. As was the case elsewhere, once the settlement was established other families came in from places such as Duxbury and Plymouth, and the town grew into some significance. In 1669 this burgeoning habitation was incorporated and named Sandwich after the town in Kent, England, from which a number of the settlers originated.

The established religion of Sandwich was, as it was throughout the colony, that of the Congregational Church. Quaker missionaries arrived peacefully enough to live and, if possible, gain converts, but they were readily condemned and persecuted as heretics. The people of early Sandwich were Puritans ("Roundheads") out of the same theological mold as Oliver Cromwell. Their intolerance was no different from that of the Anglicans in Virginia and that of the Roman Catholics in Mexico and French Canada. After the restoration of the monarchy in England, King Charles II ordered that members of the Society of Friends should not be persecuted, but it took some years for toleration of the Quakers to take hold in Sandwich. As with other evolutionary changes in American society, the acceptance of diverse beliefs did come in the eighteenth century, and today Sandwich is as proud of its Quaker heritage as it is of its Puritan.

The early economy of Sandwich was based on agriculture and whaling on Cape Cod Bay. In the early nineteenth century, a number of companies began making glass in Sandwich and fashioned beautiful and useful objects out of this ethereal material. These were among the first industrial plants in a largely agricultural-commodity-producing America. Among the reasons why the glassmaking industry flourished in Sandwich was that the town was the source of the two basic ingredients—silica (the fine sand at Sandwich) and sodium chloride (deriving salt from the sea was itself a mainstay industry for many a Cape Cod town). Although glassmaking faded away, the remaining examples of Sandwich glass today are highly valued by collectors of early Americana. In addition to glass, Sandwich factories produced stage coaches, prairie schooners, and railroad cars. One can say that the town was a "hub of America transport manufacturing" long before Detroit assumed that title.

All the early factories of Sandwich are gone, and what remains is a peaceful, charming town much beloved by its residents and those who visit. Over many years, I have found Sandwich to be one of Cape Cod's friendliest towns. Within the Main and Water streets area of the town center are a number of Sandwich attractions that you can reach on foot: Shawme Lake, with its resident population of geese and ducks eager for handouts from generous visitors; the 1637 Hoxie House, oldest home on Cape Cod; town hall; Dexter's Mill, built in the 1650s; the Sandwich Glass Museum; the Thornton W. Burgess Museum; Yesteryears Doll Museum; and the Dan'l Webster Inn, highly recommended for dining and overnight stays. Heritage Plantation, one of Cape Cod's "must see" attractions, can be reached via Grove Street from the town hall. While in the center of town, stroll Main Street and visit the lovely Congregational, Episcopal, and Roman Catholic churches. This area of Sandwich seems to have remained within the nineteenth century, with only horse-drawn carriages, ladies in long skirts and bonnets, and prudent gentlemen in stovepipe hats missing from the scene. On Route 6A, heading east, are other attractions: the state fish hatchery and game farm; the 1685 Nye Homestead; the Quaker Meeting House; and the Stephen Wing House.

Sandwich Accommodations

The Dan'l Webster Inn, Sandwich Village Center, 888–3622. *Inn.* A superb Upper Cape inn in every respect—accommodations, dining, service, atmosphere, and interior and exterior environments. In the center of Sandwich, within walking distance of attractions and a short drive of Heritage Plantation and beaches. Open all year except Christmas Day. Moderate to Expensive.

Scusset Beach Reservation, Scusset Beach Road off Route 3 (Mainland Side of Cape Cod Canal), 888–0859. *Campground.* Near Cape Cod Canal and Sandwich attractions. Campers are allowed to use Scusset State Beach as part of the daily rate. Open from mid-April to mid-October; 98 sites.

Shawme-Crowell State Forest, Route 130, 888–0351. *Camp-*

ground. Near Cape Cod Canal and Heritage Plantation in Sandwich. Open from mid-April to mid-October; 260 sites.

Wingscorton Farm Inn, 11 Wing Boulevard in East Sandwich, 888–0534. **B&B.** 1758 farmhouse that had been owned by the Wing family for six generations. Once used by the Underground Railroad to bring slaves into freedom. This is a working farm with horses, cows, sheep, chickens, and ducks. Ample farm breakfasts are served; dinner is also provided by special arrangement. Open all year. Expensive.

Shady Nook Inn, "The Old King's Highway"—Route 6A, 888–0409. **Motor Inn.** Good value; some efficiencies and cottages. Swimming pool; coffee shop. Open all year. Moderate.

Captain Ezra Nye House, 152 Main Street, 888–6142. **B&B.** 1829 sea captain's house in a lovely area of historic Sandwich. Decorated with fresh-flower bouquets. Homemade muffins a specialty for breakfast. Open all year. Moderate.

Ocean Front, 273 Phillips Road, 888–4798. **B&B.** A traditional, weathered-shingle Cape Cod home. Fine views of Cape Cod Bay and the white cliffs of Plymouth. Italian spoken here. Open mid-April to mid-October. Moderate.

The Quince Tree, 164 Main Street, 888–1371. **B&B.** A fine 1825 home in the center of town with many amenities for guests. Quince jelly, made from trees on property, served with homemade muffins and herbal teas. Open all year. Moderate.

Six Water Street, 6 Water Street, 888–6808. **B&B.** Located on Shawme Pond in center of Sandwich, within walking distance of Hoxie House and glass and doll museums and a few minutes' drive of Heritage Plantation and beaches. Home built in 1845 and well furnished. Breakfast items include johnnycake and peach muffins; wicker-basket breakfasts packed for the beach. Open all year. Moderate to Expensive.

The Earl of Sandwich Motor Manor, "The Old King's Highway"—Route 6A, 888–1415. **Motor Inn.** Fine accommodations with a Tudor feel. Open all year. Moderate.

Old Colony Motel, "The Old King's Highway"—Route 6A, 888–9716. **Motor Inn.** Good value. Swimming pool. Open all year. Moderate.

Sandy Neck Motel, "The Old King's Highway"—Route 6A, 362–3992. **Motor Inn.** Good value; located at the entrance of Sandy Neck Beach area on Cape Cod Bay. Near several restaurants. Open early April to end of November. Moderate.

Peters Pond Park, Cotuit Road, 477–1775. **Campground.** Fresh-water-lake swimming, fishing, and boating. Open mid-April to mid-October; 500 sites.

Sandwich Dining

The Dan'l Webster Inn, Sandwich Village Center, 888–3622. Fine dining, ✓ service, and environment in the heart of the oldest town on Cape Cod. Creative cookery at its finest. Excellent wine list. Live entertainment. Highly recommended. Open all year. Moderate to Expensive.

Bare Tree, "The Old King's Highway"—Route 6A, 888–6113. Superb ✓ meals served in a pleasant environment. The chefs here try new twists with fresh and unusual ingredients. Pub with entertainment adjoins. Open all year. Moderate.

Marshlands Restaurant, "The Old King's Highway"—Route 6A, 888– ✓ 9824. This little eatery is not much to look at on the outside, but inside they create gourmet breakfasts, luncheons, and dinners. A favorite of mine and many others. Open all year. Inexpensive.

Horizons on Cape Cod Bay, On Town Neck Beach in Sandwich, 888– 6166. Fresh seafood, great chowders, heaping big sandwiches, and bountiful salads. Open all year. Inexpensive.

Sandy's Restaurant, "The Old King's Highway"—Route 6A, 888–6480. Popular restaurant on the Upper Cape. Well known for good food at fair prices—seafood and meat dishes, special plates. Open all year. Inexpensive.

The First Edition, "The Old King's Highway"—Route 6A, 888–5484. This restaurant has the feel of a comfortable, old club. Delicious seafood, meat dishes, and international cuisine prepared with imagination. Open all year. Moderate.

Michael's at Sandy Neck, "The Old King's Highway"—Route 6A in West Barnstable, 362–4303. Fine food at reasonable prices. Seafood is the specialty. Open all year. Inexpensive to Moderate.

Mashpee

Town offices—Great Neck Road in Mashpee, 477–1616 Mashpee Information Center, Mashpee Rotary—Route 28, 477–0792

The following villages, with their postal zip codes, are within the town of Mashpee: Mashpee—02649; New Seabury—02649; and Popponesset Beach—02649.

Before the arrival of settlers from England, Cape Cod and the islands were inhabited by bands of native people belonging to the Wampanoag Federation. They subsisted on agriculture, fishing, and hunting. They had a culture that gave their lives great meaning and satisfaction. When the

English arrived to stay for good in the early seventeenth century, the Indians helped these newcomers to survive and encouraged them to share in the bounty of land and sea, sources perceived by them as having more than enough to provide for everyone. Land sharing was the way of the Indian, however, while exclusive land ownership was the way of the Europeans; and these two diametrically opposed concepts soon collided in bloodshed. The Indians rebelled against the incessant encroachment of the whites, and what is known in the history books as King Philips War broke out. Although the Indians came out on top in a few raids and skirmishes, the war was won by the white settlers, who possessed superior weapons. As a result of war and new diseases against which they had no immunity, the once abundant and vigorous Indian population of Cape Cod was decimated and subjugated.

Although modern-day Wampanoags live in many Cape Cod towns as individuals and families indistinct from other residents, the last remaining, significant concentration of Wampanoags continues on in the town of Mashpee. During the 1970s the Mashpee Wampanoags attempted to regain ownership of large tracts of land in the town, basing their claim on aboriginal rights and treaties made with the early settlers. Adding insult to the many injuries the Mashpee Wampanoags had suffered for so long, the courts ruled that they were not a tribe in the legal and anthropological sense and therefore could not claim ownership of the land they sought.

Mashpee today is a community of several distinct groups. There are the Wampanoag Indian families who live in or near the center of town, along Route 130, and on the adjacent roads. Within this general area there are also a number of new home developments catering to the affluent retired, summer camps for young people, and enclaves of vacation homes on fresh-water lakes.

The eastern portion of the Massachusetts Military Reservation (Otis Air Base and Camp Edwards) extends into Mashpee. At Mashpee Rotary, where Routes 28 and 151 merge, a major shopping center has been created. Within it the developers are attempting to simulate an upscale town center based on a nostalgic version of a New England–village main street. The land south of Route 28 and on Nantucket Sound has been developed into several exclusive vacation communities. The most notable of these, in architecture, landscaping, and amenities, is New Seabury. Within New Seabury are stunning, expensive vacation/retirement homes, inns, luxury boutiques, a championship golf course, beautiful beaches, and other facilities. Here also is the Popponesset Beach area, where the affluent vacationed long before New Seabury was built. Mashpee attractions include: Old Indian Meeting House, built in 1684, off Route 28; Mashpee Indian Museum, on Route 130; and the Lowell Holly Reservation, off South Sandwich Road. Swimming in the warm waters of Nantucket Sound can be enjoyed at South Cape Beach, reached via Great Oak Road (off Mashpee Rotary and past New Seabury).

Mashpee Accommodations

New Seabury Cape Cod Resort, 1 Mall Way, 477–9111. *Resort.* A luxury resort offering many quality amenities: championship golf courses (eighteen holes), ocean-side and golf-side villas, sixteen tennis courts, swimming pool, private beaches, restaurants, lounges, specialty shops, and boutiques. One of Cape Cod's finest resorts. Open all year. Expensive.

Popponesset Inn, 1 Mall Way, 477–9111. *Inn & Cottages.* Part of New Seabury resort complex; access to all facilities mentioned above. Open May through September. Expensive.

South Cape Resort & Club, Route 28, 477–4700. *Resort.* Accommodations in luxury condos. Indoor and outdoor swimming pools, tennis courts, steam room, and sauna. Open all year. Expensive.

Otis Trailer Village—Johns Pond Campground, Sandwich Road, 477–0444. *Campground.* Private lake beach; swimming, boating, fishing. Open mid-April to mid-October; 90 sites.

Mashpee Dining

The Flume, Lake Avenue, off Route 130 near Center Mashpee, 477–1456. Popular seafood restaurant within a wooded setting overlooking a pond. Open all year. Inexpensive.

Popponesset Inn, 1 Mall Way in New Seabury, 477–9111. Overlooking the ocean; seafood and beef dishes; live entertainment and dancing. Open all year. Expensive.

New Seabury Restaurant, 1 Mall Way in New Seabury, 477–9111. Excellent continental cuisine and seafood; overlooking ocean; lounge; live entertainment and dancing. Open all year. Expensive.

Ma Glockner's, Route 130 near Center Mashpee, 477–3889. Ma's specialty is roast chicken; also seafood and steak. A nice family restaurant. Open all year. Inexpensive.

Bobby Byrne's Pub, In Shopping Center at Routes 151 & 28 in Mashpee, 477–0600. British-pub atmosphere for food and drink. Live entertainment. Popular drinking and munching place. Open all year. Inexpensive.

Barnstable

County offices—off Route 6A in Barnstable Village, 362–2511 Town offices—397 Main Street in Hyannis, 775–1120 Hyannis Chamber of Commerce, 319 Barnstable Road, 775–2201 Cape Cod Chamber of Commerce Information Center at junction of Routes 132 & 6A, 362–5225.

The following villages, with their postal zip codes, are within the town of Barnstable: Barnstable—02630; West Barnstable—02668; Marstons Mills—02648; Cotuit—02635; Osterville—02655; Centerville—02632; Hyannis—02601; Hyannisport—02647; West Hyannisport—02672; Craigville—02636; Cummaquid—02637; Santuit—02635; and Wianno—02655.

Barnstable is Cape Cod's largest town. It also has within its boundaries the Cape's most diverse collection of villages. Hyannis is Cape Cod's tourism, commercial, transportation, and shopping center. More visitors come to Hyannis throughout the year than to any other Cape Cod village. Hyannis is not as aesthetically pleasing as the smaller, quainter villages, but it offers more of everything—accommodations, dining, entertainment, and shopping. Because of its central location on the Cape, Hyannis is within easy reach of other popular areas: Woods Hole to the southwest and Cape Cod National Seashore and Provincetown to the northeast. Because it is the Cape's transportation hub, all buses converge on Hyannis; plane travel is available from here to the islands, Boston, and New York; rail service is offered during the summer; and ferries run to the islands of Martha's Vineyard and Nantucket.

The Cape Cod Mall on Route 132, our largest shopping center, encompasses under one roof many well-known large stores and smaller shops in which to spend time and money on dismal days when even the gulls and terns abandon the beach. Main Street is always busy with people strolling, browsing, and enjoying the many stores, souvenir shops, and places of entertainment and dining. At the west end of Hyannis is the Cape Cod Melody Tent, *the* Cape show place featuring America's best popular talent. In and near Hyannis are a number of public beaches on the warm waters of Nantucket Sound.

Hyannis is also strongly associated in the minds of many with the Kennedy family, although some of its members reside in a private compound in exclusive Hyannisport that was the Summer White House during the late president's administration. Admirers of the Kennedy family can attend services at Saint Francis Xavier Church, where members of the clan worship on occasion, and see their homes in the compound from a boat tour of the harbor and Lewis Bay. Perhaps the most inspiring place on Cape Cod dedicated to JFK is his memorial overlooking Lewis Bay and containing the presidential seal and these words of his: "I believe that this country sail, and not lie still in the harbor."

Just west of Hyannis are the villages of Craigville, Osterville, and Cotuit. Craigville is well known to many Hyannis visitors for its superb beach on Nantucket Sound and the Craigville Conference Center, site of religious meetings and the Cape Cod Writers' Conference. At Centerville is the 1840 Mary Lincoln House. Both Osterville and Cotuit are year-round and vacation towns for the rich, although many ordinary people also live in them. Osterville, at Crosby boatyard, is where the popular, quick-responding Cat Boat was designed and built. There are several fine shops and boutiques in center Osterville to drop in on when touring. While in Osterville visit the 1795 Captain Johnathan Parker House, in which the local historical society now has a museum.

Cotuit is famous for its oysters, and these delicious treats from the sea are still harvested here and shipped to markets to the delight of gourmets. Cotuit is also where, in 1916, a sailing organization for youngsters, called the Cotuit Mosquito Club, was founded. The town itself lacks many tourist amenities, but the absence of commercialization at its center makes Cotuit a most attractive village in which to live. The Cotuit Historical Society operates the 1800 Dottridge Homestead with its period furnishings and historical artifacts. Inland from Cotuit and Osterville is the village of Marstons Mills with its architecturally superb West Parish Meetinghouse, which is located on Route 149. There's also an old-time general store in this area just before you come to scenic Route 6A in West Barnstable.

At West Barnstable is one of Cape Cod's best beaches—Sandy Neck on Cape Cod Bay—and extensive salt marshes. Barnstable Village, the administrative and political center of both the town and county, is a place of historic homes and a harbor that offers whale-watching cruises and deep-sea-fishing charters. The attractions on the Cape Cod Bay side of Barnstable include: the 1717 West Parish Meeting House; the 1644 Lothrop House & Sturgis Library—oldest public-library building in the country; Cape Cod Community College; the 1834 Barnstable County Court House; and the 1856 Thrayser Memorial Museum (U.S. Customs House from 1856 to 1913). The Barnstable Village area, including West Barnstable and Cummaquid, has several fine bed and breakfast homes and gourmet dining places. It is the opposite of frenetic, often gaudy Hyannis. There are beaches for swimming and meandering as well as antique and crafts shops along lovely Route 6A.

The early history of Barnstable was shaped by religious reformers from England who journeyed to the New World in the early seventeenth century. Their purpose was to create the Puritan utopia that existed in their minds and that, they knew, would be impossible to establish in their home country, where the established Anglican Church viewed dissent such as theirs as heresy and treason. The Reverend John Lothrop became leader of these early Puritan utopians in Barnstable. Through the force of Lothrop's vision and character, the community set down roots, grew, and prospered. Another important figure from Barnstable's history is James Otis, known during the Revolutionary War period as "The Great Advocate" and "The Patrick Henry of the North." John Adams said of Otis that he was "the spark by which the child of Independence was born."

Hyannis Accommodations

Iyanough Hills Motor Lodge, Iyanough Road—Route 132, 771–4804. *Motor Inn.* Excellent accommodations and guest amenities in a convenient location. Eighteen-hole golf course, indoor tennis, indoor swimming pool, game room, tanning booths, sun terrace, and whale-watching packages. Open all year. Moderate.

Hyannis Regency Inn, Iyanough Road—Route 132, 775–1153. *Motor Inn.* Excellent accommodations and guest amenities. Indoor swimming pool, whirlpool, sauna, steambaths, health club, efficiency suites, restaurant, and lounge. Open all year. Moderate to Expensive.

Sheraton Hyannis, Iyanough Road—Route 132, 771–3000. *Motor Inn.* Excellent accommodations and guest amenities: indoor and outdoor swimming pools, whirlpool, and tennis court; two restaurants, lounge, and live entertainment. Open all year. Expensive.

Howard Johnson's Motor Lodge, Main and Winter Streets, 775–8600. *Motor Inn.* Fine intown accommodations. Swimming pool, whirlpool, and restaurant. Open all year. Moderate.

Best Western Heritage House Motor Hotel, 259 Main Street, 775–7000. *Motor Inn.* Fine intown accommodations. Indoor and outdoor swimming pools, saunas, Jacuzzi, and whirlpool; restaurant and lounge. Open all year. Moderate.

Days Inn, Iyanough Road—Route 132, 771–6100. *Motor Inn.* Located next to the Cape Cod Mall. Good accommodations at reasonable prices; restaurant, indoor/outdoor pool, fitness center, and other amenities. Open all year. Moderate.

Hyannis Harborview Resort, 213 Ocean Street, 775–4420. *Motor Inn.* Fine accommodations, some with balconies overlooking harbor. Indoor and outdoor swimming pools, saunas, whirlpool, and exercise room; restaurant, coffee shop, and lounge. Open all year. Moderate to Expensive.

Candlelight Motor Lodge, 447 Main Street, 775–3000. *Motor Inn.* Comfortable intown accommodations offering swimming pool and lounge with entertainment. Open all year. Moderate.

Captain Gosnold Village, 230 Gosnold Street, 775–9111. *Motor Inn & Cottages.* Comfortable accommodations within walking distance of beaches and island ferries. Seasonal. Moderate.

Tara Hyannis Resort, at West End Circle, 775–7775. *Motor Inn & Resort.* Excellent accommodations and amenities. One of the most popular places of accommodation on Cape Cod. Rooms have patios or balconies. Excellent eighteen-hole golf course, tennis, indoor and outdoor swimming pools, playground, rental bikes, and health club. Fine restaurant and popular nightclub. Located across the road from the Cape Cod Melody Tent. Open all year. Expensive.

Elegance By-The-Sea, 162 Sea Street, 775-3595. *Guest House.* Elegant sea captain's home furnished with antiques. Emphasis on hospitality and guest service. Within walking distance of most in-town attractions. Open all year. Moderate.

The Inn on Sea Street, 358 Sea Street, 775-8030. *Inn.* A nice Victorian inn in the heart of town offering comfortable accommodations and gourmet breakfasts. Open all year. Moderate.

The Yachtsman Condominiums, 500 Ocean Street, 771-5454. *Apartments & Condos.* Luxury accommodations with many amenities. Private beach and swimming pool. Secluded location on the ocean front. Seasonal. Expensive.

Lewis Bay Motel and Marina, 53 South Street, 775-6633. *Motor Inn.* Comfortable accommodations overlooking harbor and Lewis Bay. Near island ferries. Short walk to downtown. Restaurants, lounges, and a marina. Seasonal. Moderate.

Holiday Inn, Iyanough Road—Route 132, 775-6600. *Motor Inn.* Fine accommodations and many amenities. Indoor swimming pool and tennis court; dining room, lounge, and live entertainment. Its Gee Willikers is an active nightclub for both rock and popular music. Open all year. Moderate to Expensive.

Hyannis Dining

Fiddlebee's, North Street, 771-6032. A family restaurant featuring an eclectic menu—clam chowder, lemon-marinated chicken wings, fried mozzarella, Cajun chicken, and Tex-Mex chili. Open all year. Inexpensive.

331 Main—Penguins Go Pasta, 331 Main Street, 775-2023. A humorous name for a superior Northern Italian restaurant in the heart of downtown Hyannis. Open all year. Moderate.

Market Place Bistro, At Village Marketplace, North and Stevens Streets, 771-7231. Fresh seafood and continental cuisine. Fine food, service, and ambience. Near Melody Tent shows. Open all year. Moderate to Expensive.

Wursthaus Restaurant, Cape Cod Mall, 771-5000. Cape Cod offshoot of the famous Wursthaus in Harvard Square, this one located within the Cape Cod Mall. German beer-hall atmosphere, fine German and American cuisine, beers and ales from all over the world. Open all year. Inexpensive to Moderate.

The Upper Crust Restaurant at Tara Hyannis Resort, West End Circle, 775-7775. An above-average restaurant within a popular Hyannis resort. American and continental cuisines. Dancing and live entertainment. Open all year. Moderate to Expensive.

As you view the architecture of Cape Cod while touring the length and breadth of this peninsula, look at the details on buildings and discover the meaning of good taste in American design. The lovely churches and meeting houses of the Congregationalists are living reminders of Cape Cod's Puritan heritage.

Mooring on the Waterfront, 230 Ocean Street at the Docks, 775–4656. A casual dining place located at a busy, interesting harbor. Seafood and beef dishes. Open all year. Moderate.

The Paddock, West Main Street Traffic Rotary, 775–7677. Victorian environment. Fresh flowers and candlelight on tables. Eclectic menu of American and continental dishes. Open mid-April to mid-November. Next to Melody Tent shows. Expensive.

Asa Bearse House, 415 Main Street, 771–4131. Fine dining in a sea captain's home or out on the patio. Cozy lounge with piano music. Open all year. Moderate.

Sam Diego's, Iyanough Road—Route 132, 771–8816. All your favorite Mexican dishes and drinks. Open all year. Inexpensive.

Bobby Byrne's Pub, Route 28 & Bearse's Way, 775–1425. British-pub atmosphere. Live entertainment. Popular drinking-and-munching place. Open all year. Inexpensive.

Up The Creek, 36 Old Colony Boulevard, 771–7866. Lobster, seafood, and steaks; cheery tavern setting. Open all year. Moderate.

Mitchell's Steak and Rib House, Iyanough Road—Route 132, 775–6700. Great chowder, steaks, and seafood. Irish music and entertainment. A popular place with visitors. Open all year. Moderate.

Fiores Restaurant, 297 North Street at Village Marketplace II, 778–4200. A fine Italian restaurant within a relaxing, tasteful environment. Open all year. Moderate.

Chef Urano's, Corner of South and Sea Streets, 771–7371. An excellent Italian restaurant where the food is expertly prepared by the chef, who is also the owner. Seasonal. Moderate.

Mildred's Chowder House, Iyanough Road—Route 132, across from Airport, 775–1045. Fantastic chowder and good seafood. Popular with families and chowder mavens alike. Open all year. Moderate.

Starbuck's, Iyanough Road—Route 132, 778–6767. Colorful and somewhat zany decor. Interesting Yuppie dishes—mesquite-grilled meats, seafood salads, and baked Brie. Open all year. Inexpensive to Moderate.

Alberto's Ristorante, Ocean Street, 778–1770. An excellent restaurant for Northern Italian cuisine and homemade pasta. Open all year. Moderate.

Hill's Seafood and Steaks, 530 West Main Street, 775–0344. A fine restaurant serving well-prepared American cuisine. Operating in Hyannis since 1939. Cape Cod clambake, roast duckling, and rib-eye teriyaki; wonderful desserts. Seasonal. Moderate.

D'Olimpio's, Route 28, 771–3220. New York City–style deli on Cape Cod. Hearty luncheon and dinner specials and ample sandwiches. Best rye bread baked on Cape Cod. Open all year. Inexpensive.

Dockside Inn, 110 School Street, 775–8636. Overlooks the harbor. Delicious chowder and seafood. Open all year. Inexpensive.

Hyannisport Accommodations

Homestead, 288 Scudder Avenue, 778–4999. **B&B.** Elegant sea captain's mansion. Private baths, fireplaces, canopy bed, and quilts. Full breakfast served. Wraparound porch. Near all Hyannis attractions and beaches. Open all year. Moderate.
Harbor Village, Marstons Avenue, 775–7581. **Cottages.** Fully furnished accommodations with fireplaces. Private beach, fishing, and canoeing. Open May to October. Moderate.
Sea Breeze by the Beach, 397 Sea Street, 775–4269. **Rooms & Cottages.** Accommodations in secluded area with flowered grounds; cottages with fireplaces. Near beach and Hyannis attractions. Open all year. Moderate.

Centerville Accommodations

Centerville Corners Motor Lodge, South Main Street and Craigville Beach Road, 775–7223. **Motor Inn.** Motel and efficiency units; indoor pool and saunas; close to Craigville Beach. Golf, tennis, and restaurants nearby. Open all year. Moderate.
Copper Beech Inn, 497 Main Street, 771–5488. **B&B.** This fine house was built by Captain Hillman Crosby in 1830. It has traditional furnishings. Breakfast is cooked on a century-old stove. Next door is the 1881 Howard Marston estate with park landscape designed by Frederick Law Olmstead. Open all year. Moderate.
Sandman Inn, 116 Hillside Drive, 362–4284. **B&B.** Family atmosphere, overlooking Lake Wequaquet, rural setting, near churches and synagogue. Walk to lake, short drive to beaches. Open all year. Moderate.

Craigville Accommodations

Trade Winds Inn, Craigville Beach Road, 775–0365. **Motor Inn.** Excellent accommodations overlooking Craigville Beach and Lake Elizabeth. Private beach, coffee room and lounge, putting green, and many other amenities. Seasonal. Expensive.
Ocean View Motel, At Craigville Beach, 775–1962. **Motor Inn.** Comfortable accommodations at one of Cape Cod's most popular beaches. Seasonal. Moderate.
Craig Village by the Sea, At Craigville Beach, 775–0350. **Cottages.** Housekeeping cottages and studio efficiency units near warmwater beach. Open May to October. Moderate.

Osterville Accommodations

East Bay Lodge, East Bay Road, 428–6961. *Inn.* Well-known and well-liked Cape Cod accommodation and dining place. Excellent in every respect—service, ambience, location, and surroundings. Open all year. Expensive.

The Osterville Fairways Country Inn, 105 Parker Road, 428–2747. *Inn.* Fine accommodations in the Cape's "ritzy" town. Convenient to golf, tennis, and village shopping. Open all year. Moderate.

Osterville Dining

East Bay Lodge, East Bay Road, 428–6961. Elegant dining environment overlooking yacht-filled East Bay. Excellent service. Gourmet selections include chateaubriand, rack of lamb, tournedos homard, oysters Moscow, veal Francaise, seafood medley, and fresh lobster prepared to your liking. Open for lunch and dinner. Open all year. Expensive.

Wimpy's, Main Street, 428–6300. Popular Osterville restaurant. Fresh swordfish and bluefish daily. Lobster pie and crab imperial. Early bird specials such as baked haddock and pork cutlets Marsala. Live musical entertainment in the lounge. Open all year. Inexpensive to Moderate.

Cotuit Accommodations

The Allen's, 60 Nickerson Lane, 428–5702. *B&B.* Comfortable accommodations in one of Cape Cod's prettiest, most tranquil towns. Full country breakfasts served. Tours to many local attractions and easy access to beaches. Open all year. Moderate.

Cotuit Harborside Guest House & Apartments, 845 Main Street, 428–6849. *Guest House.* A charming house in a lovely town offering large rooms with modern amenities. Apartments available in carriage house. Spacious lawns. Near beach, golf, and tennis. Open all year. Moderate.

Salty Dog, 451 Main Street, 428–5228. *Guest House.* Near beaches and close to attractions in Hyannis and Falmouth. Continental breakfast served. Open all year. Moderate.

Cotuit Dining

Regatta of Cotuit at the 1790 Crocker House, Route 28, 428–5715. For many years the Crocker House, located about halfway between Falmouth and Hyannis, was a highly regarded dining place. The folks who own and operate the Regatta of Falmouth are now also performing their gastronomic and hospitality wonders at the Crocker House, a colonial home of historic significance. The culinary emphasis here is on American cuisine—from the traditional to the contemporary. Among the featured traditional dishes are pheasant, partridge, buffalo tenderloin, and fresh seafood, not unfamiliar menu items to past generations but special treats in ours. There is every reason to believe that the Regatta of Cotuit will quickly establish itself as one of Cape Cod's premier restaurants. Luncheon, dinner, and Sunday brunch are served. Open all year. Expensive.

Barnstable Village Accommodations

Cobb's Cove, Powder Hill Road in Barnstable Village, 362–9356. **Inn.** Excellent accommodations in a peaceful area on Cape Cod Bay offering many quality amenities. Breakfast and dinner served. Open all year. Expensive.

Ashley Manor, "The Old King's Highway"—Route 6A, 362–8044. **B&B.** Fine, antique-filled mansion dating from 1699. Secret passage and hiding places used by Loyalists of the British crown during the American War of Independence. Manicured lawns and diverse plantings highlight a lovely environment. Open all year. All rooms have private baths; there are working fireplaces in most rooms. Amenities include fresh flowers, candy, Crabtree & Evelyn soaps, shampoos and lotions, plus wine, sherry, or port available in the living room. Full buffet breakfast every morning. Expensive.

Beechwood Inn, "The Old King's Highway"—Route 6A, 362–6618. **B&B.** Victorian house with antique furnishings. Queen-sized four-poster bed. Paintings by local artists. Home-baked breads and muffins part of breakfast menu. Rocking chairs on veranda. Open early May to November. Moderate to Expensive.

Charles Hinckley House, "The Old King's Highway"—Route 6A and Scudder Lane, 362–9924. **B&B.** A shipwright's house built in 1809. Fine accommodations inside, beautiful flowers surrounding the house. I consider the wildflowers growing in front of this historic house to be one of the loveliest floral displays on Cape Cod. Amenities include fresh-flower arrangements, chocolates, and fresh fruit. Open all year. Moderate to Expensive.

Thomas Huckins House, "The Old King's Highway"—Route 6A, 362–6379. **B&B.** Eighteenth-century house restored with many details. Furnished with antiques and reproductions. New England maple syrup and cranberry muffins are traditional items served at breakfast. Open all year. Moderate to Expensive.

The Lamb and Lion, "The Old King's Highway"—Route 6A, 362–6823. **Inn.** Comfortable accommodations. All rooms have private baths.

Fine honeymoon suite. Housekeeping units for large families. Swimming pool in atrium. Continental breakfast served. Open all year. Moderate. **Honeysuckle Hill,** "The Old King's Highway"—Route 6A, 362-8418. ***B&B.*** Victorian farmhouse with easy access to Sandy Neck Beach, marshes, village center, and cranberry bogs. Emphasis on making guests feel special. Both full and continental breakfasts—Scotch eggs and blueberry pancakes. Open all year. Moderate to Expensive.

Barnstable Village Dining

The Barnstable Tavern & Restaurant, "The Old King's Highway"— Route 6A, 362-2355. Creative cookery in a colonial setting in the heart of Barnstable Village. Changing menu; emphasis on fresh ingredients. Open all year. Moderate to Expensive.

Mattakeese Wharf, Barnstable Village Harbor, 362-4511. Fine seafood restaurant with views of the harbor. Open May to October. Moderate.

Harbor Point Restaurant, Harbor Point Road, 362-2231. Seafood and meat dishes; views of the harbor. Open May to November. Moderate.

Yarmouth

Town offices—Route 28 at Wood Road in Yarmouth, 398-2231 Yarmouth Chamber of Commerce, Route 28 in South Yarmouth, 398-5311

The following villages, with their postal zip codes, are within the town of Yarmouth: Yarmouth—02675; Yarmouth Port—02675; South Yarmouth—02664; West Yarmouth—02673; and Bass River—02664.

Sometimes, along Route 28, it is difficult to figure out where Hyannis ends and the town of Yarmouth begins, because one seems to blend into the other. The Route 28 section of West Yarmouth and South Yarmouth/ Bass River is an elongated area of family motels, restaurants, places of entertainment and amusement, and shopping centers and souvenir stores. This strip is one of Cape Cod's most popular tourist centers because of the abundance of these tourist amenities and their proximity to the warm-water beaches on Nantucket Sound. In contrast, the villages of Yarmouth and Yarmouth Port, on the Cape Cod Bay side of the peninsula, exude more history, tranquility, and the charming nostalgia of a bygone era.

The first settler of note in Yarmouth was Reverend Stephen Bachiler, who arrived from north of Boston in the late 1630s. Bachiler was a carnal sort of fellow—a womanizer in today's lingo. He was defrocked by his church, married several times, and went to England, dying there when almost a hundred years old. The first permanent settlers of "proper substance" in seventeenth-century Yarmouth were the Thachers, the Crowes (now "Crowell"), and the Howes. Anthony Thacher was the leader of this fledgling community. Quakers also settled in Yarmouth and formed their own enclaves in southern sections.

During the nineteenth century, the citizens of Yarmouth, seeking intellectual self-improvement, established lyceums where debates, lectures, and readings from literature and poetry were held. The discussion of religion or politics at these gatherings was not permitted due to their incendiary nature. In 1836 N. S. Simpkins launched his newspaper, the *Yarmouth Register*, and wasted no time in taking on the likes of Andy Jackson and Martin Van Buren. Also during the mid-nineteenth century, Amos Otis placed himself into the local history books as the man who planted a mile of elm saplings on each side of what is now Route 6A. Many decades later, when the high, thickly leafed elm branches arched over the roadway, Otis's trees and the many historic sea captains' homes behind them together formed one of the most beautiful, foliage-ensconced, mansion-dotted avenues in America.

Historical attractions in town include: the 1780 Winslow Crocker House in Yarmouth Port, Friends Meeting House in South Yarmouth, Bass Hole Viking site in Yarmouth, Captain Bangs Hallet House in Yarmouth Port, Church of the New Jerusalem in Yarmouth Port, Judah Baker Windmill in Yarmouth, the Pawkanawkut Village Indian graves in South Yarmouth, and the Yarmouth Village Pump in Yarmouth Port.

West Yarmouth Accommodations

The Manor House, 57 Maine Avenue, 771–9211. *B&B.* Comfortable accommodations overlooking Lewis Bay; close to beaches, golf, tennis, and restaurants. Open mid-May to mid-October. Inexpensive to Moderate.

Tidewater Motor Lodge, Route 28, 775–6322. *Motor Inn.* Fine accommodations near downtown Hyannis offering indoor and outdoor swimming pools, sauna, and playground; coffee shop. Open early February to late October. Moderate.

Americana Holiday Motel, Route 28, 775–5511. *Motor Inn.* Good value. Three swimming pools, sauna, whirlpool, putting green, and playground; coffee shop. Open mid-March to mid-November. Moderate.

Cape Sojourn Motel, Route 28, 775–3825. *Motor Inn.* Good value. Two swimming pools, kid's wading pool, whirlpool, putting green. Open early April to early November. Moderate.

American Host Motel, Route 28, 775–2332. *Motor Inn.* Good value. Two swimming pools, wading pool, whirlpool, putting green, miniature golf, and playground. Open mid-April to early November. Moderate.

Thunderbird Motor Lodge, Route 28, 775-2692. *Motor Inn.* Good value. Three swimming pools, his and hers saunas, Roman whirlpool baths, tennis court, putting green, and playground. Open February through November. Moderate.

The Mariner Motor Lodge, Route 28, 771-7887. *Motor Inn.* Good value. Two swimming pools, whirlpool, sauna. Open all year. Moderate.

Town 'n Country Motor Lodge, Route 28, 771-0212. *Motor Inn.* Good value. Three swimming pools, kiddie pool, his and hers saunas, Roman whirlpool baths, and putting green. Open all year. Moderate.

The Holly Tree Resort, Route 28, 771-6677. *Motor Inn.* Fine accommodations. Indoor and outdoor swimming pools, whirlpool, game room; restaurant and lounge. Open all year. Moderate.

Green Harbor on the Ocean, 182 Baxter Avenue, 771-1126. *Motor Inn.* Excellent accommodations overlooking Nantucket Sound. Swimming pool, boating, fishing, bikes, and miniature golf; landscaped lawns. Open early May to mid-October. Moderate to Expensive.

Irish Village—Cape Cod, Route 28, 771-0100. *Motor Inn/Cottages/Efficiencies.* A bit of Ireland on Cape Cod. Comfortable accommodations; tennis, indoor swimming pool, whirlpool, sauna; restaurant, Irish pub, and live entertainment; Irish gift shop. Open all year. Moderate.

Aladdin Motor Inn on Mill Creek Bay, Route 28, 775-5669. *Motor Inn.* Modern accommodations; indoor and outdoor pools, whirlpool, and saunas. Near beaches, restaurants, and downtown Hyannis. Open all year. Moderate.

Flagship Motor Inn, Route 28, 775-5155. *Motor Inn.* Good value. Two swimming pools, saunas, whirlpool, game room, and playground; coffee shop. Open all year. Moderate.

The Cove at Yarmouth Resort, Route 28, 771-3666. *Motor Inn/ Resort.* Fine accommodations. Tennis, racquetball, squash, health spa, and indoor and outdoor swimming pools; restaurant and lounge. Open all year. Moderate.

West Yarmouth Dining

Yarmouth House Restaurant, Route 28, 771-5154. Steaks, seafood, and prime rib of beef; luncheon and dinner specials. Open all year. Moderate.

Irish Village Restaurant & Pub, Route 28, 771-0100. A family restaurant for seafood, prime rib of beef, steaks, and Irish specialties. Irish gift shop and Irish entertainment. Children's menu. Open all year. Inexpensive.

Fred's Turkey House, Route 28, 775-6783. Specialties include turkey dinners, barbecue foods, fresh fish, lobster, fancy burgers, and salads. An excellent family eatery. Seasonal. Inexpensive.

Lobster Boat, Route 28, 775-0486. The specialty here is fresh New England lobster. You can get one up to four pounds. Also serves a complete menu of seafood, steaks, and prime rib of beef. Seasonal. Moderate.

Bloom's Prime Rib House, Route 28, 775–0524. Although the specialty is roast prime rib of beef, continental cuisine is also featured—rack of lamb, veal dishes, and the like. Extensive wine list. Good food and service in a cozy Victorian environment. Open all year. Moderate.

Dorsies, Route 28, 771–5898. Fine steaks, prime rib of beef, and seafood. Large salad bar. Live entertainment. Relaxing environment. Open all year. Moderate.

Johnny Yee's, Route 28, 775–1090. Wide selection of Chinese and Polynesian dishes. Johnny Yee's has the best Hawaiian/Polynesian live stage show/revue on Cape Cod. Highly recommended for a good time. Open all year. Inexpensive to Moderate.

Casa Mia, Route 28, 771–6251. Soul- and tummy-satisfying Italian food. Open all year. Moderate.

Shirdan's Country Kitchen, Route 28, 778–6844. A family restaurant offering seafood platters, steaks, salads, and chowders. Children's menu. Open all year. Inexpensive.

Surf & Turf Family Restaurant, Route 28, 778–1977. Family restaurant. Lobster, seafood, steak, and prime rib of beef. Children's menu. Seasonal. Inexpensive.

South Yarmouth/Bass River Accommodations

Blue Rock Inn, Highbank Road, 398–6962. *Motor Inn.* Blue Rock golf course; private beach, swimming pool, Jacuzzi, and whirlpool; restaurant and lounge. Open from early April to mid-November. Moderate to Expensive.

All Seasons Motor Inn, Route 28, 394–7600. *Motor Inn.* Good value. Two swimming pools, saunas, whirlpool, and exercise room; coffee shop. Open all year. Moderate.

The New Jolly Captain Resort, Route 28, 398–2253. *Motor Inn.* All suite accommodations with kitchens and private balconies or patios; swimming pool. Open all year. Expensive.

The Old Cape House, 108 Old Main Street, 398–1068. *B&B.* Romantically furnished 1815 home. English hospitality. Suites and individual rooms, one with fireplace and kitchen facility. Fresh fruit and home-baked muffins among featured goodies for breakfast. Open April through November. Moderate.

Captain Isaiah's House, 33 Pleasant Street, 394–1739. *B&B.* Restored sea captain's home. Continental breakfast with home-baked breads and cakes. Open June to September. Moderate.

Surf and Sand Beach Motel, South Shore Drive, 398–3700. *Motor Inn.* Ocean-front location and beach; suites and efficiency units. Open all year. Moderate to Expensive.

Surfcomber on the Ocean, South Shore Drive, 398–9228. *Motor Inn.* Ocean-front location. Some rooms with patios or balconies. Swimming pool and beach. Open late April to late October. Moderate to Expensive.

Brentwood Motor Inn, Route 28, 398–8812. *Motor Inn.* Motel rooms and housekeeping units. Indoor and outdoor pools, sauna, and whirlpool. Open from early April to early November. Moderate.

Cavalier Motor Lodge & Resort, Route 28, 394–6575. *Motor Inn.* Motel and efficiency units; indoor and outdoor pools, wading pool, playground, and putting green; coffee shop. Open early April to early November. Moderate.

Ambassador Motor Inn, Route 28, 394–4000. *Motor Inn.* Indoor and outdoor pools, sauna, and whirlpool; restaurant and lounge. Comfortable accommodations. Near beaches, golf, and tennis. Open all year. Moderate.

Blue Water Resort, South Shore Drive, 398–2288. *Motor Inn.* Located on the ocean. Beach, indoor pool, saunas, putting green, and tennis court; dining room and coffee shop. Live entertainment. Open all year. Expensive.

Red Jacket Beach Motor Inn, South Shore Drive, 398–6941. *Resort.* Excellent accommodations; cable television and movies; private beach, swimming pools, tennis, and putting green; dining room and lounge; and many other amenities. One of the best motor inns on the Cape. Open spring to fall. Expensive.

Riviera Beach Motor Inn, South Shore Drive, 398–2273. *Motor Inn.* Ocean-front location. Efficiency units; sailboats and swimming pools; coffee shop. Open mid-April to late October. Moderate to Expensive.

South Yarmouth/Bass River Dining

Skipper, 152 South Shore Drive, 394–7406. Views of Nantucket Sound. American and continental cuisine. Open May to October. Moderate.

Frontier Prime Rib & Lobster House, Route 28, 394–8006. Lobsters, prime rib of beef, steaks, and seafood. Children's menu. Seasonal. Inexpensive to Moderate.

J. F. Murphy's, Route 28, 398–6224. Friendly, family restaurant serving fine beef and seafood dishes. Soul food—homemade corned beef and cabbage—for the Irish on Thursday nights. Early birds specials. Open all year. Inexpensive to Moderate.

150

Kyoto, Route 28, 771-1622. Authentic Japanese cuisine. Sukiyaki prepared at your table; sushi bar; take-out orders. Open all year. Inexpensive to Moderate.

Bass River Fish Market, 15 Mill Lane, 398-6434. Broiled halibut, king-crab legs or lobster with drawn butter, broiled bluefish, and prime rib of beef. Early bird specials. Open all year. Moderate.

Yarmouth Port Accommodations

Old Yarmouth Inn, "The Old King's Highway"—Route 6A, 362-3191. *Inn.* Built in 1696 and considered the oldest inn on Cape Cod. Staying and/or dining at the Old Yarmouth Inn is like going back to a time when America was a land in the process of becoming, in contrast to one having arrived. Among its dinners are traditional roast turkey with all the trimmings, prime rib of beef, and roast leg of lamb. Open all year. Moderate.

Olde Yarmouth Manor, 4 Summer Street at "The Old King's Highway"—Route 6A, 362-5000. *Inn.* A manor house from the early nineteenth century furnished with antiques. Continental breakfast served. Open all year. Moderate.

Liberty Hill Inn, "The Old King's Highway"—Route 6A, 362-3976. *B&B.* Eighteen twenty-five Greek Revival home with easy access to beaches, restaurants, and antique shops. Full breakfasts served with many gourmet items. Open all year. Moderate.

The Village Inn, "The Old King's Highway"—Route 6A, 362-3182. *Inn.* Seventeen ninety sea captain's home. Fine rooms, spacious grounds, and screened porch; continental breakfast. Open all year. Moderate.

Colonial House Inn, "The Old King's Highway"—Route 6A, 362-4348. *Inn.* Restored sea captain's home decorated with antiques. Price of room includes continental breakfast and dinner. Open all year. Moderate.

Wedgewood Inn, "The Old King's Highway"—Route 6A, 362-5157. *Inn.* Eighteen twelve home of maritime lawyer. Near beaches and restaurants. Accommodations include continental breakfast. Open all year. Moderate to Expensive.

Yarmouth Port Dining

Anthony's Cummaquid, "The Old King's Highway"—Route 6A, 362-4501. This excellent dining place set within beautiful grounds overlooking marshes and Cape Cod Bay is the Cape Cod branch of Anthony's Pier 4 in Boston, one of America's best-liked restaurants. Superb American and continental cuisines, with emphasis on fresh seafood. The service and environment can't be topped. Extensive wine list. Open all year. Expensive.

Captain Howe's Restaurant, "The Old King's Highway"—Route 6A, 362–3775. An old sea captain's home in which good food and cheer are served in the midst of Victorian decor. Open all year. Moderate.

Colonial House Inn, "The Old King's Highway"—Route 6A, 362–4348. The cuisine of New England. The ambience of a quintessential country inn by the village green. Excellent service. Open all year. Expensive.

Bogart's Restaurant, "The Old King's Highway"—Route 6A, 362–9223. Hearty fare in 1930s setting. Daily culinary specialties. Open all year. Moderate.

✓ **La Cipollina,** "The Old King's Highway"—Route 6A, 362–4341. Superior Italian and French cuisine. Osso bucco, a rare treat, is on a menu that promises and delivers great gastronomic pleasure. Elegant environment. Candlelight and music. One of the Cape's best. Open all year. Expensive.

✓ **Chanterelle,** "The Old King's Highway"—Route 6A, 362–8195. A favorite dining place for discriminating gourmets and gourmands. Creative continental cuisine. Beautiful environment of flowers and plants. Highly recommended. Open all year. Expensive.

✓ **Cranberry Moose,** "The Old King's Highway"—Route 6A, 362–8153. Fine dining in a mid-eighteenth-century home. American cuisine with flavors à la Francaise. A culinary treat. Seasonal. Expensive.

Oliver's, "The Old King's Highway"—Route 6A, 362–6062. A casual eating and drinking place. Sandwiches and full dinners; live entertainment. Open all year. Inexpensive.

Dennis

Town offices—Main Street in South Dennis, 394–8300 Dennis Chamber of Commerce, Route 28 at Route 134 in Dennis Port, 398–3568

The following villages, with their postal zip codes, are within the town of Dennis: Dennis—02638; Dennis Port—02639; East Dennis—02641; South Dennis—02660; and West Dennis—02670.

As do Barnstable and Yarmouth, the town of Dennis extends to both coasts of the (Mid) Cape along Cape Cod Bay and Nantucket Sound. Scenic Route 6A, "The Old King's Highway," continues on through the tranquil villages of Dennis and East Dennis, with their beaches on Cape Cod Bay, many historic homes, Sesuit Harbor for deep-sea-fishing expeditions, and Scargo Lake for fresh-water angling. There are fine B&Bs, restaurants, and shops along this lovely route. Route 134 connects the Dennis villages on

DENNIS

Cape Cod Bay with those on Nantucket Sound: West Dennis, and Dennis Port. The two are on Route 28 where there is a concentration of motor inns, restaurants, shops, and amusements. The warm-water beaches of Dennis on Nantucket Sound are very popular with Cape Cod visitors. In its early days Dennis was part of Yarmouth. Among the original families who settled Dennis were the Nickersons, the Bakers, and the Searses. The first parish was established in 1721, and in 1725 Reverend Josiah Dennis became pastor of this rural, sea-oriented congregation. The reverend did such an outstanding job ministering to the spiritual and civic needs of his congregation that all the town's villages were named in his honor. East Parish, as this area of Yarmouth was known, became incorporated as the Town of Dennis in 1793. Dennis was home port to many a sea captain, and at Sesuit Harbor the Shiverick Shipyards built some of the finest packet boats, schooners, and clippers of the nineteenth century.

Historical places of interest in Dennis include: Cape Playhouse, where Lee Remick, Gertrude Lawrence, Henry Fonda, and Robert Montgomery have performed; Hokum Rocks in Dennis; Scargo Lake and Tower in Dennis; the 1801 Jericho House Museum in Dennis; the 1736 Josiah Dennis Manse; Whig Street in Dennis; Shiverick Shipyards in East Dennis South Parish; and the 1835 South Parish Congregational Church, Main Street in South Dennis.

Dennis Accommodations

The Four Chimneys Inn, "The Old King's Highway"—Route 6A, 385–6317. **B&B.** Eclectically, tastefully furnished 1881 Victorian house. Swedish spoken here. Continental breakfast. Open mid-February through October. Moderate.

Isaiah B. Hall House, 152 Whig Street, 385–9928. **B&B.** Warm, homey 1857 Greek Revival house. Near Cape Cod Playhouse, often serving as residence for performers. Art and crafts of Dorothy Gripp throughout the house. Breakfast served in dining room festooned with antiques. Open all year. Moderate.

Dennis Dining

Marshside Restaurant, 28 Bridge Street near Junction of Routes 6A and 134, 385–4010. A place for family dining. Seafood, burgers, beef and chicken dishes, and salads. Open all year. Inexpensive.

Playhouse Restaurant, Route 6A, 385–8000. Fine restaurant on the grounds of the Cape Playhouse offering elegant dining and easy access to top-star entertainment. Open all year. Moderate.

Red Pheasant Inn, Route 6A, 385–2133. A long tenure of acceptance on Cape Cod. American and continental cuisine, including game. Comfortable, with good food and service. Open all year. Moderate.

Dennis Port Accommodations

In addition to the places of accommodation listed here, Dennis Port has a large number of cottage colonies. Most of these are rented by the week, and advance reservations are essential during the months of July and August. For more information about these cottage colonies, contact the Dennis Chamber of Commerce at the address and telephone number given on page X.

Corsair Resort Motel, 41 Chase Avenue, 396–2279. *Motor Inn.* Ocean-front location with private beach; swimming pool and shuffleboard; in-room movies; free coffee. Seasonal. Moderate.

Johnathan Edwards Motel, 392 Main Street, 398–2953. *Motor Inn.* Motel rooms, efficiencies, and apartments. Swimming pool and game room; near beaches. Open all year. Moderate.

The Edgewater, Chase Avenue, 398–6922. *Motor Inn.* Fine accommodations; some efficiencies and apartments; indoor and outdoor pools; near beaches. Open end of April to mid-October. Moderate to Expensive.

The Soundings, Chase Avenue, 394–6561. *Motor Inn.* Private beach, two swimming pools, sauna, putting green, and tennis courts; coffee shop. Most units with balconies overlooking Nantucket Sound. Seasonal. Moderate to Expensive.

The Breakers Motel, Chase Avenue, 398–6905. *Motor Inn.* Many rooms with balconies overlooking Nantucket Sound. Private beach and swimming pool. Seasonal. Moderate.

The Rose Petal, 152 Sea Street, 398–3412. *B&B.* A fine old New England home with spacious rooms. Near beaches, shops, and restaurants. Serves breakfast with home-baked goodies. Open all year. Moderate.

The Colony Beach Motel, Corner of Old Wharf Road and Depot Street, 398–2217. *Motor Inn.* Motel rooms and efficiencies. Private beach and swimming pool. Seasonal. Moderate to Expensive.

Dennis Port Dining

Brass Kettle Family Restaurant, Route 28, 398–2888. Family restaurant with a varied menu. Open all year. Inexpensive.

The Ebb Tide, 88 Chase Avenue, 398-8733. Gourmet seafood specialties served in an elegant environment. Seasonal. Moderate.

The Ocean House, Chase Avenue and Depot Street, 394–0700. Excellent continental cuisine properly served in an elegant environment. Bouillabaisse, rack of lamb, and veal Oscar are among the specialties. Seasonal. Expensive.

Clancy's, Upper County Road, 394–6661. With a name like Clancy, this place could be a pub in Ireland, but it's on Cape Cod overlooking the sea. Good food in a cheery atmosphere. Irish entertainment. Open all year. Inexpensive.

West Dennis Accommodations

Lighthouse Inn, On the Beach, 398–2244. *Inn & Cottages.* A complex that includes the Bass River Light, the inn, and cottages. Dining room; outdoor pool, tennis courts, and private beach. Modified American Plan (breakfast and dinner). Open May to October. Moderate.

Beach House, On the Beach, 398–8321. *B&B.* Turn-of-the-century house with its own private beach on Nantucket Sound. Breakfast buffet in the sunroom overlooking the ocean. Open all year. Moderate.

Elmwood Inn, 57 Old Main Street, 394–2798. *B&B.* Fine Victorian house located on Bass River. Traditional wicker furniture, spacious grounds, pine groves, and a private beach. Serves full breakfasts. Moderate. Open all year.

Huntsman Motor Lodge, Route 28, 394–5415. *Motor Inn.* Family owned and operated; welcomes families. Motel and efficiency units; swimming pool. Convenient to beaches and area restaurants. Open mid-April to the end of October. Moderate.

West Dennis Dining

The Inn at West Dennis, Route 28, 394–9427. All the right stuff—gourmet cuisine and candlelight within a historic sea captain's home. Open all year. Moderate.

Lighthouse Inn, Lighthouse Road, 398–2244. Dining room overlooking the sea. Fine seafood and meat dishes. Open May to October. Moderate.

East Dennis Accommodations

Sesuit Harbor Motel, "The Old King's Highway"—Route 6A, 385–3326. *Motor Inn.* Good value. Near restaurants, bike and hiking trails, and beaches. Open all year. Moderate.

Harwich

Town offices—Main Street in Harwich, 432–0433 Harwich Chamber of Commerce, Main Street, Harwich Port, 432–1600

The following villages, with their postal zip codes, are within the town of Harwich: Harwich—02645; Harwich Port—02646; South Harwich—02661; West Harwich—02671; East Harwich—02645; North Harwich—02645; and Pleasant Lake—02645.

Many illustrious individuals have come from, or lived on, Cape Cod. In the early days this area of the Cape was dominated by strong personalities—William Nickerson of Chatham; John Wing, a Quaker from Sandwich; John Dillingham; and John Mecoy. In the later 1660s Gershom Hall built his house in South Harwich and is therefore considered one of the first settlers. In 1694 Harwich was incorporated as a town. The town was divided into South Parish and North Parish. In 1803 North Parish spun off from Harwich and became the Town of Brewster. South Parish continued on as the Town of Harwich.

As was the case in other Cape towns, Harwich became a "burnt over district" of religious denominations and splinter sects contending with each other for a larger share of available souls. The battle between theologies for souls involved Congregationalists, Baptists, New Lighters, Come Outers, and Standpatters. From before the Revolutionary War to well after the Civil War, religious contention raged between people basically cut from the same ethnic cloth on issues as diverse as who would be saved and whether or not slavery should be abolished. It is said that Come Outers, when in a trance, walked on fences and spoke in strange tongues.

Today the strange tongues spoken in Harwich are by visitors who come from all over the world; a few have been known to walk fences after downing several pops of firewater at a local pub. Harwich has fine beaches, places of accommodation, and restaurants. Two of the Cape's best resorts are here: Wychmere Harbor Hotel and Beach Club, and Wequassett Inn on Pleasant Bay in East Harwich.

The following Harwich attractions are well worth visiting: Brooks Academy Museum and the Harwich cranberry bogs. Auto or bike touring of Wychmere Harbor and the Pleasant Bay area is also recommended.

Harwich Port Accommodations

Wychmere Harbor Hotel and Beach Club, 23 Snow Inn Road, 432–1000. *Hotel/Beach Club.* An exclusive waterfront-accommodation complex. Private beach on Nantucket Sound, large swimming pool, and tennis; gourmet dining, dancing, and live entertainment. Seasonal. Expensive.

The Inn on Bank Street, 88 Bank Street, 432–3206. *B&B.* Located in peaceful area near restaurants and shops. Italian and Spanish spoken. Menu reflects health-food interests of owners. Open April to November. Moderate.

Seadar Inn by the Sea, Braddock Lane at Bank Street, 432–0264. *Motor Inn.* Good value. Nantucket Sound beach; breakfast buffet. Open mid-May to October. Moderate.

Harwich Port Dining

L'Alouette, Route 28, 430–0405. Excellent restaurant for French cuisine. A wide selection of wines. Open all year. Moderate to Expensive.
The Rexford Restaurant, Route 28, 432–9282. Family restaurant offering seafood, steaks, and extra special desserts. Seasonal. Inexpensive.
Thompson's Clam Bar, On Snow Inn Wharf on the dock at Wychmere Harbor, 432–3595. Popular seafood restaurant overlooking harbor. Children's menu. Seasonal. Moderate.
Oliver's, Route 28, 432–7677. Casual eating and drinking place. Sandwiches and full dinners; live entertainment. Open all year. Inexpensive.
The Country Cupboard, Route 28, 432–9232. Family restaurant. Seafood, steaks, chowder, salads, and sandwiches. Open all year. Inexpensive.
Sword & Shield, Route 28, 432–9763. Family restaurant. Seafood, steaks, and other popular favorites. Open all year. Inexpensive to Moderate.
Country Inn, Route 39, 432–2769. Intimate atmosphere enhanced by candlelight. Fine food featuring fresh seafood and beef; breads and pastries made on premises. Open all year. Moderate.
Brax Landing, Route 28 at Saquatucket Harbor, 432–5515. Gourmet seafood. Overlooking the harbor. Open all year. Moderate.
Cafe Elizabeth, 31 Sea Street, 432–1147. Elegant dining in a historic home overlooking Nantucket Sound. Creative menu: blini with salmon caviar and lobster melded with Irish whiskey. Highly recommended. Seasonal. Expensive.

Harwich Accommodations

Victorian Inn at Harwich, 102 Parallel Street in Harwich Center, 432–1182. *B&B.* Restored 1866 Victorian home. Comfortable accommodations in a quiet area. Continental breakfast and afternoon tea. Open all year. Moderate.

South Harwich Accommodations

Handkerchief Shoals Motel, Route 28 in South Harwich, 432–2200. *Motor Inn.* Good value. Swimming pool; near beaches. Seasonal. Moderate.

Bayberry Motel, Old County Road, 432–2937. *Motor Inn.* Good value. Spacious grounds and swimming pool; near beaches. Seasonal. Moderate.

Stone Horse Motor Inn, Route 28, 432–0662. *Motor Inn.* Good value. Some suites and efficiencies; near beaches. Seasonal. Moderate.

West Harwich Accommodations

The Commodore, 30 Earle Street, 432–1180. *Motor Inn.* Quiet area near Nantucket Sound beach. Swimming pool, putting green, and lawn games; restaurant. Open all year. Moderate to Expensive.

Lion's Head Inn, 186 Belmont Road, 432–7766. *B&B.* A sea captain's home close to two hundred years old. Antiques and traditional furnishings; interior warm and historical. Fine collection of pewter. Many excellent amenities including private woods, fresh flowers, chocolates, and wine for return guests. Gourmet items on the breakfast menu—omelets with lobster eggs and homemade muffins. Open all year. Moderate.

Tern Inn, 91 Chase Street, 432–3714. *B&B.* Comfortable accommodations in a two-hundred-year-old home within a few minutes' walk of Nantucket Sound beaches. Continental breakfasts served at a "common table." Open early April to the end of November. Moderate.

Sunny Pines Inn, 77 Main Street, 432–9628. *B&B.* Turn-of-the-century Victorian home featuring traditional Irish hospitality. Breakfasts of Irish soda bread, grilled meats, and homemade yogurt. Within walking distance of beaches, theater, and restaurants. Closed January, February, and March. Moderate.

West Harwich Dining

Bishop's Terrace, Route 28, 432–0253. Fresh seafood, prime rib of beef, and roast duckling among the specialties. Fine food and service in a 1790 sea captain's home. Also dining in the Garden Room and dancing to live music. Open all year. Expensive.

Le Chateau Renee, 278 Main Street, 432–5765. Excellent French-gourmet dining served in a romantic nineteenth-century home. Owner/chef provides a home-catering service. Open all year. Moderate to Expensive.

East Harwich Accommodations

Wequassett Inn, Route 28 on Pleasant Bay, in East Harwich near Chatham Town Line, 432–5400. *Resort.* Wequassett is superior in all respects and at the top of Cape Cod's finest. Its complex of eighteen separate buildings includes the historic Eben Ryder House and the Warren Jensen

Nickerson House. Accommodations include guest rooms, cottages, and suites with fireplaces. All guest rooms have views of Pleasant Bay, Round Cove, or the woods. There are three tennis villas within steps of five courts. Wequassett offers a heated swimming pool, a beach on Pleasant Bay, certified swimming instructors, a sailing school, boating and deep-sea fishing, a jogging path, limousine service, and a country store. The location on a secluded cove and the grounds, architecture, and landscaping are all exceptional. The main dining room is within an elegantly decorated sea captain's home with views of the water; meals are also served on a lovely garden terrace. Its cuisine is American and continental—fresh seafood and prime beef—prepared by an award-winning European chef. The luxury of Wequassett Inn is highly recommended. Open from late spring to fall. Expensive.

Brewster

Town offices—Route 6A in Brewster, 896–3701 For tourist information, call president of Brewster Board of Trade at 896–5713

The following villages, with their postal zip codes, are within the town of Brewster: Brewster—02631; East Brewster—02631; and West Brewster—02631.

Although the Town of Brewster was incorporated as late as 1803, this community was settled much earlier as the North Parish of Harwich. Brewster's claim to fame is that it was home port to many outstanding sea captains such as David Nickerson, who, it is said, brought the dauphin of France out of his revolution-torn country to New England in 1789. Several years later, Captain Elijah Cobb had his vessel taken by the French. Through Robespierre, Cobb obtained release of his ship and stayed long enough to see this disagreeable French revolutionary dispatched by his own Reign of Terror. In 1815 Captain Jeremiah Mayo offered to take Napoleon to America in his ship. Before Napoleon could make it to Mayo's vessel, the *Sally*, however, he was captured; Mayo had to depart without his prize passenger.

Brewster captains defied President Thomas Jefferson's embargo with the British during the War of 1812 by sailing out to sea and continuing on with their business. Brewster even paid a cash ransom to the captain of a British warship, as it saw no need to suffer bombardment and raiding parties in what was to many New Englanders an unpopular war. After hostilities, Brewster-captained ships sailed all over the world, making considerable fortunes for land-based merchants and investors as well as the captains themselves. Throughout the nineteenth century Brewster sea captains were paragons of adventure, commerce, and profit.

There's frenetic hurly-burly on the main streets of Cape towns in the Summer, but there are also places of beautiful solitude where one can soothe jangled nerves and create personal poetry. The Cape is one of America's oldest vacation places, but one which is constantly kept new and interesting.

Today's Brewster is a quiet, lovely town on scenic Route 6A. The heritage of the sea captains remains in the fine homes they built, many of which have been converted to charming places of accommodation and superior restaurants. Brewster is also a town of interesting attractions: Cape Cod Museum of Natural History, Sealand of Cape Cod, Drummer Boy Museum, New England Fire and History Museum, the 1834 First Parish Church, Brewster Historical Society Museum, Bassett Wild Animal Farm, and Nickerson State Park.

Brewster Accommodations

Beechcroft Inn, "The Old King's Highway"—Route 6A, 896–9534. *Inn.* This fine inn served as a church in the early 1800s. Accommodations include continental breakfast. Open all year. Moderate.

Brewster Farmhouse Inn, "The Old King's Highway"—Route 6A, 896–3426. *B&B.* Attractive, large home with many amenities. Ample continental breakfast. Swimming pool and hot tub. Open May to October. Moderate to Expensive.

The Captain Freeman Inn, 15 Breakwater Road—RR 4, 896–7481. *B&B.* Near the general store and First Parish Church, which convey small town–America feel. Eighteen sixty sea captain's home with many unique architectural details. Swimming pool; bikes. Open all year. Moderate.

The Bramble Inn, "The Old King's Highway"—Route 6A, 896–7644. *B&B.* Greek Revival home with antique furnishings. Near beaches, bike route, tennis, and shops. Excellent dining room. Closed mid-January to mid-March. Moderate.

Old Manse Inn, "The Old King's Highway"—Route 6A, 896–3149. *Inn.* Lovely decor and candlelight dining. Sleep under handmade quilts. Gourmet dining. Open all year. Moderate.

Isaiah Clark House, "The Old King's Highway"—Route 6A, 896–2223. *Inn.* Seventeen eighty sea captain's house. Fireplaces, pre-dinner get-togethers, hearty American breakfasts. Near beach and golf. Open all year. Moderate.

Ocean Edge Resort and Conference Center, "The Hilton Inn on Cape Cod Bay," One Village Drive, "The Old King's Highway"—Route 6A, (800) 221–1837 in state, (800) 626–2688 elsewhere. *Resort.* Ocean Edge is a relatively new luxury resort on Cape Cod. Guests stay in fully furnished, two- or three-bedroom villas. It has a fine restaurant, a championship golf course (one of the best on Cape Cod), tennis, and swimming pools and overlooks Cape Cod Bay beaches. Its conference center is in the restored Samuel Nickerson mansion (Fieldstone Hall), named for the founder and president of the First National Bank of Chicago. Open all year. Expensive.

Old Sea Pines Inn, "The Old King's Highway"—Route 6A, 896–6114. *Inn.* Accommodations in a turn-of-the-century mansion. Traditional amenities—front-porch rockers, wicker furniture, priscilla curtains, and brass and iron beds. Rooms with fireplaces. Continental breakfast; dinners by candlelight. Seasonal. Moderate.

Shady Knoll Campground, Off "The Old King's Highway"—Route 6A, 896–3002. *Campground.* Near beaches; playground; hot showers and laundry. Open mid-May to mid-October; 100 sites.

Sweetwater Forest, Off Route 124, 896–3773. *Campground.* Modern facilities; children's beach; pets welcome. Open all year; 250 sites.

Nickerson State Park, "The Old King's Highway"—Route 6A, 896–3491. *Campground.* Near beaches, Cape Cod National Seashore, and services within towns of Brewster and Orleans. Open mid-April to mid-October; 420 sites.

Brewster Dining

Chillingsworth, "The Old King's Highway"—Route 6A, 896–3640. Widely honored as one of the Cape's finest restaurants; many would call it "the Cape's number one dining place." The emphasis here is on the best available ingredients transformed into elegant French cuisine. Roast tenderloin of beef with truffles in burgandy sauce is among the specialties, and so is lobster in cognac sauce. Service and ambience are superior. The wine list will make oenophiles smack their lips in delight. During the 1987 summer season, Chillingsworth opened for lunch, much to the delight of patrons and newcomers. Luncheon entrees are in the Moderate price range and, considering the overall excellence of Chillingsworth, represent some of the finest dining values on the entire Cape. The setting for lunch and dinner is within a lovely estate nearly 300 years old. Dinner at Chillingsworth is Expensive. Dinners are served from Memorial Day to mid-December; luncheons, throughout the year.

High Brewster, 964 Satucket Road, 896–3636. New American cuisine served within a classic American colonial estate. Operated by the people who run Chillingsworth. Open all year. Moderate.

Chatham

Town offices—549 Main Street in Chatham, 945–2100 Chatham Chamber of Commerce, Main Street, 945–0342

The following villages, with their postal zip codes, are within the town of Chatham: Chatham—02633; North Chatham—02650; South Chatham—02659; and West Chatham—02669.

If Cape Cod is the bent arm of Massachusetts, then Chatham is its elbow. It is difficult not to fall in love with Chatham. Imagine a village of sturdy weather-and-sun-washed homes, all cedar-shingled and bespeaking innumerable generations of residents. Imagine rose-covered white fences, narrow streets that present visual delights at every step, and both sharp-edged, brilliant days and those shrouded in fogs so thick that movements a few feet away are as apparitions from the nether world. Imagine stately churches and graveyards bearing the bones of the earliest settlers, sober sea captains, and canny charlatans. Imagine the ever-present, ever-changing sea and a fickle weather defying human logic. Imagine a place where lusty fishermen still unload their catch in early afternoon and wealthy and ordinary folks from afar find peace and renewal from the uncertainties and pressures of their daily grind. All these images converge into reality in Chatham, Cape Cod at its best.

Years before the Puritans settled in Massachusetts, Samuel de Champlain, the French explorer, anchored his vessel in Stage Harbor and came ashore with his men. Champlain considered the land before him as a suitable place to establish a French habitation but was dissuaded by hostile Indians and what he considered to be too shallow a harbor with a hazardous entrance on the open Atlantic. Another important person in Chatham's history is Squanto, the English-speaking Indian who was instrumental in helping the first Pilgrims survive by showing them how to fish and farm in this new land. He also helped the Pilgrims negotiate a peace treaty with Sachem Massasoit. Squanto died in Chatham on a mission for the colonists and is buried not far from Chatham Light.

Chatham was very much the creation of William Nickerson. He bought the land from the Indian Sachem Mattaquason and then went through several years of wrangling with other colonists, the courts, and even his own son-in-law to gain lawful possession. In seventeenth-century Massachusetts William Nickerson was considered one of the most unscrupulous real estate operators in the colony. You can could also say that the man had an ambitious vision and possessed the strength and courage to make it a reality. Part of his vision was to make the lands he owned into a full-fledged, self-governing town. He applied for that status in the late 1670s. Township was not granted because Monomoy, as Chatham was called then, did not have a minister. He was, however, able to secure the designation of "constablewick," and from this legitimacy Nickerson managed his community as an unofficial town, but a town nevertheless. Through much of its early history, Chatham was largely a community of Nickerson families, and many Nickersons continue to reside in town.

CHATHAM

The people made their living from fishing and farming. It was not until 1711 that the first permanent minister, Reverend Hugh Adams, came to stay for a bit and initiate some progress. He was able to secure town status in 1712, and the name was changed from Monomoy to Chatham. Reverend Adams's life was not to remain tranquil in Chatham. He preached against the evils of strong drink and made enemies of the tavern owners. Adams was subjected to libel suits, nasty gossip, and scurrilous harassment. He relieved himself of this anguish by getting out of town and finding more agreeable parishioners in New Hampshire. New ministers came to Chatham, however, and were instrumental in helping the community gain a stronger sense of confidence and purpose.

Chatham prospered through an economy based on fishing, agriculture, transportation, and manufacturing. Today fishing continues as an important way of making money, but tourism and real estate are far more valuable to the town's economy. With regard to real estate, the circle has been completed: Chatham came into being through the wheeling and dealing of William Nickerson, and the town continues to grow and prosper through real estate transactions.

Chatham has many superb places of accommodation and restaurants. The best known of these is the Chatham Bars Inn, once a seaside lodge for wealthy Bostonians. The town is a pleasure in which to walk. There are plenty of smart shops for browsing and buying. Don't miss walking Main Street to see Chatham Light, Chatham Fish Pier, and the splendid views overlooking the harbor, Nauset Beach, and the open Atlantic beyond. Other attractions to enjoy are: the 1752 Atwood House, Railroad Museum, Godfrey Windmill, and Wight Murals. Monomoy Island National Wildlife Refuge can be visited by boat. Be sure to take in a Chatham Band concert, held each Friday evening during July and August. These concerts are among the most popular entertainment events on Cape Cod, and they are free. Also take in a theatrical performance by the Ohio University Players at the Monomoy Theater.

In January 1987 a powerful storm unexpectedly created a new attraction for tourists and a pain in the neck for local fishermen and mariners. Chatham harbor is shielded from surges of the open Atlantic by the lower end of Nauset Beach, a barrier beach. Although a barrier beach protects one body of water from another, it is essentially a frail piece of land subject to eroding by fierce winds and powerful tides. A section of Nauset Beach at Chatham harbor had been undergoing this weakening process of a number of years. When the January storm hit, the raging ocean, pushed by an unrelenting wind, tore open the land at this vulnerable point; the Atlantic flowed into the harbor. The phenomenon was somewhat similar to the legendary Dutch boy taking his finger out of the hole in the dike and letting the North Sea flood a part of Holland.

Although Chatham itself was not inundated, a new, widening access from the harbor to the open Atlantic had been created by nature. And it is a hazardous one at that, with unfamiliar, strong currents and breaking waves that cause trouble for vessels. Swimming in this area is dangerous. This new breach of the barrier beach has attracted the curious from afar. Cape Cod Aero Marine provides sightseeing flights over the area, and Art Gould's Boat Livery/The Water Taxi and Outermost Marine will take you to the breach. True to their Yankee antecedents, the entrepreneurs of Chatham have immortalized the breach at Nauset Beach on T-shirts that you can buy, if you're so inclined to pay their price.

Chatham Accommodations

Chatham Bars Inn, Shore Road, 945–0096. *Resort.* The Chatham Bars Inn is now under new management and has undergone extensive renovations. Previously it was open from spring to fall. Now the inn is also open during the winter season for the enjoyment of off-season travelers and for use as a conference center for corporations. Chatham Bars Inn, one of Cape Cod's premier resorts, exudes an exclusive but comfortable feel. It has beautiful grounds overlooking Nantucket Sound and excellent accommodations in lodge and cottages. Chatham Bars Inn has a swimming pool, salt-water beach, boats, a nine-hole golf course, and tennis courts as well as two excellent dining rooms and a lounge with live entertainment and dancing. Open all year. Expensive.

Bow Roof House, 59 Queen Anne Road, 945–1346. *Guest House.* Fine accommodations in a two-centuries-old Bow Roof house with original paneling, fireplaces, and other details. Continental breakfast served. Open all year. Moderate.

The Captain's House Inn of Chatham, 369 Old Harbor Road, 945–0127. *Inn.* Fine accommodations in a 1839 sea captain's home. Full English breakfast served. Closed December to February. Expensive.

Seafarer Motel, Route 28 and Ridgeville Road, 432–1739. *Motor Inn.* The ambience of a country inn combined with modern comforts. Swimming pool and shuffleboard. Near beaches and restaurants. Some units have kitchenettes. Open all year. Moderate.

Ye Olde Nantucket House, 2647 Main Street in South Chatham, 432–5641. *B&B.* Fine accommodations in tastefully decorated rooms. Continental breakfast served. Near beaches and restaurants. Open all year. Moderate.

The Bradford Inn, 26 Cross Street, 945–1030. *Inn & Motel.* Fine accommodations; heated swimming pool, four-poster canopy beds, fireplaces, and many other amenities. Full breakfast included in room rate and served in the sea captain's house. Open all year. Expensive.

CHATHAM

Chatham Town House Inn, 11 Library Lane, 945–2180. *Inn.* Eighteen eighty-one home in a picture-perfect part of town. Accommodations comfortable and immaculate. Excellent breakfasts and luncheons. Closed from Christmas to Washington's Birthday. Expensive.
The Queen Anne Inn, 70 Queen Anne Road, 945–0394. *Inn.* One of the best places of accommodation in Chatham in a lovely and convenient location. Well known in the area for superb food. Inn's cabin cruiser takes guests to Monomoy and Nantucket islands. Open from April through Thanksgiving. Expensive.
The Inn at the Dolphin, 352 Main Street, 945–0070. *Inn.* Located in Chatham historic district near shops, restaurants, and beaches. Spacious accommodations, most with water view. Swimming pool. Breakfast, lunch, and Sunday brunch. Open all year. Moderate.
Cyrus Kent House, 63 Cross Street, 945–9104. *B&B.* Gracious accommodations in a 1877 sea captain's home located in the village. Award-winning restoration. Continental breakfast. Open all year. Moderate.
Pleasant Bay Village, Route 28, 945–1133. *Motor Inn.* Fine accommodations in motel, efficiency units, suites, or cottages. Beautiful landscaped setting. Swimming pool. Gourmet breakfasts and poolside luncheons. Seasonal. Expensive.

Chatham Dining

Impudent Oyster, 15 Chatham Bars Avenue, 945–3545. Superb seafood and gourmet fare. Live entertainment. Open all year. Expensive.
Chatham Bars Inn, Shore Road, 945–0096. Excellent American and continental cuisine, elegant environment, fine service, and dancing. Superb water view. A special treat while in Chatham. Open all year. Expensive.
The Queen Anne Inn, 70 Queen Anne Road, 945–0394. Elegant surroundings and gourmet selections. Highly recommended. Open April through Thanksgiving. Expensive.
Chatham Wayside Inn, 512 Main Street, 945–1800. Fine food and service in a charming setting. Open all year. Moderate.
Flemings, Route 28 in South Chatham, 432–9060. Specialties of clam chowder, seafood, lobster, and chicken. Children's menu. Seasonal. Inexpensive.
Old Harbor Bakery, Old Harbor Road, 945–3433. Excellent breakfasts, sandwiches, soups, salads, and pastries. Open all year. Inexpensive.
Pate's, Route 28, 945–9777. A popular place for steaks and seafood. Open mid-April through Thanksgiving. Moderate.
Northport Seafood House, Route 28 in North Chatham, 945–9217.

Family seafood restaurant with emphasis on fresh, local catches of the day. Salad bar. Children's menu. Closed February. Inexpensive.

Orleans

Town offices—School Road in Orleans, 255–0900 Orleans Information Booth, Eldredge Parkway, 255–1386

The following villages, with their postal zip codes, are within the town of Orleans; Orleans—02653; East Orleans—02643; and South Orleans—02662.

Lovely Orleans is the "gateway town" to the Lower Cape and Cape Cod National Seashore. It is also the retailing and commercial center for this part of the Cape. In Orleans you will find many places of accommodation, restaurants, and shops. Orleans also offers Nauset Beach, one of Cape Cod's best on the open Atlantic and within the boundaries of Cape Cod National Seashore. Nauset Beach goes on for miles, all the way to Chatham; and if you need a long, solitary beach walk next to a raging surf with wheeling gulls and terns overhead, this is the place. Orleans also has swimming on Cape Cod Bay at Skaket Beach, where the water is warmer.

Among the attractions in town are: the 1834 First Universalist Meeting House, home of the Orleans Historical Society, with Indian, local-history, and lifesaving artifacts; the 1890 French Cable Museum, housing cable and transmission gear for transatlantic communications between North America and France; and the 1873 Academy Playhouse, presenting theatricals throughout the year. Take the time to do some auto or bike touring of the less-traveled roads of Orleans. Both the scenery and architecture are pleasing in any season.

Although strong evidence is lacking, it is believed that Leif Ericsson, that intrepid Viking mariner, and his longboat crew came ashore at Nauset in A.D. 1003. Bartholomew Gosnold, the English explorer, set anchor in the waters of Orleans in 1602. Gosnold is also remembered for giving this blessed peninsula its name—Cape Cod. Samuel de Champlain also sailed here in 1605. In 1644, when the first colonists settled Eastham, Orleans was part of their land grant. South Parish in Eastham was established in 1718, and this area became the Town of Orleans in 1797. All other Cape towns have either English or Indian names. Orleans has a distinctly French appellation, however, and how it came to be named remains a mystery. Among its momentous historical events was the laying of a transatlantic communications cable between Orleans and Brest, France. This project was completed in 1898 by Compagnie Francise des Cables Telegraphiques. Ironically, perhaps symbolically, the Orleans end of the cable came in near where the French explorer Champlain had landed several centuries before.

Orleans Accommodations

The Parsonage, 202 Main Street in East Orleans, 255–8217. *B&B.* Parsonage in the nineteenth century. Within walking distance of downtown shops and restaurants. En route to Nauset Beach. Fresh fruit and flowers; continental breakfast. Open all year. Moderate.

The Farmhouse at Nauset Beach, 163 Beach Road, 255–6654. *B&B.* Nineteenth-century farmhouse within a short walk of Nauset Beach; ocean-view deck. Continental breakfast served. Open all year. Moderate.

Hillbourne House, Route 28, 255–0780. *Motor Inn/Guest House/ Cottages.* Main house built at the end of the eighteenth century. Private beach and dock and lovely location; continental breakfast. Housekeeping cottages available. Open all year. Moderate.

Ship's Knees Inn, Beach Road in East Orleans, 255–1312. *Inn & Cottages.* Fine accommodations in a 150-year-old sea captain's home. Housekeeping apartment and efficiency cottages. Near Nauset Beach. Tennis court and swimming pool. Continental breakfast. Open all year. Moderate.

Seashore Park Motor Inn, Route 6, 255–2500. *Motor Inn.* Fine accommodations in a convenient location. Indoor and outdoor swimming pools, saunas, Jacuzzi, and whirlpool. Seasonal. Moderate.

The Nauset House Inn, Beach Road in East Orleans, 255–2195. *Inn.* Short distance from beautiful Nauset Beach within Cape Cod National Seashore. Accommodations include breakfast. Open beginning of April to end of October. Moderate.

Orleans Holiday Motel, Route 6A, 255–1514. *Motor Inn.* Comfortable accommodations; large swimming pool; restaurant, lounge, and live entertainment. Open all year. Moderate.

The Cove, Route 28, 255–1203. *Motor Inn.* Excellent waterfront accommodations; some efficiency units; swimming pool. Open all year. Moderate to Expensive.

Governor Prence Motor Inn, Routes 6A and 28, 255–1216. *Motor Inn.* Excellent accommodations close to downtown Orleans, beaches, and Cape Cod National Seashore attractions. Swimming pool and whirlpool; coffee shop. Seasonal. Moderate.

Olde Tavern Motel and Inn, Route 6A, 255–1565. *Motor Inn.* This eighteenth-century inn was visited by Henry David Thoreau when he trekked over the landscape of the Lower Cape. Modern units adjoin the old inn. Swimming pool. Continental breakfast. Seasonal. Moderate.

Orleans Dining

Captain Linnell House, Skaket Road, 255–3400. One of the best places on the Lower Cape for elegant dining. Continental cuisine making excellent use of fresh, local seafood. Breads and pastries made on the premises. Live entertainment and dancing. Open all year. Expensive.

Adam's Rib, Routes 6A and 28, 255–2270. A favorite family eatery (family owned and operated for more than twenty years) where the ribs are best. Open all year. Inexpensive to Moderate.

Arbor Restaurant—Binnacle Tavern, Route 28, 255–4847; 255–7901. Two restaurants at this location: Arbor serves continental dishes, such as sweetbreads, and the traditional lobster; Binnacle is a casual place for Cajun dishes, seafood, and fancy pizzas. Open all year. Inexpensive to Moderate.

Ardath's Family Restaurant, 20 West Road, 255–9779. Home-style cooking at decent prices. Open all year. Inexpensive.

The Brown Bag, Old Colony Way & West Road, 255–4431. Popular eatery with locals, serving seafood and other well-prepared dishes. Delicious chowders, soups, and homemade pastries. Casual environment. Open all year. Inexpensive to Moderate.

Off The Bay Cafe, 28 Main Street, 255–5505. Emphasis on fresh, grilled seafood, prime beef, poultry, and pasta. Live entertainment. Open all year. Inexpensive to Moderate.

Orleans Inn, Route 6A—Town Cove, 255–2222. Fine lodging and dining. Water views. Singing waiters and waitresses during the summer. Open all year. Moderate.

Robert's Restaurant, Route 6A, 240–0011. Excellent menu of American and continental favorites. Fresh seafood dishes a specialty. Sunday buffet. Dancing. Open all year. Moderate to Expensive.

Barley Neck Inn, Main Street, 255–6830. Fine wines and continental cuisine. Elegant sea captain's home. Live entertainment. Open all year. Moderate.

Land Ho, Route 6A & Cove Road, 255–5165. Popular place with locals and visitors alike. Chowders, kale soup, burgers, sandwiches, steaks, seafood, and Wellfleet oysters; luncheon and dinner specials. Open all year. Inexpensive to Moderate.

The Lobster Claw, Route 6A, 255–1800. Got a craving for lobster? This is the place. Fresh seafood and lobsters served daily. Children's menu. Open April to November. Inexpensive to Moderate.

Old Jailhouse Tavern, 28 West Road, 255–5245. Fine dining in what was once a lockup for pirates and other local malcontents. Warm and inviting architecture today. Fine food and service. Lovely surrounding grounds. Open all year. Moderate.

Eastham

Town offices—County Road in Eastham, 255-0338 Eastham Information Booth, Route 6 near Cape Cod National Seashore entrance, 255-3444

The following villages, with their postal zip codes, are within the town of Eastham: Eastham—02642; and North Eastham—02651.

Eastham, one of the first four towns established on Cape Cod, was founded in 1644 by English Pilgrims. Among the earliest settlers were the families of Thomas Prence, Edward Bangs, John Doane, John Smalley, Nicholas Snow, Richard Higgins, and Josias Cook. At that time, the Town of Plymouth was the center of government for the colony. Plymouth, though, was experiencing growing pains, and its residents were seeking a better life. A number of them looked to Cape Cod as the place where their dreams for good land and prosperity might be better achieved through hard work and sincere prayer. Eastham was settled by just such a group. But settlement was limited by government decree to those who came to America on the first three ships—*Mayflower, Fortune,* and *Anne.* The territory that today includes the towns of Orleans, Eastham, Wellfleet, Truro, and Provincetown was purchased by Puritan men from the Indians for hatchets, some of which, no doubt, were used during King Philip's War to rid Puritans of their scalps.

In Thomas Prence Eastham found an able leader. Through Prence the community prospered enough so as to be designated an official township in 1646. The community formally took the name Eastham in 1651. During the 1650s, Eastham lost territory to other burgeoning settlements such as Harwich and Chatham. Thomas Prence served as governor of Plymouth Colony but got fed up with the long commute to the mainland and decided to govern from Eastham instead. This desire to govern Plymouth Colony from home made Eastham one of the first colonial capitals in the English-speaking New World. In 1673 Prence died while still serving as governor; he was a great man, long gone but not forgotten.

Life for members of the Congregational Church improved, while local Quakers, Methodists, and Baptists faced persecution. Eastham area Indians were converted by Reverend Samuel Treat, a preacher who dramatically mixed metaphors of fire and brimstone with salvation on strict Calvinist terms. During the eighteenth century Eastham parishes became the towns of Orleans, Truro, Provincetown, and Wellfleet. With this dismemberment, Eastham diminished in size from being one of the largest towns in the colony to one of its smallest; along with this diminution, its political status evaporated. Other changes took place in Eastham, such as

171

the decline in power of the Congregational Church and the rise of the Methodists.

During the nineteenth century Eastham was home port for a number of hardy, adventurous sea captains such as Freeman Hatch, who, in 1852, sailed the clipper *Northern Light* from Boston to San Francisco in seventy-six days and six hours, a tremendous feat at that time. Today Eastham is a quiet town where tourism is one of the major industries. Eastham offers excellent beaches on both the open Atlantic and on Cape Cod Bay as well as fine places for accommodations and dining. Eastham's main attraction is Cape Cod National Seashore with its prominent Salt Pond Visitor Center, hiking and biking trails, Coast Guard Beach, and Nauset Light Beach. Other attractions include: Doane Homestead, First Encounter Beach, the 1741 Swift-Daley House, Old Cove Cemetery, the 1876 Captain Penniman House, Schoolhouse Museum, and the 1680 Eastham Windmill.

Eastham Accommodations

The Penny House, Route 6 in North Eastham, 255–6632. *B&B.* Seventeen fifty-one sea captain's house with a bow roof. Close to Salt Pond entrance to Cape Cod National Seashore. French spoken. Homemade breads and muffins at breakfast. Open all year. Moderate.

The Over Look Inn, County Road at Entrance to Cape Cod National Seashore, 255–1886. *B&B.* Operated by a Scottish couple who came to the Cape from Toronto. Queen Anne style–Victorian house furnished with antiques and Inuit (Eskimo) art from Canada. Substantial Scottish breakfasts served. Open all year. Moderate to Expensive.

Sheraton Ocean Park Inn and Resort, Route 6, 255–5000. *Motor Inn/Resort.* One of the best places of accommodation on the Lower Cape. Two swimming pools, saunas, whirlpools, tennis courts, and bikes; restaurant, lounge, and live entertainment. Shuttle service to ocean beach. Open all year. Moderate to Expensive.

Whalewalk Inn, 169 Bridge Road, 255–0617. *B&B.* An 1830s estate offering fine accommodations and gourmet breakfasts. Open April to November. Expensive.

Captain's Quarters Motel, Route 6, 255–5686. *Motor Inn.* Fine accommodations; swimming pool; continental breakfast. Seasonal. Moderate.

Viking Shores, Route 6, 255–3200. *Motor Inn.* Fine accommodations; swimming pool, tennis courts, and bikes. Open early April to end of November. Moderate.

Eastham Ocean View Motel, Route 6, 255–1600. *Motor Inn.* Good value and many amenities—pool, bikes, in-room movies. Open from early April to end of October. Moderate.

Atlantic Oaks Campground, Route 6, Half Mile North of Cape Cod National Seashore Entrance, 255-1437. *Campground.* Many modern conveniences, including cable television hookups. Near Cape Cod National Seashore attractions. Open May 1 to November 1; 100 sites.

Eastham Dining

The Gristmill, Route 6, 240-0635. A lovely restaurant in an eighteenth-century tavern serving fine seafood and meat dishes. Open April through Indian summer. Moderate.

Eastham Lobster Pool, Route 6 in North Eastham, 255-9706. Shore-dinner specialties of lobster, clams, seafood, and such. Open April through November. Moderate.

Flipper's Family Restaurant, Route 6, across from the Wellfleet Drive-In; on the Eastham/Wellfleet Town Line, 255-1914. Seafood and meat dishes at reasonable prices near Cape Cod National Seashore, Massachusetts Audubon Sanctuary, and flea market. Seasonal. Inexpensive.

Ocean Garden Restaurant, Sheraton Ocean Park Inn, Route 6, 255-5000. Fine traditional American and gourmet continental food. Dancing and entertainment. One of the best nightclub shows on Cape Cod. Open all year. Moderate to Expensive.

Lori's Family Restaurant, Town Center Shopping Plaza—Route 6, 255-4803. Emphasis on re-creating home cooking in a restaurant. Fine dining with a small-town feel. Open all year. Inexpensive.

Demetri's Sandpiper, Route 6, 255-9913. Delicious Greek salads and other Greek specialties. Also lobster, seafood, steaks, and chicken. Open all year. Moderate.

Pilgrim Kitchen, Route 6, 255-4318. Quality family restaurant serving seafood and meat dishes. Seasonal. Inexpensive.

Wellfleet

Town offices—Main Street in Wellfleet, 349-3708 Wellfleet Chamber of Commerce, P.O. Box 571, Route 6, Wellfleet, 349-2500.

The following villages, with their postal zip codes, are within the town of Wellfleet: Wellfleet—02667; and South Wellfleet—02663.

Straddling the Cape from the bay to the open Atlantic, Wellfleet is largely an unspoiled town with pockets of commercialization along Route 6. Despite its obvious "down home" Yankee demeanor, it has become a fashionable "in" vacation place for psychiatrists, lawyers, professors, and artists. There's a joke that goes: "If you are in bad need for your shrink, don't go to Park Avenue. Look on the beaches of Wellfleet." Wellfleet is coming close to rivalling Provincetown as a center for art galleries and the outstanding talents they exhibit.

Wellfleet is a favorite Cape town not because of this *noveau* sophistication, however, but because of its splendid natural environment—high sand-and-clay cliffs overlooking the broad sweep of the open Atlantic; extensive salt marshes rich with birds and water fowl; the mystical White Cedar Trail at Marconi Station; warm-water beaches on Cape Cod Bay; the abundance of marine life and the satisfying hikes within the Massachusetts Audubon Sanctuary and on the Great Island Trail; the pleasing architecture of center Wellfleet; and meandering roads that take you through pristine areas of woods, sand, glacial kettle holes, and marshes. Some of the most glorious sunsets can be seen from the wharfs and beaches at Wellfleet Harbor. The air seems fresher and more relaxing on the Cape Cod Bay side of Wellfleet than at most other places on this peninsula. Wellfleet also offers: Cape Cod National Seashore; Marconi Wireless Station Site; First Congregational church, containing a clock that strikes ship's time; Wellfleet Historical Society Museum; and the circa-1700 Samuel Rider House.

In the seventeenth century Wellfleet was part of Eastham and known as Billingsgate. The community, incorporated as the Town of Wellfleet in 1763, was said to be named after the Wallfleet oyster beds of England. In fact the oyster beds of Wellfleet provided the town with a mainstay of its economy. In 1987 Wellfleet's shellfish industry generated ten million dollars. Because of its excellent harbor on Cape Cod Bay, Wellfleet also became a major center for New England whaling, commercial fishing, and their allied industries of salt making, ships' stores, and the like.

In the 1870s a Wellfleet captain, Lorenzo Dow Baker, first brought unspoiled, green bananas to the United States in his schooner, the *Telegraph.* From this beginning, and with financing from Elisha Hopkins, his brother-in-law and also a Wellfleet resident, the L. D. Baker Company was established in 1881. This enterprise became the Boston Fruit Company in 1885 and then the United Fruit Company in 1899. United Fruit, a giant and powerful corporation in its time, was synonymous with the best and the worst of American involvement with the countries of Central America. In its early days, however, the American banana business was better appreciated by some in the tropics. In 1905 Captain Baker was honored by Jamaica for having done more for that island in three decades than the British had accomplished there since the empire took possession. Baker was also a visionary entrepreneur in the tourist trade, which was booming in the late-nineteenth century. In 1886 he opened the Chequesset Inn, which was considered the best place to stay in Wellfleet at that time.

One of Wellfleet's most momentous events occurred in 1903 on the cliffs overlooking the open Atlantic. Here Guglielmo Marconi transmitted the first transatlantic message by wireless telegraph. Also in Wellfleet, the past and the present have converged with the on-going salvage operation of the eighteenth-century pirate ship *Whidah*. Though lying deep in Atlantic waters, its broken hulk is surrendering to divers millions of dollars worth of treasure.

Wellfleet Accommodations

The Inn at Duck Creek, Main Street, 349–7369. *Inn.* Excellent accommodations in a fine country inn. Near center of village and Cape Cod Bay beaches. Acres of salt marsh and a duck pond near the inn. Continental breakfast served. Excellent dining at its restaurants, Sweet Seasons and the Tavern Room; lounge with live entertainment. Highly recommended. Seasonal. Moderate.

The Even' Tide, Route 6, 349–3410. *Motor Inn.* Good value. Indoor swimming pool. In quiet location and near Cape Cod National Seashore attractions. Cottages also available. Open all year. Moderate.

Billingsgate Motel, Mayo Beach Road, 349–3924. *Motor Inn.* Fine accommodations at Wellfleet Harbor. Open May to September. Expensive.

Southfleet Motor Inn, Route 6, 349–3580. *Motor Inn.* Fine accommodations. Indoor and outdoor swimming pools, saunas, and playground. Open early March to end of October. Moderate.

Wellfleet Motel, Route 6, 349–3535. *Motor Inn.* Fine accommodations; swimming pool and whirlpool; coffee shop. Open all year. Expensive.

Paine's Campground, Route 6 in South Wellfleet, 349–3007. *Campground.* Near Cape Cod Bay beaches and Cape Cod National Seashore attractions. Open mid-May to October; 150 sites.

Wellfleet Dining

Bayside Lobster Hut, Commercial Street, 349–6333. Terrific lobster; chowder, scallops, and shrimp; raw bar. Seasonal. Inexpensive to Moderate.

Van Rensselaer's, Route 6, opposite Marconi Station (Cape Cod National Seashore), 349–2127. Seafood and prime rib of beef. Seasonal. Inexpensive to Moderate.

Aesop's Tables, Main Street, in the Center of Town, 349–6450. Highly regarded Lower Cape dining place within a historic sea captain's home. Attractive interior decor with original art. Creative American/continental cuisine; innovative seafood dishes. Live entertainment in the lounge. Open May to October. Moderate to Expensive.

175

Rookie's Family Restaurant, Route 6, 349–2688. South Wellfleet institution featuring favorite Italian foods, seafood, and steaks. Open April to October. Inexpensive.

The Book Store Seafood Restaurant, Kendrick Avenue, 349–3154. Creatively prepared and presented seafood and meat dishes. Casual, relaxed setting. Seasonal. Inexpensive to Moderate.

Sweet Seasons Restaurant, East Main Street, 349–6353. At the Inn at Duck Creek. Continental handling of duck, seafood, veal, and beef. Vegetarian dishes. Delicious food in the midst of casual elegance. Seasonal. Moderate to Expensive.

The Tavern Room Restaurant & Lounge, East Main Street, 349–7369. Popular eating and drinking place in the Inn at Duck Creek. You may find your shrink here, because so many of them vacation in Wellfleet. Lobster, seafood dishes, steaks, Cajun chicken, and great desserts. This is also the place for live entertainment in Wellfleet—piano, jazz, pop, or whatever in the lounge. Seasonal. Moderate to Expensive.

Serena's Restaurant, Route 6, South Wellfleet, 349–9370. Family restaurant serving seafood and Italian cuisine. Seasonal. Inexpensive to Moderate.

Captain Higgins Seafood Restaurant, On the Pier at Wellfleet Harbor, 349–6027. Delicious seafood, lobster, shrimp, steaks, and chicken. Terrific location overlooking beautiful Wellfleet Harbor. Children's menu. Open mid-June to mid-September. Inexpensive to Moderate.

The Wellfleet Oyster House, East Main Street, 349–2134. Fine dining on seafood, steak, curries, paella, and Wellfleet oysters served in a 1750 home. Open March through November; weekends the rest of the year. Moderate.

✓ **Cielo's,** East Main Street, 349–2108. Superb gourmet fare. Environment casual and relaxing, perfect for savoring the culinary art created in the kitchen. Seasonal. Expensive.

Truro

Town offices—Town Hall Road in Truro, 349–3860 Truro Chamber of Commerce, P.O. Box 26, Route 6 and Head of Meadow Road, North Truro, 487–1288 and 487–9208.

The following villages, with their postal zip codes, are within the town of Truro: Truro—02666; and North Truro—02652.

When one thinks of Truro, the austere but compelling paintings of Edward Hopper come to mind—wind-swept sand dunes crested with stands of bent beach grass, solitary lighthouses, and beach cabins. Except for the strip of tourist cottages along Route 6A, Truro is one of Cape Cod's least commercial towns. It is a place of long, lonely beaches and of sand dunes that seem to undulate far in every direction. Some individuals who highly prize their solitude happily live in cabins tucked between sand dunes, far from the continuous parade of tourists speeding back and forth along Route 6 between Wellfleet and Provincetown.

Truro's fine beaches on the open Atlantic and on Cape Cod Bay include Head of the Meadow Beach, which is part of Cape Cod National Seashore. It is in Truro that you best see the effects of the wind and sea on the Cape Cod landscape. In the Highland Light area, the cliffs are eroding; the high ground is pulling back from the edge of the sea. At Pamet River Harbor and along the beaches on Truro's Cape Cod Bay side, in contrast, land is building up and pushing out to sea. The strong northeast winds are the great transporters of soil from one side to the other. Among Truro's interesting attractions are: the 1827 Bell Church, Truro Historical Museum at Highland Light, and the Jenny Lind Tower.

When the Pilgrims first came into the waters of America in 1620, they considered the possibility of establishing a settlement in the area of what is now the Town of Truro, called Pamet in its early days. The exhausted among them wanted to stay, but others felt it was more prudent to continue on with the hope that an even more commodious place would be found. While these *Mayflower* Pilgrims were on land here, however, they found their first fresh water at what is now called Pilgrim Spring and a cache of Indian corn at a place called Corn Hill; they used the corn for their first crop of grain grown in America. Permanent settlers arrived at the close of the seventeenth century when a group of Pilgrims from Eastham known as the "Pamet Proprietors" negotiated a land deal with the local Indians. In 1705 the growing community was named Dangerfield because of the many ships that were wrecked in this area over the years. In 1709 it became a town in its own right and was renamed Truro after a town on the Cornish coast in England.

Farming, fishing, and whaling, along with the related industries they spawned, were how Truro people made their livelihoods. After the wars with Great Britain, Pamet River Harbor flourished with activity—wharfs, shipbuilding, salt works, chandleries, sail lofts, fish processing and packing plants, and financial institutions that provided capital and insurance for seafaring ventures. As Truro entered the second half of the nineteenth century, however, the town, a maker of substantial profits from the fisheries and maritime industries, began to decline, as was also the case with many other communities along the New England coast. In 1860 the Union Company of Truro, the commercial heart and soul of the town in which many of the locals had invested their capital, went bust. This calamity was like a person being gunned down at the knees, not fatal but utterly crippling. What was once a bustling, frenetic town brimming with optimism and generating substantial profits became a quiet place passed over by economic progress.

To present year-round and summer residents, that passing of economic progress saved the town from the many evils of material success. Besides, what is left is a very beautiful and tranquil place existing in close harmony with nature. As there are few human-made attractions in Truro, the best way to experience its many-faceted beauty is to wander over back roads, beaches, and rough trails without a precise plan. Expect to see wonders at every turn.

Truro Accommodations

The majority of Truro accommodations are located in the North Truro and Beach Point areas. Most of these places are cottage colonies either with their own private beaches on Cape Cod Bay or within easy access of beaches. These cottage colonies are on Route 6A close to Provincetown and to Cape Cod National Seashore attractions. Many cottage colonies rent their units by the week, and advance reservations are essential for the months of July and August. For more information on renting a cottage in Truro, contact the Chamber of Commerce at the address or telephone number on page 176.

Parker House, Shore Route 6A, 349–3358. *B&B.* A comfortable home located near Cape Cod Bay beaches and Cape Cod National Seashore. Open all year. Moderate.

Sea Gull Motel, Shore Route 6A in North Truro, 487–9070. *Motor Inn.* Good value. Cape Cod Bay location. Private beach. Seasonal. Moderate.

Crow's Nest Motel, Shore Route 6A in North Truro, 487–9031. *Motor Inn.* Motel and efficiency units. Private beach on Cape Cod Bay; sun deck. Open April to November. Moderate.

Seaside Village Motel, Shore Route 6A in North Truro, 487–1215. *Motor Inn & Cottages.* Fine ocean-front accommodations; private beach and sun deck. Seasonal. Moderate.

Horton's Trailer Park & Camping Resort, Route 6A in North Truro to South Highland Road, 487–1220. *Campground.* Near Cape Cod Bay beaches, Provincetown, and Cape Cod National Seashore attractions. Open first week in April to mid-October; 216 sites.

North Truro Camping Area, Route 6 in North Truro to Highland Road East, 487–1847. *Campground.* Near Cape Cod Bay beaches, Provincetown, and Cape Cod National Seashore attractions. Seasonal; 350 sites.

North of Highland Camping Area, Route 6 in North Truro to Head of Meadow Road, 487–1191. *Campground.* Near Cape Cod Bay beaches,

Provincetown, and Cape Cod National Seashore attractions. Open end of May to first week in September; 237 sites.

Outer Reach Motel, Shore Route 6A in North Truro, 487–9090. *Motor Inn.* Fine accommodations with views of Cape Cod Bay. Children welcome. Tennis, swimming pool, and shuffleboard. Access to ocean beach. Seasonal. Moderate.

Truro Dining

Whitman House, County Road in North Truro, 487–1740. Fine restaurant serving beef and seafood selections. Old Cape Cod decor. Open first of April to mid-December. Moderate.

The Blacksmith Shop, Truro Center, 349–6554. Rustic environment and setting capturing some of the tranquil spirit of Truro. Excellent meat and seafood dishes sauced creatively. Open from Memorial Day through September; weekends the rest of the year. Moderate.

Gepetto, Route 6 and Highland Road in North Truro, 487–1100. Fine Italian food and roast prime rib of beef. Salad bar. Seasonal. Moderate.

Provincetown

Town offices—Bradford Street, 487–2662 Provincetown Chamber of Commerce, P.O. Box 1017, 307 Commercial Street, Provincetown, 487–9007

Provincetown is complete unto itself. It's postal zip code is 02657.

Trying to describe Provincetown is to risk running out of adjectives. It is historic, established, family, gay, tasteful, outrageous, gaudy, subdued, beautiful, kinky, responsible, carefree, religious, nonbelieving, and so on. To put it succinctly, Provincetown is Cape Cod's most colorful and fascinating town. The irony is that it was founded by starchy Puritans. If bodies do turn in their graves at the onset of unpleasant news, those of Provincetown's original Puritans must be continuously spinning like tops.

Provincetown today is an amalgamation of many different kinds of people. You have descendants of the early settlers, newcomer WASPs, fishermen, merchants, professionals, Jews, Portuguese-American families, homosexuals, artists, writers, craftspersons, family-trust-account supported persons, indigent persons, naturalists, profiteers, gourmet chefs, fast-food operators, actors, town characters who should be actors, cheaters, and followers of *veritas*. Somehow this bouillabaisse of humanity lives in peace together, each faction respecting differences and each contributing to the richness that makes Provincetown a truly special place in America.

Provincetown is at the narrowest part of Cape Cod at land's end. It is

An irresistible attraction to the sea is genetically inbred in all ages; for we do have the sea in our blood. On the edge of Cape Cod waters a deep longing is satisfied.

surrounded by sea on three sides. You can't go any farther unless you fly or sail away. In a world where just about everything is relative, the absolute of being at the end of something does have its appeal and no doubt contributes to the attractiveness of Provincetown.

Provincetown has long been a favorite refuge for creative people, from Eugene O'Neill to Norman Mailer. It was also home to Admiral Donald B. MacMillan, the famous Arctic explorer.

Provincetown has the largest number of art galleries on Cape Cod, and they display contemporary paintings, prints, and sculptures by established and new artists. There is a large number of shops selling excellent crafts and jewelry, cheap souvenirs, unique fashions, and Army and Navy castoffs. Commercial, Provincetown's main street, is flanked on both sides by shops, restaurants, places of accommodation, bars, and night spots. Commercial Street is usually packed thick with people during the summer, which makes it difficult and time-consuming to negotiate by car. There are, however, parking lots off Commercial Street, on adjacent streets, and next to MacMillan Wharf. Commercial Street, with its restaurants, nightclubs and bars, is bustling with people until the early morning hours. The center of Provincetown is where Commercial Street, MacMillan Wharf (the waterfront area), and Town Hall converge. Bradford Street, which runs parallel to Commercial, also has many places for accommodations, dining, and parking.

The highest point in town is the Pilgrim Monument, which, on a clear day, can be seen from the Massachusetts mainland. MacMillan Wharf has several operations providing whale-watching adventures, sightseeing cruises, and deep-sea-fishing trips. Daily ferry boats from Boston and Plymouth also come into the dock area. Most of the land of Provincetown is within Cape Cod National Seashore. Two excellent beaches are here, Herring Cove and Race Point, as well as a visitor's center offering information on biking, hiking, and sand-dune-vehicle and horseback-riding trails. Among Provincetown's many attractions are: oldest cemetery in Provincetown; Mayflower Compact Memorial (historic bas-relief plaque) at town hall; Heritage Museum, housed in what was an 1860 Methodist church; the Pilgrim Monument and Museum; and the 1764 Seth Nickerson House, the oldest house in Provincetown. If you get bored in Provincetown, look into the mirror for the cause.

The historical importance of Provincetown should be known to every American. Here, in 1620, the *Mayflower* Pilgrims sailed into American waters after an arduous voyage across the Atlantic. During their brief stay here, the Pilgrim fathers created and signed the Mayflower Compact, an agreement whereby a free people would govern themselves and from which the fullness of American liberty would eventually emerge.

During the early seventeenth century, when the Pilgrims were establishing towns along the south shore of Massachusetts and in areas on Cape Cod, Provincetown, because of its remoteness from governmental authority, became a place where traders, seamen, and fishermen plying the Atlantic would come ashore to drink themselves silly, gamble until anything of worth was won or lost, and revel in diverse entertainments. Law, order, sobriety, and religion had to wait until 1727, when the righteous colonists were enough in control of the community to create an official township.

In succeeding years Provincetown, with its excellent harbor on the open Atlantic, became a thriving center for the whaling industry, ranking behind only Nantucket and New Bedford in importance. It was through whaling that the first Portuguese settlers came to Provincetown. From the Azores, the Canaries, and the Cape Verdes, they volunteered as replacements for English crew members who were either lost at sea or who had jumped ship in foreign ports. Provincetown has long been as much a Portuguese town as it has been a Yankee one. During its days as a primary port for the fleets that fished the Grand Banks, Provincetown also attracted fishing families from Cape Breton Island, Nova Scotia. Some of their descendants also continue to live in this land's-end community. The last whaling vessel to operate out of Provincetown was the *Charles W. Morgan*. She completed her final voyage in 1921 and can today be seen lovingly restored as the "center piece" vessel at Mystic Seaport in Connecticut. Although whaling has disappeared, Provincetown continues to be a major fishing port, with most of the fleet owned and operated by Portuguese mariners. Today's Provincetown fishery accounts for approximately eleven million pounds, all of it landed at MacMillan Wharf.

The first art colony in America began in Provincetown. Its impetus came in 1899 from the portrait painter Charles W. Hawthorne, who established the Cape Cod School of Art. This locus of excellence attracted talented artists from throughout North America. A summer stint of painting in Provincetown became an important credential that helped to open many a gallery door to new talent. Today the Provincetown Art Association, located on Commercial Street, carries on this tradition with exhibitions and courses. The large concentration of art galleries in Provincetown is another result of what Hawthorne set in motion at the turn of the century.

The cultural high point of Provincetown came in this century when the Provincetown Players, with their Playhouse on the Wharf, were established. Eugene O'Neill, Sinclair Lewis, and John Dos Passos, now considered immortals in American theater and literature, were among many individuals who contributed their talents and learned the intricacies of their crafts in Provincetown. Over the years, valiant attempts to resurrect the Playhouse on the Wharf have met with success and disappointment. The potential for a Phoenixlike rise will become reality only when the right convergence of vision, talent, and money is finally put together.

Provincetown Accommodations

Provincetown Inn, 1 Commercial Street, 487–9500. *Motor Inn.* Top-quality accommodation at land's end offering many amenities: indoor pool and private beach; restaurant, lounge, and live entertainment. Open all year. Expensive.

Bradford Gardens Inn, 178 Bradford Street, 487–1616. *B&B.* Owners originally from Ottawa. Home built in 1820 and located at the center of everything in Provincetown. French spoken here. Ample breakfasts feature many gourmet specialties. Open April to October. Moderate to Expensive.

The Masthead, 31–41 Commercial Street, 487–0523. *Motel & Cottages.* Waterfront location with harbor views, private beach, luxury kitchens, and sun deck. Mooring and launch services. Open all year. Moderate to Expensive.

Ship's Bell Inn, 586 Commercial Street, 487–1674. *Motor Inn.* Private beach, secluded patio; some units with kitchens. Near all downtown attractions. Open May to November. Moderate to Expensive.

Holiday Inn, Shore Route 6A and Snail Road, 487–1711. *Motor Inn.* Fine accommodations; restaurant, lounge, and live entertainment; swimming pool. Near beaches. Open all year. Moderate to Expensive.

Cape Colony Inn, Shore Route 6A, 487–1755. *Motor Inn.* Fine accommodations near all attractions. Open beginning of April to end of October. Moderate.

Tides Motor Inn, Shore Route 6A, 487–1045. *Motor Inn.* Fine accommodations with patios or balconies; private beach on Cape Cod Bay; swimming pool, shuffleboard, and badminton; coffee shop. Seasonal. Moderate.

The Breakwater, Shore Route 6A, 487–1134. *Motor Inn & Cottages.* Uncongested area overlooking Cape Cod Bay; sun deck. Open from May to October. Moderate.

Watermark Inn, 603 Commercial Street, 487–2506. *Luxury Suites.* Ocean views, private beach, and many amenities. Open all year. Expensive.

Somerset House, 378 Commercial Street, 487–0383. *Inn.* Beautiful interior environment—classical music, fresh flowers, paintings, and modern guest rooms. Near all downtown attractions. Seasonal. Moderate.

Surfside Inn, 543 Commercial Street, 487–1726. *Motor Inn.* Fine accommodations; private beach and swimming pool; within walking distance of all downtown attractions. Seasonal. Moderate to Expensive.

Ocean's Inn, 386-L Commercial Street, 487–0358. *Inn.* Fine accommodations in central location; indoor pool, patio, and sun deck; lounge and dining room. Open all year. Moderate.

Best Western—Chateau Motor Inn, Bradford Street West, 487–1286. *Motor Inn.* Excellent accommodations; beautiful grounds and views of Cape Cod Bay and sand dunes; swimming pool. Near all attractions. Seasonal; opens in May. Moderate.

Sandcastle Resort, Shore Route 6A, 487–9300. *Motor Inn.* All efficiency units, many with private balconies; indoor and outdoor swimming pools, tennis court, and private beach; restaurant and lounge. Open April to November. Moderate.

Elephant Walk Inn, 156 Bradford Street, 487–2543. *Inn.* Turn-of-the-century inn. Spacious rooms and sun deck; morning coffee. Open all year. Moderate.

Hargood House Apartments, 493–A Commercial Street, 487–1324. *Luxury Suites.* Suites with living room and kitchen, some with private deck or patio. Cape Cod Bay location; near beaches and downtown attractions. One of the finest accommodations in Provincetown. Open all year. Moderate to Expensive.

Beach Point Club, Shore Route 6A, 487–1048. *Motor Inn & Cottages.* On the shore of Cape Cod Bay. Swimming pool and private beach. Not far from downtown attractions. Seasonal. Moderate.

Anchor Inn, 175 Commercial Street, 487–0432. *Beach House.* Comfortable accommodations with water view; private beach. Open all year. Moderate.

Shamrock Motel & Cottages, 49 Bradford Street, 487–1133. *Motor Inn & Cottages.* Comfortable accommodations near beaches and downtown attractions. Seasonal. Moderate.

Bradford House and Motel, 41 Bradford Street, 487–0173. *Motor Inn.* Accommodations in motel and Victorian-style guest house; swimming pool; sun deck overlooking town and harbor. Open mid-May to late October. Moderate.

Angel's Landing, 353–355 Commercial Street, 487–1420. *Apartments & Studios.* Comfortable, spacious accommodations near beaches and downtown attractions; sun deck. Seasonal. Moderate.

Mayflower Colony, Shore Route 6A, 487–1916. *Cottages.* Fully equipped housekeeping cottages located near beaches, Cape Cod National Seashore, and downtown attractions. Seasonal. Moderate.

Coastal Acres Camping Court, Bradford Street, 487–1700. *Campground.* Near Cape Cod National Seashore, Cape Cod Bay beaches, and downtown attractions. Open April 1 to November 1; 180 sites.

Dune's Edge Campground, Route 6 to left on Road Marker 116, 487–9815. *Campground.* Near Cape Cod National Seashore, Cape Cod Bay beaches, and downtown attractions. Open May 1 to end of September; 100 sites.

Provincetown Dining

Napi's, 7 Freeman Street, 487–1145. Excellent cuisine—eclectic continental and American—in an elegant place. Open all year. Expensive.

The Red Inn, 15 Commercial Street, 487–0050. Good food three times a day. Super views of Cape Cod Bay. Open all year. Inexpensive to Moderate.

Grand Central Cafe, 5 Masonic Place, 487–9116. Steaks, prime rib of beef, seafood, and salads served in intimate dining rooms and in garden. Seasonal. Moderate.

Vorelli's, 226 Commercial Street, 487–2778. A feast for the hungry. Homemade lobster stew; marinated calamari salad; and veal as scalloppini, parmigiana, melenzana, and artichoke. Seafood tetrazzini—shrimp, lobster, and scallops sautéed in garlic butter, oil, fresh mushrooms, tomato wedges, and black olives and laced with white wine. Seasonal. Moderate.

The Boatslip Restaurant, 161 Commercial Street, 487–1669. American cuisine, grilled steaks, and seafood. Dining with waterfront views. Excellent live entertainment and shows. Open April through October. Moderate.

The Moors, Bradford Street in West Provincetown, 487–0840. Portuguese specialties: Espada Cozida, a marinated, grilled swordfish; Galinha a moda da Maderia, chicken breast sautéed with herbs in a Madeira wine sauce; and Bife Portuguese, beef tournedos rubbed with garlic and spices, topped with smoked ham, and then grilled. Live entertainment in the lounge. Seasonal. Moderate.

The Terrace, 133 Bradford Street, 487–0598. Gourmet cuisine, fine service, and elegant environment. Good value. Seasonal. Moderate to Expensive.

Weathering Heights, 30 Shank Painter Road, 487–9259. Fine entrees such as grilled pork tenderloins, seafood dishes, prime rib, and kabobs. Open April to October. Moderate.

Pepe's Wharf, 371–373 Commercial Street, 487–0670. One of Provincetown's finest gourmet restaurants. In business for more than twenty years. Many unusual dishes such as zuppa di pesce and steak Budapest. Panoramic views of the harbor and Cape Cod Bay. Open May to October. Expensive.

Anna Restaurant, At the Painted Lady Inn, 186 Commercial Street, 487–1443. Home of the original "Death by Chocolate." American and continental cuisine. Sunday brunch. Seasonal. Moderate.

Basil's, 350 Bradford Street, 487–3368. Grilled swordfish steak, steamed mussels with leeks and cream, and veal parmesan among the specialties. Live entertainment in Tulips Lounge. Open April to end of November. Moderate.

Snug Harbor, 157 Commercial Street, 487–2276. Cajun-style food and New Orleans *bonhomie.* Unusual drinks (for New England, that is)—fresh mint julep, Cajun martini, sazerac, and Creole cocktail; these drinks also served without alcohol. Seasonal. Moderate.

Landmark Inn Restaurant, 404 Commercial Street, 487–9319. Specialties of New England seafood and baked lobsters but also champagne Chateaubriand. Sea captain's mansion. Open April to December. Moderate.

Provincetown Beef and Lobster House, 247 Commercial Street, 487–0900. Baby back ribs, seafood, steaks, and lobster among the specialties. Dining out on the deck overlooking the harbor. Seasonal. Moderate.

Different Ducks, 135 Bradford Street, 487–9648. Eggs and omelets; burgers, salads, and chicken club sandwiches; seafood, pasta, and steaks. Live entertainers. Open all year. Inexpensive to Moderate.

Sea View Restaurant, 183 Commercial Street, 487–0773. Seafood dinners and lobsters. Traditional clambake suppers—steamed clams, lobster, corn on the cob, salad, potato, and watermelon. On the waterfront. Early bird specials. Seasonal. Inexpensive to Moderate.

Plain and Fancy, 334 Commercial Street, 487–0147. In business close to thirty years. Seafood and meat dishes, Italian food, and low-calorie meals. Seasonal. Inexpensive to Moderate.

The Mews, 359 Commercial Street, 487–1500. Continental specialties— veal Pomidori and seafood cataplana—served in a casual environment overlooking boats bobbing in the harbor. Open mid-February to mid-November. Expensive.

Cafe Blase, 328 Commercial Street, 487–9465. Gourmet pizza and burgers, quiche, seafood, fancy sandwiches, and Italian coffees. Sidewalk dining in the Parisian manner. Seasonal. Inexpensive to Moderate.

Index